NARRATIVES OF SHIPWRECKS

OF

THE ROYAL NAVY:

BETWEEN 1793 AND 1849.

COMPILED

PRINCIPALLY FROM OFFICIAL DOCUMENTS IN
THE ADMIRALTY,

BY

WILLIAM O. S. GILLY.

WITH A PREFACE

BY

WILLIAM STEPHEN GILLY, D.D.

VICAR OF NORHAM AND CANON OF DURHAM.

LONDON:

JOHN W. PARKER, WEST STRAND.

M DCCC L.

NARRATIVES OF SHIPWRECKS

OF

THE ROYAL NAVY.

CONTENTS.

ADVERTISEMENT.

SOME time ago a friend suggested that a selection of the most interesting naval shipwrecks might be made from the official documents of the Admiralty, in illustration of the discipline and heroism displayed by British seamen under the most trying circumstances of danger: permission to search the records was accordingly asked, and most kindly granted by the Lords Commissioners of the Admiralty, and the present volume is the result.

The Author is well aware that the task of preparing these materials for publication might have fallen into better hands; and whilst he gratefully acknowledges his obligations to the Lords Commissioners of the Admiralty, for allowing him to have access to their Records, he desires also to express his most cordial thanks for the assistance he has received from those friends, who have kindly revised and improved his pages as they passed through the press. Without such aid, his own literary inexperience would have left the work more defective than it is. He is especially indebted to some naval friends for correcting his errors in the use of nautical terms and descriptions.

A list of all the shipwrecks that have occurred in the Royal Navy since the year 1793 has been appended to this volume, in the hope that it may be useful as a table of reference. The ships are classed, first, under the initial letter of their names; and secondly, they are arranged in chronological order as regards the time of their wreck.

W. O. S. G.

PREFACE.

A T the request of my son, the Author of this volume,
I have undertaken to write the Preface, and to
say a few words on the very peculiar and noble traits
of character, which distinguish the British seaman on all
trying occasions, and especially in the terrible hour of
shipwreck.

Many circumstances have combined to make me take
a warm interest in all that concerns the navy. In early
life, having passed several months in a line-of-battle ship
during the war with France, I was an eye-witness of
scenes and events, which called forth some of those
qualities that are illustrated in the following pages.
For the restoration of my health, in the year 1811, I
was advised to try the effects of sea air and a change of
climate, and was glad to accept the opportunity offered
me, by the captain of an eighty-gun ship, to take a cruise
with him off the southern parts of the French coast.

On one occasion, in a severe tempest in the Bay of
Biscay, a flash of lightning struck the ship and set her
on fire. The calmness with which orders were given
and obeyed, and the rapidity with which the fire was
extinguished, without the least hurry or confusion, made
a deep impression on me. This was afterwards increased
by the conduct of the crew in a severe gale of wind,

when it was necessary to navigate one of the narrow channels, by which the squadron that blockaded Rochelle and Rochfort was frequently endangered. The vessel had to pass between two rocks, so near that a biscuit could have been thrown from the deck on either. An old quarter-master was at the wheel; the captain stood by to con and to direct his steering. At one fearful crisis, every blast threatened to shiver a sail, or to carry away a spar, and a single false movement of the helmsman, or the slightest want of steadiness or of obedience on the part of any man on duty, would have been fatal to the life of every one on board.

> As they drifted on their path
> There was silence deep as death,
> And the boldest held his breath
> For a time.

When the danger was over, the captain thanked the officers and men for their conduct, and gave a snuff-box with five guineas in it to the quarter-master, in admiration of his steady head and iron nerves.

I mention these incidents in my early experience as a sort of apology for a landsman's presumption, in venturing to write this Preface to a series of nautical details. In after years, the death of a dear brother, a lieutenant in the navy, who lost his life in a generous attempt to save a vessel from shipwreck on the coast of Sussex, moved me to a still deeper concern for those whose employment is 'in the great waters.'

My early observation of the hazards of a sailor's career, and my brother's sudden call to his last account, in the awful perils of a storm at sea, taught me to reflect with painful solemnity on the many thousand instances, in which our naval protectors are summoned in a moment, prepared or unprepared, to stand before the throne of the Eternal. Often have I asked myself and others, Can nothing be done to elevate the hopes, and to place the fortitude of these men on a firmer foundation than that of mere animal courage, or the instinct of discipline? The present is an opportunity of pleading for the sailor which I should be sorry to lose, and of suggesting something, which may establish his good conduct on a basis more durable, and more certain, than even the well-known courage and discipline of a British tar.

I shall begin by noticing the extraordinary displays of self-possession, self-devotion, and endurance, which shed lustre on our naval service; and I will close my remarks with hints for the improvement of these noble qualities.

The intrepidity and mental resources of a brave man are more discernible in the hour of patient suffering, than in that of daring action: and the contents of this volume form a record of heroic doings and endurances, which exhibits the British seaman as a true specimen of the national character. Duty is his watchword, and the leading principle by which he is governed. Nelson knew the spirits he had to deal with, when he hoisted the memorable signal, 'England expects every man to do his duty.' He was well aware that the men who could patiently and calmly face the toil and danger of a blockading fleet, day and night, on the stormy waves of the Bay of Biscay, or on the lee shores of the Mediterranean, such as his fleet had had to encounter, wanted no other stimulus, in the presence of the enemy, than

that which he so confidently applied. Napoleon found
to his cost, on the field of Waterloo, that the word *Glory*
had no longer any power to launch his battalions success-
fully against troops, who had learnt in the British school
of duty and obedience to confront death, not only in the
impetuous battle-charge, but in the more trying season
of long endurance in the Lines of Torres Vedras. Men
who can wait, and bear and forbear, and remain steadily
at their post under every provocation to leave it, are
invincible opponents. The cool determination which
resisted the onset, and withstood the furious rush of the
French Guards, was part and parcel of the same character which made heroes of the comrades of Nelson.
To obey implicitly, and to feel that no quality is superior
to that of obedience,—to wait for your commander's
word,—to keep order,—to preserve presence of mind,—
to consider yourself one of many, who are to follow the
same rule, and to act in unison with each other,—to
regulate your movements according to the demands of
the common safety,—to consider your honour to be as
much at stake in submitting to a command to remain
stationary and not to stir, as to dash forward,—these are
the peculiarities, which constitute the substantial excel-
lence of the national character; and the shipwrecks of
the Royal Navy illustrate this national character even
more than the battles of the Nile and of Trafalgar. The
perils of a shipwreck are so much beyond those of a
battle, that the loss of life, when the St. George, the
Defence, and the Hero, were wrecked in the North Seas,
in 1811, was far greater than that on the part of the
English in any naval action of late years. In order to

place the qualities of obedience and endurance—so characteristic of the British seaman—in the strongest light, and to show by contrast that the possession of them is the greatest security in danger, whilst the want of them ensures destruction, I commend the following statement to the attention of all who shall read this volume.

In the year 1816 two stately vessels were sailing on the ocean, in all the pride of perfect equipment and of glorious enterprise. The one was an English frigate, the Alceste, having on board our ambassador to China; the other was a French frigate, the Medusa, taking out the suite of a governor for one of the colonies of France on the coast of Africa. The importance of the mission on which each ship was despatched, and the value of the freight, would seem to assure us that the Alceste and the Medusa were officered and manned by the best crews that could be selected. Two nations, rivals in science and civilization, who had lately been contending for the empire of the world, and in the course of that contest had exhibited the most heroic examples of promptitude and courage, were nautically represented, we may suppose, by the élite who walked the decks of the Alceste and the Medusa. If any calamity should happen to either, it could not be attributed to a failure of that brilliant gallantry, which the English and French had equally displayed on the most trying occasions.

But a calamity of the most fearful nature did befal both, out of which the Alceste's crew were delivered with life and honour untouched, when that of the Medusa sank under a catastrophe, which has become a proverb and a bye-word to mariners. Both ships were

wrecked. For an account of the good conduct, of the
calm and resolute endurance, and of the admirable
discipline to which, under Providence, the preservation
of the crew of the Alceste is to be attributed, see pages
204—226 of this volume. A total relaxation of discipline, an absence of all order, precaution, and presence
of mind, and a contemptible disregard of everything and
of everybody but self, in the hour of common danger,
filled up the full measure of horrors poured out upon the
guilty crew of the Medusa. She struck on a sand-bank
under circumstances which admitted of the hope of saving all on board. The shore was at no great distance,
and the weather was not so boisterous as to threaten the
speedy destruction of the ship when the accident first
happened.

There were six boats of different dimensions available
to take off a portion of the passengers and crew : there
was time and there was opportunity for the construction
of a raft to receive the remainder. But the scene of
confusion began among officers and men at the crisis,
when an ordinary exercise of forethought and composure
would have been the preservation of all. Every man
was left to shift for himself, and every man did shift for
himself, in that selfish or bewildered manner which increased the general disaster. The captain was not
among the last, but among the first to scramble into a
boat; and the boats pushed off from the sides of the
frigate, before they had taken in as many as each was
capable of holding. Reproaches, recrimination, and
scuffling took the place of order and of the word of
command, both in the ship and in the boats, when tran-

quillity and order were indispensable for the common
safety.

When the raft had received the miserable remnant,
one hundred and fifty in number, for whom the boats
had no room, or would make no room, it was found,
when it was too late to correct the evil, that this last
refuge of a despairing and disorderly multitude had been
put together with so little care and skill, and was so ill
provided with necessaries, that the planking was insecure;
there was not space enough for protection from the
waves, and charts, instruments, spars, sails, and stores
were all deficient. A few casks of wine and some biscuits, enough for a single meal only, were all the provision made for their sustenance. The rush and scramble
from the wreck had been accomplished with so little
attention to discipline, that the raft had not a single
naval officer to take charge of her. At first, the boats
took the raft in tow, but in a short time, though the sea
was calm and the coast was known to be within fifteen
leagues, the boats cast off the tow-lines: and in not one
of the six was there a sufficient sense of duty, or of
humanity left, to induce the crew to remain by the floating planks—the forlorn hope of one hundred and fifty of
their comrades and fellow-countrymen! Nay, it is related
by the narrators of the wreck of the Medusa, that the
atrocious cry resounded from one boat to another, ' *Nous
les abandonnons !'*—'we leave them to their fate,'—
until one by one all the tow-lines were cast off. During
the long interval of seventeen days, the raft struggled
with the waves. A small pocket compass was the only
guide of the unhappy men, who lost even this in one of

the reckless quarrels, which ensued every hour for a better
place on the raft or a morsel of biscuit. On the first
night twelve men were jammed between the timbers, and
died under the agonies of crushed and mangled limbs.
On the second night more were drowned, and some were
smothered by the pressure towards the centre of the raft.
Common suffering, instead of softening, hardened the
hearts of the survivors against each other. Some of
them drank wine till they were in a frenzy of intoxication, and attempted to cut the ropes which kept the raft
together. A general fight ensued, many were killed, and
many were cast into the sea during the struggle ; and
thus perished from sixty to sixty-five. On the third day
portions of the bodies of the dead were devoured by some
of the survivors. On the fourth night another quarrel
and another fight, with more bloodshed, broke out. On
the fifth morning, thirty only out of the one hundred
and fifty were alive. Two of these were flung to the
waves for stealing wine: a boy died, and twenty-seven
remained, not to comfort and to assist each other, but to
hold a council of destruction, and to determine who
should be victims for the preservation of the rest. At
this hideous council twelve were pronounced too weak to
outlive much more suffering, and that they might not
needlessly consume any part of the remaining stock of
provisions, such as it was, (flying fish mixed with human
flesh,) these twelve helpless wretches were deliberately
thrown into the sea. The *fifteen,* who thus provided for
their own safety by the sacrifice of their weaker comrades, were rescued on the seventeenth day after the
wreck by a brig, sent out in quest of the wreck of the

Medusa by the six boats, which reached the shore in safety, and which might have been the means of saving all on the raft, had not the crews been totally lost to every sentiment of generosity and humanity, when they cast off the tow-lines.

In fact, from the very first of the calamity which befel the Medusa, discipline, presence of mind, and every generous feeling, were at an end: and the abandonment of the ship and of the raft, the terrible loss of life, the cannibalism, the cruelty, the sufferings, and all the disgraceful and inhuman proceedings, which have branded the modern Medusa with a name of infamy worse than that of the Gorgon,—the monster after which she was called, —originated in the want of that order and prompt obedience, which the pages of this volume are intended to record, to the honour of British seamen.

In the history of no less than forty shipwrecks narrated in this memorial of naval heroism,—of passive heroism, the most difficult to be exercised of all sorts of heroism,— there are very few instances of misconduct, and none resembling that on board the Medusa.

This contrast is marked and stated, not in an invidious spirit towards the French, but because there is no example on record, which furnishes such a comparison between the safety which depends on cool and orderly behaviour in the season of peril, and the terrible catastrophe which is hastened and aggravated by want of firmness, and confusion.

'It is impossible,' said a writer in the *Quarterly Review*, of October, 1817, 'not to be struck with the extraordinary difference of conduct in the officers and

crew of the Medusa and the Alceste, wrecked nearly about
the same time.   In the one case, all the people were kept
together in a perfect state of discipline and subordination,
and brought safely home from the opposite side of the
globe ; in the other, every one seems to have been left
to shift for himself, and the greater part perished in the
horrible way we have seen.' *

I have brought the comparison between the two
wrecks again under notice to show, that as certainly as
discipline and good order tend to insure safety on perilous
occasions, so, inevitably, do confusion and want of discipline lead to destruction.   In the one case, intrepidity
and obedience prompted expedients and resources : in
the other case, consternation was followed by despair,
and despair aggravated the catastrophe with tenfold
horrors.

It is not to be concealed, that occasional instances of
insubordination and pusillanimity have occurred in the
British navy.   Some such appear in this narrative, and
they invariably have produced their own punishment, by
leading always to disaster, and often to death ; and they
serve as beacons to point out the fatal consequences of
misconduct, under circumstances either of drunkenness,
disobedience, panic, selfishness, or confusion.

The selfish cowardice, noticed in page 94, on the part of
the men in charge of the jolly-boat of the Athenienne,
and of some of the crew of the launch of the Boreas,
(see p. 136,) and the tumult, intoxication, and desertion

---

* See also an elaborate article on the same subject in the *Edin-
burgh Review*, September, 1818.   No. 60.

of the majority of the crew of the Penelope, which were
followed by the prolonged sufferings and painful deaths
of the culprits, (see pp. 200—204,) are but a few dark
spots in the shipwrecks of the Royal Navy, to set off
by contrast the many bright pages, which describe innumerable traits of character that do honour to human
nature.

As a direction to some of these noble traits, every one
of which will make the reader warm to the name of a
British sailor: and, if he be one himself, will bring the
blood from his heart to his face in a glow of emulation
and honest pride,—I ask him to turn for examples of
perfect discipline to pages 13, 23, 63, 70, 71, 75, 110, 173,
188, 194, 216, 223, 229, 231, 268, 269, 278, 279, 280.
Here he will behold the portraits of men on the brink
of destruction, steady, ' as if they were moving from one
ship to another in any of the Queen's ports,' and unmoved by images of death under the most appalling
forms; and he will say, ' Lo ! these are triumphs of order
and subordination, and examples of such resolute defiance
of the terrors of the last enemy, when covered with the
shadow of death, that no exploits in battle can exhibit
fortitude that will compare with them.'

For instances of generous thought for others, of self-
devotion and of disregard of personal safety, I refer the
reader to pages 58, 59, 67, 68, 69, 96, 128, 129, 169, 186,
190, 194, 231, 234, 269, 270.

In the long list of heroes, which these references to
examples of indomitable courage and unhesitating self-
devotion will unfold, it is almost wrong to mark out one
more than another for observation, and yet the following

stand so prominently forward in the front rank of heroism, that it is impossible to refrain from noticing them. Captain Lydiard sacrificed his life in his desperate endeavour to rescue a boy from the wreck of the Anson, (pp. 128, 129.) Captain Temple, of the Crescent, and more than two hundred of his crew, displayed a noble disregard of themselves, when they permitted the jolly-boat, their own last hope of escape, to take off as many as it would hold, and leave them to perish. There was no rushing, no struggling, to get away from the sinking ship, but with orderly care they helped the boat to push off, bade her God speed, and calmly waited their fate, (p. 153.) The resolution of Captain Bertram, of the Persian, to brave the danger of taking some men off a raft into his over-crowded gig, was generously followed by the crews of the other boats, who threw their clothing and provisions overboard to make room for the additional weight, (p. 191.)

I may refer also to the magnanimous contest between Captain Baker, of the Drake, and his officers and men, each insisting on being the last to make his way from the ship to a rock (p. 231), and which ended in Captain Baker refusing to stir until he had seen every man clear of the wreck. A second struggle for precedency in glorious self-devotion took place, when the same commander declared, that all his crew should pass from the rock to the mainland, by help of a line, before he himself would consult his own safety, (p. 234.) The rope broke, and the last means of communication between the rock and the shore was severed, while the captain of the Drake and three of his companions were waiting their turn to escape. They met their fate with intrepid composure, (p. 235.) Lieutenant Smith, of the Magpie, offered another memorable example, when his schooner was upset in a squall, and he took to his boat with seven men. The boat capsized, and while the struggling crew were endeavouring to right her, they were attacked by sharks. The lieutenant himself had both his legs bitten off; but when his body was convulsed with agony, his mind retained and exercised all its energies, and his last words were expressive of dying consideration for others. ' Tell the admiral, if you survive,' said he, to a lad named Wilson, ' that my men have done their duty, and that no blame is attached to them. I have but one favour to ask, and that is, that he will promote Meldrum to be a gunner,' (p. 270.) And richly did Meldrum deserve the distinction. When all in the boat had perished but himself and another, a brig hove in sight, but did not seem to notice the speck on the ocean. Meldrum sprang overboard, and swam towards the ship, and was thus the means of saving his companion's life as well as his own.

In a volume like this, ' the dangers of the seas' come before the reader in such rapid succession, that he has scarcely time to think of the many other awful perils and sufferings, besides those of wind and storm, which put the mariner's fortitude to the test. The narratives in pages 2, 3, 9, 36, 69, 70, 113, 115, present to view the horrors of a ship on fire.

In pages 12, 169, 171, 196, 226, 242, we learn something of the terrible consequences of being exposed to fogs and mist, ice and snow. In page 27, we have a vivid picture of a combination of these terrors ; and in

b 3

pages 217, 268, the most appalling of all the dangers a
sailor has to encounter is brought in view.

We will hope that the rigours and perils of the
blockade system, which occasioned so fearful a loss of
life at different periods of the late war, but especially in
the disastrous year 1811, are at end for ever. From
page 154 to 159, and from 168 to 186, the accounts of
the loss of life in the Baltic and North Seas alone occur
in fearful succession ; and the magnanimity with which
hundreds, nay, thousands of our bravest officers and men
met death on that most perilous of all services, has rendered the names of British blockading ships memorable
in the annals of hardship, hardihood, and suffering.
Many invaluable lives perished from the inclemency of
the weather ; men were frozen to death at their posts.
It is recorded of one devoted officer, Lieutenant Topping, that rushing on deck in anxiety for his ship, without
giving himself time to put on his clothes, 'in fifteen
minutes he fell upon the deck a corpse, stricken by the
piercing blast and driving snow,' (p. 169.)

In page 174, we read of the bodies of the dead, victims to the cold and tempest, piled up by the survivors
in rows one above another, on the deck of the St.
George, to serve as a shelter against the violence of
the waves and weather. 'In the fourth row lay the
bodies of the Admiral and his friend Captain Guion ;'
and out of a crew of 750, seven only were saved.

The Defence, the consort of the St. George, was cast
away in the same storm: out of her complement of 600,
six was the small remnant of survivors. This ship might
probably have escaped, but her gallant captain (Atkins)

said, ' I will never desert my admiral in the hour of
danger and distress,' (p. 175.)

An instance of obedience and discipline, worthy of
particular mention, occurred before the St. George went
down. A few men asked leave to attempt to reach the
shore in the yawl. Permission was at first granted, but
afterwards withdrawn, and the men returned to their
posts without a murmur. 'As if Providence had rewarded their implicit obedience and reliance upon their
officers,' says the narrative (p. 173), 'two of these men
were of the few (seven) that were saved.'

The question now arises, to what are we to attribute
the extraordinary display of cool determination manifested by British seamen, in such trials of nerve as are
described in the following pages? The series of shipwrecks extends from 1793 to 1847, a period of fifty-four
years; and tragic scenes are described, many of them far
exceeding the imaginary terrors of fiction, and all of
them equal in horror to anything that the Drama,
Romance, or Poetry has attempted to delineate.

We rise from the perusal with scarcely any other impression upon our minds than that of wonder and admiration, at the extraordinary self-command exercised when
death was staring every man in the face. Doubtless there
are some instances of misbehaviour, and of lack of firmness: it could not be otherwise. 'When the stormy
wind ariseth, and they are carried up to the heaven and
down again to the deep, their soul melteth because of
their trouble. They reel to and fro, and stagger like a
drunken man, and are at their wit's end.' But such
examples are so few in the British navy, that we have
little on this score wherewith to reproach our seamen.

To what, then, are we to attribute the manly bearing of British seamen, when the planks of their ship tremble under their feet, and the waves are yawning to swallow them up!

First.—To the early training which almost all our youth receive, in one way or other. It begins at school. The first principles of generosity, as of obedience and order, are taught in our schools: whether in the national and parochial schools, or at Westminster, Eton, and Harrow, and other schools of a higher order, where in his very games the boy learns to exercise presence of mind, daring, and self-command. In our streets and play-grounds, where the humblest or the proudest are at their sports, the germ of the manly spirit is discernible in emulous contention as to who shall bear and forbear, remain at his post, give and take, with most patience and good-humour.

Foreigners have allowed that there is nothing like an English school to discipline a lad for the high places, or rough places, of after-life; and that our mixed schools of every grade are the seminaries, where one learns to lead, and another to follow, in the path of honour and duty.

Secondly.—To the habit which prevails so universally in this country, of giving place to those to whom deference is due, and of looking up to those, who are above us in station, with ungrudging respect and confidence. This goes with the man into all the walks of life. Some attribute it to the aristocratic feeling, which is said to be stronger in England than elsewhere: but it may be more justly traced to that good sense, which is at work in all orders of our people, and which understands when to obey and to hearken. In the seaman it displays itself in a predisposition to regard his officer as one worthy of his confidence, and whom it is his safety as well as duty to obey in the hour of danger. And this confidence is justified by the almost unfailing manner, in which the officer shows himself deserving of the trust reposed in him, and takes the lead in the very front of danger, and exhibits in moments of doubt and difficulty all the resources of a cool and collected mind, at the very juncture when life and death depend upon his composure.

The leadership to which a British tar is accustomed, and which ever responds to his own confiding spirit, is one of the primary causes of his endurance and daring. His officer is the first to advance, the foremost to encounter, the last to hesitate, and the most willing to take more than his share of danger and of suffering; and this inspires the men with an emulation to do likewise.

Conduct such as that displayed by the captains and officers of the Queen Charlotte (pp. 37 and 41), of the Hindostan (p. 71), of the Athenienne (p. 96), of the Anson (p. 128), of the Dædalus (p. 189), could not fail of producing a sort of instinctive effect upon a ship's crew. Under the command of officers who never flinch from their duty, who share their last biscuit with the lowest cabin-boy, and who will not move from the vessel when it is sinking under them, until every other man has taken his seat in the boat, or planted his foot on the raft that is to carry him from the wreck, where can be the quailing heart or the unready hand?

Thirdly.—The blockading service has had much to do

in training our seamen for passive heroism and enduring
fortitude. During the long war with France, it was a
service wherein all those qualities were called into action,
which are of most value in sudden emergencies. Vigilance, promptitude, patience, and endurance, were tried
to the utmost in the course of those wintry months, and
tempestuous seasons, when single ships, squadrons, and
fleets were cruising off the enemy's coast, and every man
on board was perpetually exposed to something that put
his temper or his nerves to the test. Then was the time
to learn when to keep a sharp look-out, to be on the
alert in handling the gear of a vessel, to respond to the
word of command at the instant, to do things at the
right point of time, to hold life at a moment's purchase,
and to stare death in the face without flinching. It was
a hard and rigorous school; but if proficiency in readiness and fortitude was to be attained anywhere, it was in
the blockading service, and there the heart of oak was
tried, and the seaman was trained for the exercise of that
discipline, of which this Record of Naval Shipwrecks
presents so complete a picture.

But we will hope that the principal cause, to which we
may ascribe the good conduct of our sailors in the trying
hour, when there seems to be a span only between life and
death, is the religious feeling which they bring with them
to their ship from their homes, whether from the cabin on
the sea-shore, or the cottage on the hill-side. The scene
described in page 115, and the anecdote of the poor boy,
in whose hand was found an open Bible when his corpse
was cast on shore, show the power of religious feeling in
the soul of the sailor. It may be a very imperfect feeling,

but the sailor has it; and even in its imperfection it has
a strong hold on his mind. From the first outbreak of the
Revolution, the French sailor entered the service of his
country as a volunteer or a conscript, embued with infidel
notions; or to say the least, with the religious indifference
which had become so common in France. Not so the
English sailor. He was not one of the fools to say in
his heart, 'There is no God!' It is not easy to define
the nature of that awe which fills the mind of a religious
mariner; but most certainly those 'who see the works of
the Lord and his wonders in the deep,' face danger more
steadily, under the solemn belief that there is a ruling
power to control the waters, and to say to the winds,
'Peace! be still.' They are predisposed to 'cry unto
the Lord in their trouble,' and to implore Him to 'make
the storm a calm, so that the waves thereof may be still:'
and this fear of God, which is before their eyes, has its influence in making them willing to adopt every expedient
proposed to them by their officers for their common
safety. Under this higher impulse, the spirit of obedience works in them more confidingly; and humbled
before the Supreme Power, they are prepared to yield
submission to every intellect superior to their own. Now
if there be a feeling of this kind already at work for
good in the minds of our seamen, it is of the utmost
importance to strengthen it,* to give it a sure direction,

---

* In September, 1849, five colliers were wrecked off the Gunfleet
Sands. The crews were saved, and the following extract from the
Ipswich Express, copied into the *Times* of the 12th of December,
contains a proof of the strong hold which religious awe has on the
minds of seamen :—' Yesterday (Monday) afternoon, the united crews,

and to make it run in a deeper and a broader channel,
by all the appliances of instruction and education.

To the credit of the official Boards, under whose ad-
ministrative authority provision is made for the religious
and educational improvement of men and boys in the
Navy, very much has been done lately to secure this great
object. Within my own memory few seamen could read,
still fewer could write, but now the majority of them can
do both, and they respond largely to the instruction they
receive, by their intelligence and good conduct. There
is no more imposing sight than that of the crew of a man-
of-war, when assembled for divine service ; and if the
chaplain be a clergyman, who applies himself zealously
to his duties, he has a congregation before him, who
show by their attentive looks, that they are under the
power of religious impressions. Almost all ships commanded by post-captains have chaplains and naval in-
structors, and where there is no chaplain, the commanding officer is expected to read prayers on Sundays. In

---

amounting to about thirty men, had a free passage to Ipswich by the
River Queen. The scene on board was of the most extraordinary
and affecting description. The rough, weather-beaten seamen, who
had gone through the perils of that night with undaunted courage,
were, in the review of it, completely overwhelmed with gratitude to
God for His mercy in granting them deliverance. For the most part
they were in the fore cabin of the steamer, and at one time all would
be on their knees in devout prayer and thanksgiving to God, then a
suitable hymn would be read, and the voices of those who had been
saved from the yawning ocean would presently sound it forth in
solemn thanks to God. From port to port they were entirely occupied in these devotional exercises, and the effect of them, and indeed
the whole scene, upon several hardy sons of ocean who were on
board, will never be forgotten.'

port the crews of the Queen's ships have the opportunity
of observing the sacred day, either on board the flag-ship,
the ordinary, or in the dockyard chapel. I believe every
ship in the navy is provided with a library; and first,
second, third, fourth, and fifth-rates have schoolmasters.
To men and boys desirous of entering the service, the
preference is given to those who can read and write;
and an admirable regulation has lately been adopted,
which will contribute further to advance our navy in the
intellectual scale. Boys are entered as naval apprentices,
to the number of one hundred each, at Devonport, Portsmouth, Sheerness, and Cork. They remain for one year
on board the flag-ship, under a systematic course of education, and are then drafted into sea-going ships. The
happy effects produced by mental cultivation were felt
in an especial degree, when the Discovery ships, under
Captain, now Sir Edward Parry, were blocked up with
ice, and had to pass so many dismal days and nights in
the Polar Sea. A school was established both in the
Hecla and Fury, under able superintendence; and men,
whose time would have hung heavily during their icy
imprisonment, were kept in good humour and cheerfulness by the intellectual occupations in which they were
engaged. Captain Parry's remarks in attestation of the
moral effect produced by this means, and on the uninterrupted good order which prevailed among his men, are
cited in page 243 of this work.

It would add greatly to the intellectual and spiritual
improvement of our seamen, if a Chaplain-general were
appointed to take the oversight of the religious instruction, and an *Examiner* to direct the secular instruction,

of the Navy. The former should exercise authority similar to that of an archdeacon, and the functions of the latter should resemble those of her Majesty's Inspectors of Schools. The impulse given to parochial education by the latter is beyond all calculation; and the difference of ecclesiastical discipline in a diocese, where there are active archdeacons and where there are not, is a matter of well ascertained fact.

The duties of a chaplain-general[*] should be to visit the naval posts, and to go on board the Queen's ships, (especially before they are despatched on foreign service,) for the purpose of reporting and advising. He should look out for and recommend competent chaplains,—consult with admirals and captains on the best mode of securing the regular performance of the sacred offices, —make inquiry into the state of the ship-libraries, keep them well supplied with religious books and tracts, and direct observation generally to the spiritual wants of

---

[*] His duties would be similar to those described in the following letter from a clergyman in one of the colonies, though more general in their extent:—'My own duties are pretty much those you would suppose. I visit the emigrant ships *immediately* on their coming into port, and am often on board before they drop anchor. I then inquire for the members of the Church of England, and for such others as may require the services of a Church of England clergyman; and having assembled them together, inquire as to the occurrences on the voyage, whether they have had schools, and a regular Sunday or daily service, whether there are children to be baptized, and a thousand other matters of a like nature, which it would be but tiring you to detail. We then appoint an hour for holding a thanksgiving service for their preservation from the perils of the sea, and their safe arrival in the colony. This service consists in the proper service for the day, with a short sermon suited to the occasion.'

ships and ports. He would thus be of infinite use in
making religion an object of more and more thought-
fulness to those, who take an interest in the comfort and
good conduct of the Navy: two things which always go
together.

If an Inspector of all the naval schools and schoolmasters were appointed (Professor Mosely has now the
inspection of the Dockyard Schools,) he should consider
it to be part of his office to look to the libraries, and to
recommend elementary books. His periodical examina-
tions would be likely to stir up the same spirit of emulation on board ship, which has been the result in our
towns and villages, where the schools are visited by persons appointed by the Committee of Privy Council on
Education. I am satisfied with throwing out these sug-
gestions without dwelling further upon them, under the
persuasion that every practical hint of the kind will be
well considered, and acted upon (if it commend itself
to their judgment,) by those who preside over naval
affairs, and who have at heart the mental improvement
of our seamen.

I have another suggestion to make, which is meant
not for those only, who are officially interested in the
condition of the navy, but for all who love and value it.
The merchant service, the fisheries, and the coasting
trade are the nurseries of the navy. Every shipmate
and every boatman on the sea and on the river ought,
therefore, to come in for a share of our sympathy, because he belongs to a class to which the Queen's ships
must look for a supply of men. But none are exposed
to more trials than they, and especially in the larger

ports. Many of them come home from a voyage of
danger and deprivation, full of excitement, and become
victims of plunder and temptation ; and the man who
last week was impressed, by the perils of the tempest,
with the terrors of the Lord, and was inclined to fear
God and to serve him, is waylaid by unfeeling wretches,
who first entice him into scenes of profligacy and blas-
phemy, and then cast him off, robbed of his money,
seared in his conscience, and in a miserable condition
of soul and body. Many benevolent efforts have been
made to protect and fortify some of those who are thus
beset, and to reclaim such as are not utterly lost ; and
associations have been formed for the purpose of affording temporary relief and instruction to seamen, who
might otherwise become outcasts, and perish in want
and ignorance. I allude to such institutions as the
' Sailor's Home,' or ' Destitute Sailor's Asylum,' in
London, for the reception of seamen who have squan-
dered or have been despoiled of their earnings after
their return from a foreign voyage, or who are disabled
for employment by illness, age, or accident. There is
also ' The Floating Chapel,' opened to invite and enable
mariners to avail themselves of the opportunity of
attending Divine service, (under the Thames Church
Missionary Society,) which moves from one thickly
populated sailors' locality to another. The establishment
of a district church and minister in a large sea-port
parish, like that of St. Mary's, Devonport, to relieve the
necessities of a district crowded with mariners, and rife
with all the snares and temptations which entrap a

sailor, and endanger his bodily and spiritual safety, is another undertaking worthy of notice.

Institutions like these must depend principally on public and voluntary support. There is much need for them in all our principal sea-ports; for who require them more than the men who are perpetually exposed to the double shipwreck of body and soul? The members of these and similar institutions are instrumental in preserving some from ruin—in restoring others to character and employment, to usefulness, to self-estimation, and to religious feeling; and in making both our merchant and naval service an example to the world of subordination and patient endurance.

The promoters of these institutions are not satisfied with providing a remedy for the evil which exists, but they do much to prevent the ills of irreligion and immorality, by supplying seamen with instructive and devotional books, and by employing agents to go among them and to tell them where the offices of religion are performed. The countenance which admirals and captains; prelates and lords of the Admiralty, have given to them, are the best warrant for their necessity and usefulness. A short notice of 'The Swan' and its Tender, will not be thought out of place in this volume.

'The Swan' is a large cutter of about 140 tons. On her bows she bears an inscription which describes her as 'The Thames Church.' She conveys a clergyman and a floating sanctuary from one pool in the river to another, to carry the Word of God to those who do not seek for it themselves. Hers is a missionary voyage. She is freighted with Bibles and Testaments and Prayer-books, and religious tracts. She runs along-side colliers, outward-bound vessels, and emigrant ships especially, that the services, the consolation, and the instruction of the Church may be offered as a parting gift to those, who are taking a last leave of their native shores, and are saying farewell to weeping friends and kindred.

There is also a Tender, called ' The Little Thames Church,' which sails lower down the river, as occasion may require, fraught on the same holy errand. One extract from the last Report of the ' Thames Church Mission Society,' which is patronized by the Archbishop of Canterbury and the Bishops of London and Winchester, will suffice to explain the nature of her mission.

' Sunday, February 24, Long Reach. Morning service. The congregation was 128 seamen. Afternoon, Bible class, 62. Evening service, 132,—total 322. One of the captains observed that there was a great change for the better, which he was rejoiced to see: ' For,' said he, ' about four years ago I attended a service, and found that I was the only sailor that had come from the fleet; but this morning so crowded was the church, that I had some difficulty in getting a seat.' '

It is by means such as these, which as a Christian nation we are bound to provide, that we might hope, not only to keep alive, but to improve the noble spirit which distinguishes the British Navy.

The discipline which now prevails would be established on the highest principle of obedience and action. The endurance, which now bears suffering with fortitude, would learn to submit to severer trials under the sanction of a higher teaching, and patience would have her perfect work. The courage and steadiness of a brave crew would receive an accession of energy from the hope that is set before them. The allegiance, which they owe to their Sovereign, would be strengthened by a sense of the more sacred duty which they owe to Him, by whom kings reign and rulers govern : and committing themselves habitually to the protection of Providence, they would face deprivation, fatigue, and danger with unshaken composure,—with a hand for any toil, and a heart for any fate.

WILLIAM STEPHEN GILLY.

Durham, Oct. 28, 1850.

SHIPWRECKS

OF

THE ROYAL NAVY.

Roll on, thou deep and dark blue ocean—roll!
Ten thousand fleets sweep over thee in vain;
Man marks the earth with ruin—his control
Stops with the shore;—upon the watery plain
The wrecks are all thy deed, nor doth remain
A shadow of man's ravage, save his own,
When, for a moment, like a drop of rain,
He sinks into thy depths with bubbling groan,
Without a grave, unknell'd, uncoffin'd, and unknown.
                              BYRON's *Childe Harold*.

IN the Preface to this work it has been stated that it is
not our intention to give a detailed account of every
wreck that has happened in the Royal Navy from the
year 1793, to the present time, but only of a few of those
which appear to be most interesting. We therefore pass
over the first two years, giving only a catalogue of the
wrecks that occurred during that time; because the
calamities that befel the British Navy in 1793 and 1794
were but slight in comparison with those of a later date.
The first loss that we have to record is that of the BOYNE,
of 98 guns, bearing the flag of Vice-Admiral Peyton, and
commanded by Captain George Grey. This ship took fire
as she lay at anchor at Spithead, on the 1st of May, 1795.
The origin of the fire has never been correctly ascertained; but it is supposed that some of the lighted paper

B

from the cartridges of the marines, as they were exercising and firing on the windward side of the poop, flew through the quarter gallery into the admiral's cabin, and set fire to the papers or other inflammable materials that were lying there. Be this as it may, the flames burst through the poop before the fire was discovered, and, notwithstanding the united efforts of both officers and men, they soon wrapt the vessel in a blaze fore and aft.

Upon the discovery of the fire, all the boats from the different ships put out to the Boyne's assistance, and the crew, with the exception of eleven, were saved.

The Boyne's guns, being loaded, went off as they became heated, and much injury would have been done to the shipping and those on board, had not the Port-Admiral, Sir William Parker, made signals for the vessels most in danger to get under weigh. As it was, two men were killed, and one wounded on board the Queen Charlotte.

About half-past one in the afternoon, the burning ship parted from her cables, and blew up with a dreadful explosion. At the time of the accident, Admiral Peyton and Captain Grey were attending a court martial in Portsmouth Harbour.

The next catastrophe which we have to describe, was of a far more appalling nature, and one which long threw a gloom over the inhabitants of Plymouth and the neighbourhood.

The AMPHION frigate had been obliged to put into Plymouth for repairs, and, on the 22nd Sept., 1796, was lying alongside of a sheer-hulk taking in her bowsprit, within a few yards of the dockyard jetty. The ship, being on the eve of sailing, was crowded with more than an hundred men, women, and children, above her usual complement. It was about four o'clock in the afternoon that a violent shock, like an earthquake, was felt at

Stonehouse and Plymouth. The sky towards the dock appeared red, as if from fire, and in a moment the streets were crowded with the inhabitants, each asking his neighbour what had occurred. When the confusion had somewhat abated, it was announced that the Amphion had blown up, and then every one hastened to the dock, where a most heart-rending scene presented itself. Strewed in all directions were pieces of broken timber, spars, and rigging, whilst the deck of the hulk, to which the frigate had been lashed, was red with blood, and covered with mangled limbs and lifeless trunks, all blackened with powder. The frigate had been originally manned from Plymouth ; and as the mutilated forms were collected together and carried to the hospital, fathers, mothers, brothers, and sisters flocked to the gates, in their anxiety to discover if their relatives were numbered amongst the dying or the dead.

From the suddenness of the catastrophe, no accurate account can of course be given ; but the following particulars were collected from the survivors.

The captain, Israel Pellew, was at dinner in his cabin, with Captain Swaffield of the Overyssel, a Dutch 64, and the first lieutenant of the Amphion, when in an instant they were all violently thrown against the carlings of the upper deck. Captain Pellew had sufficient presence of mind to rush to the cabin window before a second explosion followed, by which he was blown into the water ; he was soon, however, picked up by a boat, and was found to have sustained but little injury.

The first lieutenant, who followed his example, escaped in a similar manner. Unfortunately, Captain Swaffield perished, in all probability having been stunned either by the first blow he received against the carlings, or by coming in contact with some part of the hulk. His body was found a month afterwards, with the skull fractured, apparently crushed between the sides of the two vessels.

At the moment of the explosion, the sentinel at the cabin door was looking at his watch, when it was dashed from his hands and he was stunned : he knew nothing more until he found himself safe on shore, and comparatively unhurt. The escape of the boatswain was also very remarkable ; he was standing on the cathead, directing the men in rigging out the jib-boom, when he felt himself suddenly carried off his feet into the air: he then fell into the sea senseless ; and on recovering his consciousness, he found that he had got entangled amongst the rigging, and that his arm was broken. He contrived to extricate himself, though with some difficulty, and he was soon picked up by a boat, without further injury.

The preservation of a child was no less singular : in the terror of the moment, the mother had grasped it in her arms, but, horrible to relate, the lower part of her body was blown to pieces, whilst the upper part remained unhurt, and it was discovered with the arms still clasping the living child to the lifeless bosom.

Till then we had not wept—
But well our gushing hearts might say,
That there a *Mother* slept !
For her pale arms a babe had prest
With such a wreathing grasp,
The fire had pass'd o'er that fond breast,
Yet not undone the clasp.
Deep in her bosom lay his head,
With half-shut violet eye—
He had known little of her dread,
Nought of her agony.
Oh ! human love, whose yearning heart,
Through all things vainly true,
So stamps upon thy mortal part
Its passionate adieu:

Surely thou hast another lot,
There is some home for thee,
Where thou shalt rest, rememb'ring not
The moaning of the sea.—Mrs. Hemans.

The exact complement of the Amphion was 215, but from the crowded state of her decks at the time of the accident, it is supposed that 300, out of 310 or 312 persons, perished with the ship.

The captain, two lieutenants, a boatswain, three or four seamen, a marine, one woman, and the child were all that were saved.

The cause of this unfortunate event was never clearly known ; but it was conjectured that the gunner might have let fall some powder near the fore-magazine, which accidentally igniting, had communicated with the magazine itself. The gunner had been suspected of stealing the powder, and on that day he is said to have been intoxicated, and was probably less careful than usual. He was amongst the numbers who perished.

The loss of the TRIBUNE frigate, in November of the following year, is too interesting to be omitted.

At about eight o'clock on the morning of the 16th of November, 1797, the harbour of Halifax was discovered, and as a strong wind blew from the east-south-east, Captain Scory Barker proposed to the master to lie to, until a pilot came on board. The master replied that there was no necessity for such a measure, as the wind was favourable, and he was perfectly well acquainted with the passage. The captain confiding in this assurance, went below, and the master took charge of the ship.

Towards noon they approached so near the Thrum Cape shoals, that the master became alarmed and sent for Mr. Galvin, one of the master's mates. The message was scarcely delivered, before the man in the main-chains sung out, ' By the mark five.' In a few minutes after the ship struck.

Signals of distress were immediately made, and as speedily answered by the military posts, and the ships in the harbour.

Some boats put out from the harbour to the assistance of the Tribune, and Mr. Rackum, boatswain of the Ordinary, succeeded in reaching her in a boat from the dockyard, but all the other boats were forced to put back, —the wind was blowing so hard directly against them.

The ship continued to beat until eight o'clock, P.M., when all the guns having been thrown overboard (except one, retained for signals), and all means taken to lighten her, she began to heave, and in about an hour after she swung off the shoal,—not, however, without having lost her rudder.

She was then found to have seven feet of water in the hold; the chain pumps were instantly manned, and every exertion made to save the vessel. At first these efforts seemed to be successful, but by ten o'clock the gale had increased to a frightful violence, and the water was gaining on them so fast that little hope remained. The ship was driving rapidly towards the rocky coast, against which she must have been dashed to pieces had she kept afloat a few minutes longer, but she gave a lurch and went down, rose again for an instant, and with another lurch sank, and all was over,—and there were nearly two hundred and fifty human beings struggling with the waves.

Of all the crew twelve only were saved.

Mr. Galvin, the master's mate, was below, directing the working of the pumps, when the ship went down; he was washed up the hatchway, and thence into the sea; he then struck out for the shrouds, but was seized by three of his drowning comrades. To extricate himself

from their grasp, he dived for a few seconds, which caused
them to let go their hold. He reached the shrouds,
which were crowded with people, and then climbed to
the main-top. Ten men had taken refuge in the foretop, and about a hundred persons altogether are supposed
by Mr. Galvin to have been clinging to the shrouds, tops,
and other parts of the rigging; but the long November
night, the intense cold, and the fierce gale, finished the
work that the waves had left undone; and one by one
the poor creatures let go their hold, frozen or exhausted,
and dropped into the foaming sea.

About forty persons were clinging to the mainmast
when it fell over, and all were lost, except Mr. Galvin
and nine others, who had strength enough left to enable
them to gain the top, which rested on the mainyard,
being fortunately sustained by a part of the rigging.
But of the ten who regained the maintop, four only,
including Mr. Galvin, survived the night. Of the ten
in the foretop, six perished, three from exhaustion, and
three were washed way.

Here we cannot refrain from relating an instance of
the coolness which is so often characteristic of the British
sailor. Amongst those who survived in the foretop were
two seamen, Robert Dunlap, and Daniel Munroe; the
latter disappeared in the night, and his companion concluded that he had been washed away with the others.
About two hours, however, after he had been missed, Munroe, to the surprise of Dunlap, thrust his head through
the lubber's hole. Dunlap asked where he had been.

' Been,' said Munroe; ' I've been cruizing, d'ye see,
in search of a better berth.'

After swimming about the wreck for a considerable
time, he had returned to the fore-shrouds, and crawling
in at the cat-harpings, had been sleeping there more than
an hour.

When the morning dawned, there were only eight men still alive on the rigging, and no effort was made to rescue them until about eleven o'clock, A.M., when a boy of thirteen years of age put out alone, in a small skiff from Herring Cove, to their assistance, thus setting a noble example of humanity and heroism to older and more experienced men, who should have been leaders, and not followers, on such an occasion. With great courage and skill, and at the peril of his life, he reached the wreck, and backing his skiff close to the foretop, carried off two of the people. Upon this occasion, also, a noble instance of the magnanimity of the true British tar was displayed.

Munroe and Dunlap, who, during the night, had preserved their strength and spirits, and had done everything in their power to sustain their less fortunate comrades, refused to quit the wreck until the other two men, who were so exhausted as to be unable to make any effort for their own safety, were taken on shore. They accordingly lifted them into the skiff, and the gallant boy rowed them off in triumph to the Cove, and deposited them in safety in the nearest cottage.

He again put off in his skiff, but this time all his efforts were unavailing, and he was obliged to return. His gallant example, however, had the effect of inducing others to make the attempt, and the six survivors were conveyed to the shore in large boats.

Before concluding this chapter, we will briefly relate another catastrophe, somewhat similar to that of the Amphion, but which affords a still more remarkable instance of the preservation of four individuals, from one of whom the following particulars were ascertained:—

It appears that the RESISTANCE, of 44 guns, Captain Edward Pakenham, had anchored in the Straits of Banca, on the 23rd of July, 1798. Between three and four o'clock in the morning of the 24th, the ship was struck by lightning: the electric fluid must have penetrated and set fire to some part of the vessel near to the magazine, as she blew up with a fearful violence a few moments after the flash. Thomas Scott, a seaman, one of the few survivors, stated that he was lying asleep on the starboard side of the quarter-deck, when being suddenly awakened by a bright blaze, and the sensation of scorching heat, he found his hair and clothes were on fire. A tremendous explosion immediately followed, and he became insensible. He supposed that some minutes must have elapsed before he recovered, when he found himself, with many of his comrades, struggling in the waves amongst pieces of the wreck. The Resistance had sunk, but the hammock netting was just above water on the starboard side, and with much difficulty Scott and the other survivors contrived to reach it. When they were able to look around them, they found that twelve men alone remained of a crew of above three hundred, including the marines. The calmness of the weather enabled the unfortunate sufferers to construct a raft with the pieces of timber that were floating about; but most of the men were so much bruised and burnt as to be unable to assist in the work. The raft was finished about one o'clock, P.M., but in a very rough and insecure manner. Part of the mainsail attached to the mast of the jolly-boat served them for a sail, and they committed themselves to the care of Providence upon this frail raft, and made for the nearest shore, which was the low land of Sumatra, about three leagues distant.

About seven o'clock in the evening, a gale sprung up, the sea ran high, and the lashings of the raft began to give way, the planks which formed the platform were washed off, and in a short time the mast and sail were also carried away. An anchor-stock which formed part of the raft had separated, and was floating away; but although it was at some distance, Scott proposed to swim for it, and encouraging three others to follow his example, they all reached it in safety. In about an hour afterwards they lost sight of their companions on the raft, and never saw them more. The four men upon the anchor-stock gained the shore, and they then fell into the hands of the Malays.

Thomas Scott was twice sold as a slave, but was at length released, at the request of Major Taylor, the governor of Malacca, who, hearing that four British seamen were captives at Lingan, sent to the Sultan to beg his assistance in procuring their liberty. Thomas Scott returned with Major Taylor's messenger to Malacca, from whence he sailed to England: the other three men had been previously released by the Sultan's orders, and conveyed to Penang.

THE PROSERPINE.

ON Monday, January the 28th, 1799, His Majesty's frigate Proserpine, 28 guns, commanded by Captain James Wallis, sailed from Yarmouth to Cuxhaven. She had on board the Hon. Thomas Grenville, who was the bearer of important despatches for the Court of Berlin. On Wednesday, the 30th, the ship was off Heligoland, and there took in a pilot for the Elbe. The day being fine, with a fair wind from the N.N.E., the Proserpine's course was steered for the Réd Buoy, where she anchored for the night. It was then perceived that the two other buoys at the entrance of the river had been removed: a consultation was therefore held with the pilots, in the presence of Mr. Grenville, as to the practicability of proceeding up the river in the absence of the buoys. The Heligoland pilot, and the two belonging to the ship, were unanimous in declaring that there was not the slightest difficulty or danger in ascending the river ; they professed the most perfect knowledge of the passage, and assured Captain Wallis they had no fear of carrying the vessel to Cuxhaven, provided only he would proceed between half ebb and half flood tide ; for in that case they should be able to see the sands and to recognise their marks.

The next morning (31st), the Proserpine was got under weigh, and proceeded up the river, having the Prince of Wales packet, which had accompanied her from Yarmouth, standing on ahead.

At four o'clock in the afternoon, when they were within four miles of Cuxhaven, the weather became very thick, and some snow fell, so that Captain Wallis was obliged to anchor.

At nine o'clock, P.M., the wind changed to east by south, blowing a violent gale, accompanied by a heavy fall of snow, which made it impossible to see beyond a few feet from the ship ; and what was still worse, the tide and the wind brought such large masses of ice against the ship, that, with all hands upon deck, it was with the greatest difficulty they prevented the cables being cut, and were able to preserve their station till daylight.

By eight o'clock next morning, the flood tide had carried up most of the ice, and left a passage clear below the ship, while all above it was blocked up. The Prince of Wales packet had gone on shore during the night ; and, warned by her fate, Captain Wallis determined to retreat out of the Elbe. Mr. Grenville was very anxious to be put on shore as speedily as possible, his mission being of much importance ; but the river was so completely blocked up above them, that there seemed no

possibility of effecting a landing at Cuxhaven : Captain
Wallis therefore got his ship under weigh, and stood out
to sea, intending to land Mr. Grenville on the nearest
part of the coast of Jutland, if it were practicable.

The pilots were congratulating the captain on the
frigate's getting safely out of the river, and clear of the
sands, and the people had been allowed to go to breakfast,
on the supposition that all danger was past, when the
vessel struck upon Scharhorn Sand, with Newark Island
bearing south by east, at half-past nine o'clock, A.M.

As it was blowing a very strong gale of wind, the
Proserpine struck with great force, though she carried no
other canvass than her foretopmast stay-sail. Upon
sounding there was found to be only ten feet of water
under the fore part of her keel.

The boats were immediately lowered to carry out an
anchor, but the ice was returning upon them so fast that
this was found impossible, and the boats were hoisted on
board again. All hands were then employed to shore
the ship up, and make her heel towards the bank, to
prevent her falling into the stream, which would have
been certain destruction. Happily this object was
effected ; for as the tide ebbed, she lay towards the bank.

The next tide, however, brought down such huge
masses of ice that the shores were carried away—the
copper was torn from the starboard quarter, and the rudder
cut in two, the lower part lying on the ice under the
counter.

Notwithstanding all these disasters, Captain Wallis
still hoped to get the ship off at high water, and to
effect this, they proceeded to lighten her by throwing
most of her guns and part of her stores overboard,
all of which were borne up on the ice. One party
was employed in hoisting out the provisions, another in
starting the casks of wine and spirits ; and such were the

good discipline and right feeling of the men, that not one instance of intoxication occurred.

At ten o'clock on Friday night, they abandoned all hope of saving the vessel ; it was then high water, yet the heavy gale from the south-east so kept back the tide, that upon sounding, they found three feet less water than there had been in the morning, when the ship first struck.

The situation of the crew was dreadful. When the tide ebbed, they expected every moment that the ship would be driven to pieces by the ice. The cold was intense, and the darkness such that it was almost impossible to distinguish one another upon deck ; and the snow, falling very thick, was driven against their faces by the wind, and froze upon them as it fell.

There was no possibility of keeping up warmth and circulation in their bodies, for the frozen snow and ice made the deck so slippery they could scarcely stand, much less walk about quickly, and all they could do was, to try to screen themselves as much as possible from the pitiless blast. Thus the night was spent in anxious fears for the future, and dread of immediate destruction. But morning came at last, though with little comfort to the sufferers, for the wind had increased, the ice was up to the cabin windows, the stern-post was found to be broken in two, and the ship otherwise seriously damaged.

In this state they could not long remain. Mr. Grenville and some of the officers proposed to Captain Wallis that the crew should make an attempt to get over the ice to Newark Island, as the only means of preserving their lives.*

---

* Newark Island is the highest point of one of those long ridges of sand which abound on the south and south-eastern coasts of the North Sea, formed by the deposits of ages from the rivers that empty themselves into the German Ocean, acted upon by the alternate ebb and flow of the tide, till they assume a form

At first, Captain Wallis was inclined to reject the proposal ; he saw all the danger attending such an attempt ; and it appeared to him, that they could scarcely expect to succeed in crossing the ice through a dense fog and heavy snow-storm, without any knowledge of the way, without a guide, and exhausted as they were by mental and bodily suffering, and benumbed with cold.

On the other hand, he confessed that the plan presented a hope of safety, and that it was their only hope. The ship's company were unanimous in wishing to adopt it, and therefore Captain Wallis finally consented.

The people then set heartily to work to consider the difficulties of the undertaking, and the best means of meeting them. It was determined that they should be divided into four companies, each headed by an officer ; that the strongest of the men should carry planks, to be laid down in the most dangerous places by way of assistance to the less able and active of the party ; and that others should hold a long line of extended rope, to be instantly available in case of any one falling between the blocks of ice.

When all these measures were decided upon, and every man had provided himself with what was most essential for his safety and sustenance, they began their perilous journey at half-past one o'clock, P.M. By three o'clock, every one had left the ship, except Captain Wallis, and he then followed the party, accompanied by Lieutenant Ridley, of the Marines.

To describe the dangers and difficulties the crew of the

---

and establish a position and a name. Upon Newark Island is a village and light-house, situated a few miles from Cuxhaven, and accessible at low water by the sand. The sand ridge takes a north-westerly direction from Newark Island, and extends about six miles further. It was on the extremity of the north-western bank that the Proserpine was wrecked.

Proserpine had to encounter is almost impossible. The
snow was still falling heavily, driving against their faces,
and adhering to their hair and eyebrows, where in a
few minutes it became solid pieces of ice. Sometimes
they had to clamber over huge blocks of ice, and at
other times were obliged to plunge through snow and
water reaching to their middle.

As the wind blew from the direction in which they
were proceeding, the large flakes of snow were driven
into their eyes, and prevented them from seeing many
yards in advance. This caused them to deviate from
their proper course, and to travel in a direction which, if
continued, would have carried them off the shoal and
field of ice into the sea, or at least have taken them so
far from any place of shelter, as to have left them to
perish in the ice and snow during the night.

This dreadful calamity was, however, prevented, by one
of the party having in his possession a pocket compass.
Fortunately, bearings had been taken previous to their
leaving the wreck. The course they were pursuing was
examined, and to their surprise it was discovered that
they had been deviating widely from the direct line
which they ought to have pursued. This, however, enabled the party to correct the march, and after a toilsome
journey of six miles, they at length reached Newark.

In the course of their hazardous journey, a striking
instance was afforded of the inscrutable ways of Providence. Two females were on board the Proserpine
when she was stranded,—one a strong healthy woman,
accustomed to the hardships of a maritime life: the
other exactly the reverse, weak and delicate, had never
been twelve hours on board a ship until the evening
previous to the frigate's sailing from Yarmouth. Her
husband had been lately impressed, and she had come
on board for the purpose of taking farewell. Owing

to a sudden change of the weather, and the urgency of the mission for which the Proserpine had been despatched, she had been unable to quit the ship. The poor creature was upon the eve of her confinement, and naturally being but ill prepared to combat with the inconvenience of a ship at sea, in the course of the day she was delivered of a dead child. The reader can well imagine the sufferings endured by this helpless woman, with but one of her own sex to tend her, in a vessel tossed about in the stormy seas of the Northern Ocean.

But this was little compared with what she had yet to undergo. Before many hours the frigate stranded: the night was passed in torture of mind and body, and then was she compelled, with others, to quit the ship, and travel through masses of snow and ice, and to combat with the bitter north wind, hail, and sleet.

. It may well be supposed that her strength, already weakened by the sufferings she had undergone, was totally unprepared to bear up against a trial from which the strongest of the crew might have shrunk ; but it turned out otherwise. The robust, healthy woman, with her feeble companion, left the wreck together, the former bearing in her arms an infant of nine months old. No doubt many a ready arm was stretched forth to assist them in their perilsome journey. But man could have done but little against the piercing winter's blast with which they had to contend. Before they had proceeded half the distance, the child was frozen in its mother's arms, and ere long the mother herself sunk on the snow, fell into a state of stupor, and died. Not so the delicate invalid ; sustained by help from above, she still pursued her way, and ere long gained with others the hospitable shore. The inhabitants of the village received the strangers with great kindness, and did everything in their power to alleviate their sufferings. The ship's company were distributed amongst them for the night, but the poverty of the place afforded them little more than shelter.

The next morning a general muster was made, and it was ascertained that, of the whole company, twelve seamen, a woman, and her child, only were missing; these had either been frozen to death, or had died from the effects of cold, and the loss was small when compared with the hardships they had suffered. Several men had their legs and fingers frozen, but through proper medical treatment they all recovered. ·

The storm lasted without intermission till the night of the 5th, and during that time the crew of the Proserpine were suffering much from the want of necessary food, clothing, &c. Provisions were so scarce that they were all put upon short allowance; and their scanty store being nearly exhausted, it became absolutely necessary that part of them should proceed to Cuxhaven.

They learnt that at low water it was possible to get to Cuxhaven on foot; and as some of the islanders offered their services as guides, and the tide served, it was settled that the first lieutenant and half the officers and men should start with the guides on the morning of the 6th.

Mr. Grenville being very anxious to proceed on his mission to Berlin, determined to accompany the party, with the secretary to the embassy, and some of the servants; and they accordingly all set off at eight o'clock in the morning, the severity of the weather having somewhat abated.

Great as had been the difficulties they had encountered in their passage from the Proserpine to Newark Island, the dangers of their present expedition, over sand and ice, were nearly as formidable. At one part of their journey they found themselves on the banks of a river. The guides had assured them it was only a very narrow stream, and would most probably be frozen over: it proved, however, to be a river of considerable width; the ice was broken and floating upon it in large masses; the tide, too, was rising, and altogether the passage presented a formidable appearance. There was little time for deliberation, so the word was given to push forward, and the next moment they were up to their waists in the water, struggling against the tide and the large flakes of ice, which swept against them with such force that they had great difficulty in keeping their footing.

But through the mercy of Providence they all reached the opposite bank in safety, and before evening they arrived at Cuxhaven, without the loss of a single mán. Many of them were more or less frost-bitten, but by rubbing the parts affected with snow, circulation was restored.

We must now return to Captain Wallis and the officers and men who had remained with him at Newark, in hopes of being able to save some of the stores from the frigate.

On Friday, the 8th, Mr. Anthony, the master, volunteered with a party to endeavour to ascertain the state of the vessel, and if possible to bring away some bread, of which they were in much need.

They had great difficulty in reaching the ship, which they found lying on her beam ends, with seven feet and a half of water in her hold, having her quarter-deck separated six feet from her gangway, and apparently only kept together by the vast quantity of ice which surrounded her.

From this report, it was deemed unadvisable to make any more expeditions to the ship; but on the 10th, the clearness of the day induced Mr. Anthony, in company with the surgeon, a midshipman, the boatswain, and two seamen, to go off a second time.

Those who remained at Newark anxiously expected the return of the party, but they came not. Evening advanced, the tide was flowing, and at last it was too late for them to cross the sands and ice till the next ebb. The watchers were obliged to content themselves with the hope that Mr. Anthony and his party had found it safe and practicable to remain on board the frigate till morning. But during the night a violent storm arose, which increased the anxiety of Captain Wallis for the safety of his people; and this anxiety became deep distress, when in the morning he gazed wistfully towards the wreck, and saw nothing but the foaming waters, and moving fields of ice. Not a vestige of the frigate was visible. We cannot better describe Captain Wallis's feelings on this occasion than by quoting his own words, when he communicated the intelligence to Vice-Admiral Archibald Dickson.

'They got on board,' says Captain Wallis, 'but unfortunately neglected, until too late in the tide, to return, which left them no alternative but that of remaining on board till next day. About ten o'clock at night the wind came on at S.S.E., and blew a most violent storm; the tide, though at the neap, rose to an uncommon height, the ice got in motion, the velocity of which swept the wreck to destruction, (for in the morning not a vestige of her was to be seen,) and with it, I am miserably afraid, went the above unfortunate officers and men,—and if so, their loss will be a great one to the service, as, in their different departments, they were a great acquisition to it.

'The only hope I have is, that Providence which has so bountifully assisted us in our recent dangers and difficulties, may be extended towards them, so as to preserve their lives, by means of boat or otherwise; but I am very sorry to say my hopes are founded on the most distant degree of human probability. This melancholy accident happening so unexpectedly, added to my other misfortunes, has given so severe a shock to my health and spirits, as to prevent me hitherto undertaking the journey to Cuxhaven, where the survivors of the ship's company now are, except a few who are here with me, with whom I shall set out as soon as we are able.'

It is now necessary that we should follow the proceedings of Mr. Anthony and his party.

They reached the wreck at ten o'clock on Sunday morning; but, being busily occupied in collecting what stores they could, they neglected to watch the tide, and whilst they were thus employed, the time passed over, and the waves rolling between them and their temporary home at Newark; they were obliged to wait till the next day's ebb. During the night, as we have stated, the wind changed to the S.S.E.: it blew a violent gale, and the tide rose to such an unusual height, that it floated the ship, and the ice that had stuck to her, without the men on board being aware of it. The next morning, to their horror and dismay, they found the vessel drifting out to the ocean. We can scarcely imagine a situation more terrible than that in which these unfortunate men were placed. They were in all six persons, four officers and two seamen, and these few hands had to manage a frigate of 28 guns, which was actually going to pieces, and it was impossible to conjecture how long she might swim. She was merely buoyed up on the sea by the fields of ice that surrounded her; and if the ice were to break away, in all probability she would not hold together for an hour.

Mr. Anthony and his companions did not, however, give way to despair, nor lose time in useless repining. They set to work immediately, to avoid the danger as far as circumstances would permit.

Their first care was to drop the lead between two of the masses of ice, and they found that the ship was floatine in eleven fathoms. They then fired several guns, to give warning of their situation. By turns they worked at the pumps, and, in order to lighten the vessel, threw all the remaining guns, except four, overboard—a labour of no small magnitude for six men to perform.

Their next object was to get up the tackles for hoisting out the boat, in case of their getting into clear water, or being obliged to quit the wreck.

There was one advantage in all this hard labour, to which most of them were unaccustomed : it prevented their suffering so much as they otherwise must have done from the extreme cold ; and in one respect they were better off than their comrades at Newark, for they had plenty of provisions on board. So passed the first day on the wreck.

The next morning, Tuesday, the 12th, at about eleven o'clock, land was descried on their lee, on which they fired several guns, and hauled the colours on the main-rigging, union downwards, as a signal of distress. An hour afterwards the ship struck on a rock off the island of Baltrum, about a mile and a-half distant from the shore.

Mr. Anthony and his companions then tried to launch the cutter, but they were obliged to give up the attempt, as the sea was not sufficiently clear of ice ; they therefore remained on board another night.

The next morning, however, they hoisted out the boat, and pulled towards the shore ; but they had not gone more than half way, when they were surrounded by fields of ice, so that they were obliged to get upon the ice, and drag the boat with them.

About noon they had reached to within a cable's length of the shore, and here they were compelled to leave the boat : they were all completely exhausted, and found it impossible to drag her any further. They themselves had to leap from one piece of ice to another, often falling into the water; and it was at the imminent risk of their lives that they at last gained the beach.

They were tolerably well received by the inhabitants, who took them to their houses, and allowed them to seek that repose which they so much needed.

The next day the islanders, unable to resist the temptation of plunder, took to their boats, and made off to the ship, which they ransacked, and carried off all the arms, stores, and provisions of every kind. In vain Mr. Anthony protested against this base conduct : it was as much as he could do to persuade them to spare some part of the provisions for himself and his friends.

The party were obliged to remain at Baltrum amongst their rapacious hosts until Saturday, the 16th, when they deemed that the ice was sufficiently cleared away to allow of their sailing for Cuxhaven ; they accordingly secured the cutter and took their departure. As there was not the remotest chance of getting the Proserpine afloat again, they abandoned her to the island plunderers. They reached Cuxhaven about the 22nd, and there they found Lieutenant Wright and those who had accompanied him from Newark.

On the following day, Captain Wallis arrived, with the rest of the ship's company, the sick and wounded. We can imagine the joy and gratitude with which Captain Wallis received the announcement of the safe arrival of Mr. Anthony and his friends, whom he had deplored as lost.

Thus were the crew of the Proserpine, with the exception of thirteen persons, brought once more together after three weeks endurance of innumerable hardships, and having been exposed to many perils. Never was the Almighty hand of Providence more visibly displayed than in the protection afforded to these gallant fellows; and never did men do more to help themselves than they did. We cannot but admire the calm courage they evinced throughout that long and dismal night when almost certain destruction awaited them ; as well as their obedience and cheerful alacrity through their toilsome march from the wreck to Newark, and again from Newark to Cuxhaven. Nor must we forget the fortitude displayed by Mr. Anthony and his companions, when they were a second time wrecked in the Proserpine.

Throughout the history of their dangers and sufferings from cold and hunger, and the other evils attending a shipwreck on such an inhospitable shore and in such a climate, there is no mention of one single instance of murmuring, discontent, or disobedience of orders.

When the Elbe was again navigable and free from ice, the crew embarked in different packets and sailed for England, where they all arrived without further disasters.

THE SCEPTRE.

EARLY in the spring of 1799, a large convoy of transports and merchantmen sailed from the Cape of Good
Hope, with troops and stores for the siege of Seringapatam.
The Sceptre, 64 guns, commanded by Captain Valentine
Edwards, was appointed to the sole charge of the convoy, and to take Sir David Baird and the whole of the
84th regiment on board. The Sceptre may, perhaps, have
been the only king's ship then at the Cape; it is certain
that she had been an unusual length of time on that
station, and had become so weak and leaky as to be
hardly seaworthy, when she was dispatched on this important service.

Happily, the insecure state of the vessel induced extreme watchfulness on the part of both officers and men,
and all went on well till she had made about two-thirds
of her way, when one night a brisk gale sprung up,
which increased in violence so rapidly, that the officers
of the watch felt some anxiety on account of the unusual
strain upon the ship. Captain Edwards ordered the well
to be sounded, and the result confirming his apprehensions, the pumps were manned in an incredibly short
time, every one on board being aroused to a sense of
danger.

Lieutenant the Honourable Alexander Jones had been
relieved from the first watch, and had retired to his berth
about an hour before without any misgivings. He was
suddenly awakened by the alarming cry that the ship
was sinking, and the call of ' all hands.' He sprang up,
and in a few moments joined the group of officers, naval

and military, assembled on the quarter-deck. Anxiety was depicted on every countenance; for although the pumps were worked incessantly, the soldiers taking their turn with the sailors, the water was still gaining on them fast; and even whilst the men relieved each other, it rose several inches. But when human efforts were un-availing, the hand of Providence was stretched out to save. The wind fell as suddenly as it had risen, and after many hours of hard labour, the water was got under, and the vessel was considered comparatively safe.

Had the Sceptre gone down that night, hundreds and hundreds of England's best and bravest defenders must have sunk into a watery grave, and in all probability the enemy's ships, which were hovering upon the track of the convoy, would have got possession of the transports and merchantmen; and even the success of our arms in India might have been seriously affected.

A few weeks after the gale we have mentioned, the Sceptre and her convoy arrived safely at Bombay. She was there put into dock and repaired, and was strengthened by having large timbers, technically termed riders, bolted diagonally on either side, fore and aft.

When again fit for sea, she returned to Table Bay, and anchored there about the middle of October.

On the 1st of November, the captain and officers gave a ball to the inhabitants of Cape Town, and on that night the ship presented an appearance of unusual gaiety; mirth and music resounded on all sides; in place of the stern voice of command, the laugh, the jest, and the soft tones of woman's voice were heard; whilst many a light footstep glided over the decks of the old ship.

C

The lamps shone o'er fair women and brave men;
A thousand hearts beat happily; and when
Music arose with its voluptuous swell,
Soft eyes looked love to eyes that spake again,
And all went merry as a marriage bell.

CHILDE HAROLD.

The night was calm and beautiful, and as the guests left the ship, little did they think of the fearful doom that was so soon to overwhelm many of those whose hands they had clasped for the last time.

The weather continued perfectly calm till the evening of the 4th of November, when some ominous looking clouds indicated an approaching storm.

In addition to the Sceptre there remained in the Bay the Jupiter of 50 guns, the Oldenburg, a Danish 64 gun ship, and several other vessels. On the morning of the 5th, a strong gale blew from the north-west, but no danger was apprehended, and the ship, dressed in flags, and with the royal standard hoisted, fired her salute at noon in commemoration of the Gunpowder Treason.

The gale had increased considerably by two o'clock, and as Table Bay affords no shelter from a north-west wind, the captain took every precaution to make all secure; the topmasts were struck, and the fore and main-yards were lowered to ease the ship. But half-an-hour had not elapsed before the violence of the storm was such, that the ship parted from her best bower cable; the sheet anchor was immediately let go, and the cable veered away to twenty-eight fathoms. The storm gathered strength, and at half-past six the whole fury of the elements seemed to be concentrated in one terrific blast.

Orders were given to let go the anchor, with two of the forecastle guns attached; but even this proved insufficient to hold the ship.

One of the boats was then hoisted out, in order to communicate with the Jupiter, and procure the end of a cable from her, but in a few minutes the boat upset and was lost, with all her crew. For some hours signal guns of distress had been fired, and the ensign had been hoisted downwards, but no help could reach the vessel : in that tempestuous sea no boat could live. Some of the officers who had gone on shore the previous evening were standing on the beach, unable to render any assistance to their comrades, and compelled to remain inactive spectators of the harrowing scene, and to behold their brave ship foundering at her anchors.

About eight o'clock, loud above the howling of the tempest and the booming of the minute gun, arose the wild cry of *fire :* and thick smoke was discernible from the shore, issuing from the hatches. Now were the opposing elements of air, fire, and water combined for the destruction of the ill-fated ship. For an instant, all stood paralysed ; but it was only for an instant. Again the voices of the officers were raised in command, and every man was ready at his post.

The smoke came up from the hatches in such dense volumes, that all attempts to go below to extinguish the fire were abortive. Each man felt that his last hour was come,—there was not a shadow of hope that their lives could be saved ; it was but a choice of death by fire or water : to quit the ship must be fatal ; they had seen the boat and its crew swallowed up by the yawning waves, when the tempest raged less fiercely than now, and she was too far from the shore to afford even a ray of hope that the strongest swimmer might gain the beach. On the other hand, to remain on board was to encounter a still more terrible death—a burning funeral pile amidst the waters. While they hesitated in doubt and horror,

c 2

one of their fears was relieved,—the heavy sea that washed incessantly over the wreck extinguished the fire. The ship continued to drive at the mercy of the waves till about ten o'clock, when she stranded, broadside to the shore, heeling on her port side towards the sea.

The captain then ordered the main and mizen masts to be cut away, and the foremast soon afterwards went by the board. At this juncture, a man of the name of Connolly, a favourite with both officers and crew, volunteered to jump overboard with a deep-sea line attached to his body, in order to form a communication between the ship and the shore. He made but a few strokes ere he was borne away by the eddy and drowned.

The ship being lightened by the falling of the masts, righted herself and got clear off the ground : there appeared some slight chance of preservation, and every heart was buoyed up with hope that she might be thrown high enough upon the beach to enable the people on shore to render them some assistance.

She was driven nearer and nearer to the land—voices became more and more audible, so as even to be recognised—in a few minutes more, the perishing crew might be safe—when a heavy sea struck the ship, the orlop deck gave way, and the port side fell in—many were swept away,—those who had the power to do so, retreated to the starboard side.

A most heartrending scene must that have been ! The people were so benumbed with cold and exhaustion, and paralysed by fear, that many of them could no longer cling to the ropes and spars for support, and every wave that broke over the wreck, washed away its victims.

Many in despair leaped overboard, and attempted to swim to shore, but the eddy caused by the wreck was so

strong, that they were carried out to sea ; and in spite of
the attempts made by those on board to rescue them,
they all perished. Mr. Tucker, a midshipman, lost his
life in the endeavour to reach the bow of the ship.

About half an hour later the poop was washed away,
and carried towards the shore. Seventy or eighty men
who were upon it seemed likely to be saved from the
surrounding destruction. The people on the beach
crowded to the spot where they would probably be
driven, that they might render every possible assistance ;
but what was their horror to see a tremendous wave
strike the poop, capsize it, and turn it over and over,
whilst every one of those who clung to it perished !

But the terrors of that awful night were not yet
exhausted. The wreck, to which the remaining officers
and men were clinging, heeled towards the shore ; but
when the gale increased and blew with redoubled force,
it heeled off again, rent fore and aft, and parted in two
places—before the main-chains, and abaft the fore-chains
—and then all disappeared from the eyes of the awe-
stricken spectators on the beach.

High above the crash of timbers and the roaring of
the blast, rose the despairing cry of hundreds of human
beings who perished in the waters, and whose mutilated
forms, with the fragments of the wreck, strewed the
beach for miles on the following morning.

Thirty or forty seamen and marines still clung to the
bow, the sea breaking over them incessantly ; they kept
their hold, however, in the fond hope that the signal gun
remaining, might by its weight prevent the bow from
being capsized ; but the timbers, unable to resist the
fury of the tempest, suddenly parted,—the gun reeled
from side to side, and the unhappy men shared the fate
of their companions. It has been said that during that
awful time, whilst threatened with instant death, many

of these men were in a stupor, with their hands locked
in the chain plates.

Among the incidents connected with the wreck, it is
related that Mr. Buddle, a midshipman, (one of the few
who escaped,) was cast upon the waves almost insensible.
He had not strength to strike out for the beach, and he
therefore merely tried to keep himself above water.
This proved to be the means of saving his life, for he
floated in a direction parallel with the shore, and avoided
the huge pieces of wreck by which all his companions
who made directly for land (excepting three) were dashed
to pieces.

Mr. Buddle was nearly exhausted, when he caught
hold of a small piece of timber that was floating near
him; a nail which projected from it wounded him on the
breast; he fainted, and did not recover his senses until he
found himself lying on the beach upon a heap of dead
bodies. He attempted in vain to rise; for though he
felt no pain, his left leg was broken, his knee cut almost
half through, and his body much bruised. In this state
he was discovered, and carried by some persons to a large
fire until further assistance could be obtained, and he was
then conveyed to the hospital.

One of the officers of the Sceptre, who is still alive,
and who happened to be on shore at the time this terrible
catastrophe occurred, declares, that nothing imagination
could conceive ever equalled the horrors of that night.
When the first signals of distress were made from the
Sceptre, the whole population of Cape Town, with the
officers and soldiers of the garrison, crowded down to the
beach, in the vain hope of being able to afford some
assistance. The night was bitterly cold; the wind blew
with terrific violence, and the sea, lashed into fury, broke
with a deafening roar upon the beach. As night approached, and darkness hid the vessel from their sight,

the feelings of the agonized spectators became almost insupportable. The booming of the guns alone told that the ship still lived among the raging waters; whilst ever and anon a piercing shriek announced that the work of death had begun.

All along the beach large fires were lighted, as beacons to guide those who might be cast upon the shore. At length the ship was driven nearer, and again she became visible from the land. She appeared, says an eye-witness (before mentioned), like a huge castle looming in the distance. The hopes of the spectators revived as she heeled on towards them, and they all stood ready to give assistance whenever it should be available. At one moment, a fearful crash was heard—next, a piercing shriek, and the flash of the torches waved in the air displayed the struggling forms of the drowning seamen, tossed to and fro upon the waves amongst masses of the wreck, which, in many instances, killed those whom the waters would have spared.

The only help that the people on shore could render to the unhappy sufferers was, to watch the opportunity when the waves brought a body near to the land, and then to rush into the water, holding one another at arm's length, and to grasp the exhausted creature before he was borne back by the receding wave.

In this manner forty-seven men were saved, together with Mr. Shaw, a master's mate, and two midshipmen, of the names of Spinks and Buddle, before-mentioned. Six officers had fortunately been on shore at the time; all the others, with the captain, were lost on the wreck, together with about three hundred and ninety-one seamen and marines.

The people of Cape Town and the troops were employed the whole night in searching for the dead, amongst whom they discovered the son of Captain Edwards, with one hand grasping an open Bible, which was pressed to his bosom, the parting gift, perhaps, of a fond mother, who had taught the boy to revere in life that sacred volume, from which he parted not in death.

Three waggon-loads of the dead were next morning taken to a place near the hospital, and there buried. About one hundred bodies, shockingly mangled, were buried in one pit on the beach. The remains of all the officers (with the exception of Captain Edwards) were found, and were interred the following Sunday with military honours.

The reader may be interested by being informed of a few of the providential escapes which were experienced by Lieutenant Jones (now Rear-Admiral Jones), one of the few survivors of the catastrophe above described. This officer had been midshipman of the Providence, discovery-ship, commanded by Captain William Broughton, which vessel, after many dangerous vicissitudes, was finally wrecked among the Japanese islands. Mr. Jones having faced all the dangers consequent on such a trying position, with difficulty escaped a watery grave, by taking refuge, with the rest of the officers and crew, on board the tender which accompanied this ill-fated ship. This great addition to her small complement, and her want of accommodation, produced a virulent disease amongst the crew, from which Mr. Jones did not escape. On arrival at Macao, Mr. Jones was ordered a passage, with his surviving shipmates and crew of the Providence, to England, in the Swift, sloop of war, selected to convoy a large fleet of Indiamen. The evening before their departure, it was found that the accommodation in the Swift was not sufficient for the supernumeraries, and, consequently, Mr. Jones and Lord George Stuart (also a midshipman of the Providence) were, by order of Captain Broughton, distributed among the merchant ships, the former to the Carnatic, the latter to the Duke of Buccleugh. The Swift and her convoy sailed on the morrow. They had not proceeded far, before a succession of violent typhoons overtook them, which scattered and disabled the Indiamen, most of which were obliged to return to India; but the Swift foundered: she was seen for a short time struggling with the elements, and making signals of distress—a moment more, and she disappeared for ever.

Mr. Jones, arriving at the Cape of Good Hope, was detained by Rear Admiral Pringle, and employed to communicate with his flag-ship, the Tremendous, then in a state of mutiny, the mutineers having put her officers ashore. His courage on this occasion was much lauded, as it was believed by all, and expected by himself, that he would have been thrown overboard. Harmony was at length restored on board the Tremendous, and six of the mutineers were executed. As a reward for his services, Mr. Jones was appointed acting lieutenant of the Sceptre : his preservation, and the part he acted on that occasion, have already been described.

When lieutenant of the Ajax, attached to the fleet under Sir J. Borlase Warren, lying in Vigo Bay, he was sent with a boat's crew to the assistance of the Tartarus, sloop of war, which ship was then driving to leeward in a gale on a rocky shore. So inevitable appeared her destruction, that the officers and crew had abandoned her, after letting go an anchor, to retard her expected crash against the rocks. At this critical moment, whilst held by only one strand of the cable, Lieutenant Jones's boat (although nearly swamped by the frequent shipping of seas) neared the ship; and this officer, watching an opportunity, sprung on board with his intrepid crew, and, by almost superhuman exertions, succeeded in hauling her a-head. She had just reached the point of

safety, when her officers and crew, who witnessed her
more favourable position, brought about by Lieutenant
Jones's courage and perseverance, returned on board, and
Lieutenant Jones and his gallant followers rejoined their
ship amidst the cheers of the fleet. For this service
Lieutenant Jones was sent for by the commander-in-
chief, and thanked by him on the quarter-deck of his
flag-ship.

As lieutenant of the Naiad, this officer had the misfortune to be involved in a serious quarrel with his superior
officer (Lieutenant Dean), and on that person using very
abusive, and unofficer-like language, Lieutenant Jones
struck him. A court martial being held, Lieutenant
Jones was sentenced to be hanged ; but, in consideration
of the very provoking language used by Lieutenant
Dean, and Lieutenant Jones's previous irreproachable
conduct, his Majesty George the Third was graciously
pleased to pardon him, and restore him to his former
position in the Navy, while Lieutenant Dean was dis-
missed the service.

THE QUEEN CHARLOTTE.

ONE of the greatest calamities that ever befel a ship belonging to the British Navy was the destruction of the Queen Charlotte of 100 guns, launched in 1790. She was the sister-ship to the Royal George, and was destined to a no less tragical fate. Her first cruise was with the fleet fitted out against Spain; Lord Howe, the commander-in-chief, being on board of her; and she carried his flag on the 1st of June.

She was afterwards sent to the Mediterranean, under the command of Captain James Todd, and bearing the flag of Vice-Admiral Lord Keith. Before entering upon our narrative, we may be permitted to apologize for any inaccuracy, or lack of incident, that may be apparent in the following account, by stating that the official reports of the disaster are so vague and imperfect, that it is almost impossible to give the details of it as fully as we could wish; and so many years have elapsed since the event, that we cannot obtain information from private sources.

On the 16th of March, 1800, Lord Keith, with Lieutenant Stewart, and four other persons, having landed at Leghorn, directed Captain Todd to proceed in the Queen Charlotte to reconnoitre the Island of Cabrera, about thirty miles from Leghorn, then in possession of the French, and which it was his lordship's intention to attack.

At four o'clock on the morning of the 17th, the men who were washing the decks stowed some hay close aft to the admiral's cabin, near a match-tub, in which it was usual to keep a match burning, for the purpose of firing signals. At six o'clock, when the men were in the act of

removing the hay, a portion of it was discovered to have
ignited. Not a moment was lost in giving the alarm,
and those at hand used every means in their power to
extinguish the slumbering element; but the fire had
been smouldering for some time before it was discovered.
The water thrown upon it from the buckets was useless
—the flames bursting forth with such violence that they
baffled the most strenuous efforts to overcome them. Such
was the posture of affairs when the captain, officers, and
men, alarmed by the cry of fire, rushed from all parts of
the ship to the scene of conflagration. It would be no
easy task to describe the feelings of a number of human
beings thus suddenly and awfully awakened to the perils
of their situation. For the moment, no doubt, fear pre-
dominated over every other feeling, and a degree of confusion ensued. Nor can this be regarded with astonishment, when we remember that of all the dangers to which
a sailor is familiarized in his hazardous profession, none
is so fraught with horror as a fire at sea.

The battle has no terror for him : he rushes to the
conflict excited by the cheers of his comrades and the
hopes of victory—

> Though fore and aft the blood-stained deck,
>   Should lifeless trunks appear,
> Or should the vessel float a wreck,
>   The sailor knows no fear.

He glories in the stormy sea, and in 'the wild wind's
roar:' they fill him with a fierce delight, while with steady
hand and steadfast heart he obeys the voice of his commander ; he trusts to his good ship, and 'laughs at the
storm and the battle.'

But how differently does he feel, when roused from his
deep slumber by the cry of fire. He rushes upon deck,
but half awake, to meet an enemy far more terrible than

any he has yet encountered. He finds himself enveloped in a suffocating smoke—here and there gleams a lurid flame—the fire becomes gradually more vivid : it rises higher and higher ; grows brighter and brighter. In vain he looks for help,—beneath, nothing meets his eye but the boundless waste of waters, that can avail so little to quench those flames ; above, the pathless fields of air, that serve but to increase their fury. The insidious enemy quietly but surely creeps onward, and the sailor knows but too well, that if not speedily arrested, the flames must reach the powder magazine, and then a few smouldering fragments strewed upon the waters will alone remain of the gallant ship and her living freight.

Such was the hideous form in which death presented itself to the minds of the crew of the Queen Charlotte, who now anxiously turned their eyes to their captain and officers, in the hope that, as on former occasions, their example and assistance might enable them to avert the threatened danger. Nor was their confidence misplaced.

Captain Todd and his first lieutenant (Mr. Bainbridge) stood upon the quarter-deck, displaying a calmness and self-possession of which the effects were soon felt throughout the vessel, and restored order among the ship's company.

They went among the people, calming their fears, and encouraging them to increased exertion, neither of them seeming for a moment to think of his own safety in comparison with that of his companions in danger.

All that man could do in such a case was done ; but human foresight and presence of mind were of no avail against the irresistible power of that relentless enemy.

The flames darted up the mainmast, reached the boats upon the boom, and now wrapped in wreathing fires the whole of the quarter-deck, from whence all had been driven save the captain and first lieutenant, who still nobly kept their posts.

Amongst those who more particularly distinguished themselves on this occasion (where all did their duty) was Lieutenant the Hon. G. H. L. Dundas. This officer was roused from his sleep by the sentinel announcing to him that the ship was on fire. Springing from his cot, he hastily put on some clothes and attempted to ascend the after hatchway, but was driven back by the smoke. He then went to the main hatchway, and had almost reached the top of the ladder, when he was so overpowered, that he fell exhausted upon the middle deck.

When he had in some degree recovered, he rushed to the fore hatchway and thence to the forecastle, where he found the first lieutenant, some petty officers, and the greater part of the ship's company. These were endeavouring to haul up the mainsail which was in flames. The carpenter, seeing Lieutenant Dundas, suggested that he might direct some of the men to sluice the lower decks, and secure the hatchways, to prevent the fire reaching that part of the ship.

Mr. Dundas collected about seventy men, who volunteered to accompany him, and descended to the lower decks. The ports were opened, the cocks turned, and water thrown upon the decks. All the hammocks were cleared away, and as many people as could be spared were employed in heaving water upon the burning wood, rigging, and spars, which kept falling down the hatchways. The gratings were fastened down and covered over with wet blankets and hammocks. In this way the lower deck was kept free from fire for some time, until at length it broke out in both of the transom cabins, and burnt forward with great rapidity. Mr. Dundas and his party did not leave that part of ship, till several of the middle guns came through the deck.

At nine o'clock, finding it impossible to remain longer below, he got out of one of the starboard lower deck ports, and reached the forecastle, followed by most of the officers and men who had been with him. On the forecastle, about 250 men were drawing water, and throwing it upon the fire as far aft as possible.

For nearly four hours every exertion was made to subdue the flames. Officers and men behaved with heroic courage and self-possession ; but in spite of their almost superhuman efforts, the flames rolled on, and the destruction of the ship became inevitable.

> With fruitless toil the crew oppose the flame,
> No art can now the spreading mischief tame.

And many of that gallant company verified the poet's description : almost maddened by the intense heat, they sprung overboard and perished.

> Some, when the flames could be no more withstood,
> By wild despair directed, 'midst the flood,
> Themselves in haste from the tall vessel threw,
> And from a dry to liquid ruin flew.
> Sad choice of death, when those who shun the fire,
> Must to as fierce an element retire.

Lieut. Archibald Duff, who had been alarmed by the firing of guns, attempted to get out of the ward-room door, but was driven back by the smoke. He at last succeeded in scrambling out of the quarter gallery, and reached the poop, from whence he jumped into the sea, and was picked up by the launch, when in the act of casting off the tow-rope. He had hardly left the ship when the mizen-mast fell over the side, by which great numbers were thrown into the water, and left struggling in the waves; for, as the launch had only one oar, and neither sail nor mast, she drifted much faster than the men could swim, and many, whom those on board her would gladly have saved, perished within a few feet of the boat.

At length a ray of hope dawned upon the anxious survivors : vessels and boats were seen coming towards them from Leghorn ; and as they neared the ship, every heart beat quicker, and every hand was nerved with increased strength. But the boats' crews, alarmed by the explosion of the guns, which were most of them shotted, refused to approach nearer, and hove to. Seeing their hesitation, the crew of the Queen Charlotte gave them three cheers to encourage them. The English cheers seemed to have the desired effect, for again the boats pulled towards the hapless vessel ; but it was afterwards discovered that this renewed activity was entirely owing to the persuasions of Lieut. Stewart and other English officers who were in the boats.

Lord Keith, who was watching with intense anxiety the destruction of his noble ship, used every possible effort to induce the Tuscans to put to sea ; but his entreaties, backed as they were by the commands of the governor and other authorities, had no influence save with a few only, and even these, when they did venture to the rescue, were with great difficulty prevailed upon to approach the vessel. A boat from an American ship presented a striking contrast. She was manned by three men only, who, in their generous ardour to save the lives of their fellow-creatures, came alongside too incautiously, so that the wretched sufferers from the burning deck leaped into the boat in such numbers that she capsized, and every one of them perished. The fire had now advanced so rapidly that it was impossible to bear the heat on the forecastle, and most of the people got on to the bowsprit and jib-boom. The latter, however, gave way under the pressure, and numbers were precipitated into the water and drowned.

The boats, headed by Lieutenant Stewart, approached about ten o'clock, and the people continued dropping into them from the ship for some time. Captain Todd and Mr. Bainbridge continued to the last to give orders for the safety of those who remained alive.

Lieutenant Duff gives the following account of the closing scene :—

'Lieutenant Stewart's ardour in the cause of humanity was only equalled by his judgment in affording relief. When he reached the Queen Charlotte, he dropped his tartane under the bows, where almost all the remaining crew had taken refuge. Little more than an hour had elapsed, after this assistance was given, before the ship blew up. All that had been left unburnt immediately sunk down by the stern, but when the ponderous contents of the hold had been washed away, she for an instant recovered her buoyancy, and was suddenly seen to emerge almost her whole length from the deep, and then, turning over, she floated on the surface, with her burnished copper glistening in the sun.'

Such was the fate of the Queen Charlotte, which, excepting the Ville de Paris, was the largest ship in the British navy.

With the gallant vessel perished six hundred and seventy-three of her men and officers ; amongst whom were Captain Todd and Lieutenant Bainbridge. These two officers, with heroic self-devotion, remained to share the fate of their ship, occupied to the last in endeavouring to save the lives of the men.

Before Captain Todd fell a victim to the flames, he had the presence of mind to write the particulars of the melancholy event, and to give copies of his account to several of the sailors, charging them to deliver it to the admiral if they should be so fortunate as to escape.*

The following daring exploit is related of Lieutenant Bainbridge in James's *Naval History*. We transcribe it as affording a striking example of the union of undaunted courage with endurance in the character of a British sailor.

"On the evening of the 21st of December, the British hired 10 gun cutter, Lady Nelson, while off Carbareta Point, was surrounded and engaged by two or three French privateers, and some gun vessels, in sight of the 100 gun ship, Queen Charlotte, and the 36 gun frigate Emerald, lying in Gibraltar Bay. Vice-Admiral Lord Keith, whose flag was flying on board the former ship, immediately ordered the boats of the two to row towards the combatants, in the hope that it might encourage the Lady Nelson to resist, until she could approach near enough to be covered by the guns of the ships. Before the boats could get up, however, the Lady Nelson had been captured, and was in tow by two of the privateers.

"Notwithstanding this, Lieutenant Bainbridge, in the Queen Charlotte's barge, with sixteen men, ran alongside, and boarded with the greatest impetuosity; and after a sharp conflict, carried the Lady Nelson, taking as prisoners seven French officers and twenty-seven men,— six or seven others having been killed or knocked overboard in the scuffle. Lieutenant Bainbridge was severely wounded in the head by the stroke of a sabre, and slightly in other places."

We have seen how, a few months afterwards, this brave officer patiently anticipated death in a more terrible form on board the Queen Charlotte.

---

* *Naval Chronicle*, vol. iii. p. 302.

THE INVINCIBLE.

THE Invincible, of 74 guns, bearing the flag of Rear-Admiral Totty, and commanded by Captain Rennie, sailed from Yarmouth on the morning of the 16th of March, 1801, to join the · fleet of Admiral Sir Hyde Parker in the Baltic.

The master and the pilot were both considered very skilful mariners of those seas, and their orders were to navigate the ship into the North Sea, and to put her in the way of joining the fleet to the northward, as soon as she had cleared all the shoals.

About half-past two o'clock, P.M., of the same day, the Invincible, going at the rate of nine knots an hour, struck violently upon a sand-bank, and before the sails could be furled, she was fast aground in little more than three fathoms water.

The pilot and master assured Captain Rennie that there was no danger, and that the ship must have struck upon a lately formed knowl. In order to lighten her as much as possible, the yards and topmasts were struck, and some of the provisions thrown overboard, and then strong hopes were entertained that she would float off the bank with the next tide.

During this time she lay tolerably quiet, and the water gained but little upon the pumps. Every means was used to draw the attention of vessels passing near—guns were fired, and signals hoisted ; but they remained unanswered until about five o'clock, P.M., when a cutter was observed scudding towards Yarmouth Roads, as if to inform Admiral Dickson of the situation of the Invincible. As the ship remained easy, neither the officers nor men suspected that the danger was imminent, and they performed their duty with the same regularity as if the ship were proceeding under ordinary circumstances.

All went on well until about half-past five, P.M., when the wind freshened, and the vessel began to beat the ground with such violence, that it was thought necessary to cut away the masts. The ship at this time dropped from three and a half into seventeen fathoms. She was then brought to with her bower anchor, and there appeared every probability of her getting safely off till about nine o'clock, when the flood-tide was making; she then lost her rudder, became unmanageable, and was driven back upon the rock.

Fortunately a fishing-smack had come near the Invincible a short time before, and Admiral Totty learnt from her master that the ship had struck upon Hammond's knowl; whereupon the admiral requested that the smack might be anchored as near as possible, so as to be ready in case of emergency.

In the meantime, the ship continued to strike with increasing violence, and the water gained considerably upon the pumps. At ten o'clock, the wind rose, and again the ship swung off into deep water, and the only prospect of saving her was by pumping and baling till daylight. Both officers and men laboured incessantly at the pumps, but all to no purpose, for unfortunately the Invincible was an old ship (built in the year 1766), and the water gained fast upon them in spite of all their efforts. Admiral Totty, seeing there was no hope of saving the ship, ordered Captain Rennie to send all the boys, and the least able of the crew and passengers, on board the smack, and to make arrangements for the rest of the crew to leave the ship at day-break, or sooner, if possible.

A boat was lowered, into which the admiral and his secretary immediately descended, with as many others as she would carry, and they reached the smack in safety.

Two other boats were also lowered and filled with people, but they were less fortunate than the admiral's, for before they reached the smack, the tide being to windward and against them, they were carried out to sea, and all on board would inevitably have perished, if they had not been picked up by a collier, which conveyed them in safety to Yarmouth.

The fishing-smack, with the admiral on board, remained at anchor during the night, without being able to afford the slightest assistance to the crew of the Invincible. At daybreak, as soon as the tide permitted, the cable of the smack was cut, and she stretched under the stern of the ship, endeavouring by all possible means to get alongside of her, but before that could be accomplished, the ill-fated vessel began to sink. About sixty men jumped into the launch, but they had only just time to clear the poop, when the gallant ship went down with four hundred men.

> And first one universal shriek there rush'd,
>   Louder than the loud ocean, like a crash
> Of echoing thunder, and then all was hush'd,
>   Save the wild wind and the remorseless dash
> Of billows: but at intervals there gushed,
>   Accompanied with a convulsive splash,
> A solitary shriek, the bubbling cry
> Of some strong swimmer in his agony.
>   LORD BYRON.

'The horror of the scene,' writes Admiral Totty, 'and the screams of the unhappy sufferers, at the moment the ship went down, exceed all power of description. Numbers who were struggling with the waves attempted to lay hold of the launch, but the boat was already overladen, and, for the safety of those who were in her, the drowning wretches were beaten off, and, soon exhausted, they perished in the waves.'

Captain Rennie remained in his ship till she sank. He then attempted to swim to the launch, and by great exertion got within reach of her oars, when, too much exhausted to make any further effort, he was seen to raise his hands as if in supplication to Heaven, then putting them before his face, sank into his watery grave. All the other commissioned officers, with the exception of Lieutenants Robert Tucker and Charles Quart, perished.

Captain Rennie had distinguished himself, when a lieutenant, at the Helder ; and Admiral Mitchell had mentioned him in such high terms of commendation in his public despatches, that he was made a post-captain. After remaining for some time unemployed, he was appointed to the Invincible, and proud of his first command, full of life and hope, he had just put to sea when this melancholy catastrophe closed a career that held out such bright prospects for the future.

We must not be supposed to have more feeling for an officer than for the men before the mast. If we dwell with peculiar sorrow upon the loss of a brave commander, like Captain Rennie, it is not that we are indifferent to the fate of the four hundred gallant men who perished with him; but there is something in human nature that compels even the most generous spirit to speak more of the loss of a man in a responsible station than others ; and one reason for this may be, that our hopes under God, for the safety of our fleets and our armies, rest on our brave and efficient commanders.

No one can read such records of British seamen, as appear in this volume, without joining heart and soul in the sentiment expressed by the poet :—

> To them your dearest rights you owe ;
> In peace, then, would you starve them ?
> What say ye, Britain's sons ?   Oh, no !
> Protect them and preserve them ;

Shield them from poverty and pain;
'Tis policy to do it:
Or when grim war shall come again,
Oh, Britons! ye may rue it.

Lieutenant Robert Tucker, who was saved in the launch, accompanied Rear-Admiral Totty to the Baltic and West Indies in the Zealous, 74. He was subsequently promoted, and appointed to the Surinam in 1803.

Whilst the Surinam was on the West India station, Captain Tucker rendered good service to the French garrison at Jacquemel; and on returning from thence, his ship sprung her foremast, and was in other respects so much damaged, that he was obliged to put in at Curaçoa. Whilst refitting, he received private information that Great Britain and Holland would ere long be declared enemies. He therefore made every effort to hasten his departure, and get his ship ready for sea; and he had warped her to the head of the harbour, when a prize schooner which he had despatched to Commodore Hood returned from that officer, with orders for his future guidance. The officer on board the schooner incautiously permitted his vessel to touch at the government wharf, when some of the crew, having the opportunity imprudently afforded them, jumped on shore, and reported that the British had already commenced hostilities.

Upon this the Surinam was detained, and Captain Tucker was ordered on shore, and informed that he must consider himself a prisoner of war. At first he was not put under strict surveillance, and he therefore employed the weary hours in taking plans of the forts and batteries of the island. His occupation, however, was soon discovered, and highly disapproved by the authorities, who immediately placed him in close confinement in a room of the barracks.

On the first night of his captivity two musket-balls were fired into his room, one of which struck a table at which he had been seated a few moments before. These murderous attempts were frequently repeated during his imprisonment, and he must inevitably have been shot in his bed, had he not taken the precaution of constantly moving its position, and thus baffled the treacherous designs of his cowardly assailants.

A friendly warning was given to him, that where bullets failed, *poison* might succeed; and he was thenceforth obliged to watch most narrowly, lest it should be administered in his food. In this wretched state of suspense, he lingered for four months, when happily he and his officers were released in exchange for nine Dutch clergymen.

We regret that our pen should have to record such treachery as that we have described. We ask, and others have asked, were these soldiers and gaolers free men and Christians, or were they slaves and heathens? It must, however, be remembered that politics ran very high at that time; and in this particular instance, at the outbreak of a war, men's minds were half frantic, and we must not judge of the character of a nation by the isolated acts of a petty colonial government.

THE GRAPPLER.

CHAUSSEY, or Choyé, is a group of islets lying off the coast of Normandy, about twenty miles from Jersey, and nine from Granville. They stretch north, east, and west, and cover a space of nearly twelve miles. The principal of them is called the Maitre Isle, and is the resort of a few French fishermen during the summer, but being only a rock, and totally devoid of vegetation, its inhabitants are entirely dependent on the neighbouring shores for all the necessaries of life, excepting what their nets may produce. At the time of which we are writing, the winter of 1803, this group of islets was in the hands of the English, and was the scene of the wreck of the Grappler in that year.

On the 23rd December, 1803, Lieutenant Abel Thomas, commanding His Majesty's brig Grappler, then stationed at Guernsey, was directed by Admiral Sir James Saumarez to proceed, with some French prisoners on board, to Granville, in Normandy, and there to set them at liberty; after which he was to touch at the islands of Chaussey, on his return to Guernsey, in order to supply twelve French prisoners who were on the Maitre Isle with fifteen days' provisions.

On the evening of the 23rd,—the same day that they sailed from Guernsey,—the Grappler anchored off the north side of Chaussey, but a heavy gale of wind which came on during the night rendered her position so dangerous, that Lieutenant Thomas thought it advisable either to return to Guernsey, or to run into one of the small harbours formed among the rocks, which afford a safe shelter during the severest gales, but are by no means easy of access, and are available only to small

D

vessels, and with the aid of an experienced pilot. Into
one of these natural harbours, Lieutenant Thomas, by
the advice of his pilot, determined to run the Grappler,
and succeeded in anchoring her in safety under the
Maitre Isle. There they remained four or five days,
keeping a sharp look-out by day from the top of one of
the adjacent rocks, to guard against a surprise from the
enemy's cruizers; while for their better security at night,
a guard-boat was stationed at the entrance of the harbour. As the weather still continued too boisterous to
trust the brig with safety on a lee shore, her commander
determined to return to Guernsey, and offered his
prisoners the alternative of returning with him, or remaining with their countrymen at Chaussey. As they
all chose to remain, they were promptly landed, and
furnished with a boat and a week's supply of provisions,
in addition to what had already been left for the use of
the inhabitants. To enable his prisoners to land with
greater security at Granville, Lieutenant Thomas read
aloud and sealed in their presence a letter, addressed by
Sir James Saumarez to the Commissary of Marine at
that port, containing an explanation of his reasons
for liberating these Frenchmen,—with his hopes that
the French authorities would act in the same manner
towards any English who might fall into their hands,—
and entrusted it to one of them, with another letter from
himself, in which he stated how he had been prevented
from conveying them to Granville in his own vessel, and
begged that any English prisoners who chanced to be at
that place might be sent to one of the Channel Islands.
The sequel will show in what manner this courtesy and
generosity were repaid by the French government.

At six, A.M., December 30th, all was in readiness for the
Grappler to leave the harbour. The anchor was up, and
the vessel was riding between wind and tide, with a hawser

made fast to the rocks. Unfortunately, the hawser either broke or slipped while they were in the act of close reefing the topsails, and the brig cast to port. She drifted about three or four hundred yards, and struck at last on a half-tide rock, from which all their efforts were unavailing to haul her off again, and at low water she bilged, and parted in two abreast the chess tree.

Lieutenant Thomas, foreseeing the inevitable loss of the brig, had ordered the master to proceed with the cutter and eight men to Jersey for assistance ; and he was directing the crew in their endeavours to mount some guns upon a small rocky islet, to which they had already carried the greater part of the provisions, small arms, and ammunition, when the look-out man, who had been stationed on the summit of the rock, reported that several small craft were steering towards them. Upon receiving this intelligence, the commander and pilot repaired to the high ground, and after carefully examining the appearance of the vessels, agreed that they were merely fishing boats, and considered that it would be imprudent to let them depart before assistance had been procured from Jersey, as, in case there were no ships of war at that place, these boats might possibly be hired to carry the men and stores to Jersey. With this object in view, Lieutenant Thomas pushed off in the jolly boat, accompanied by the French fishermen's small boat which had come to the assistance of the Grappler's crew.

In order to approach the supposed fishing boats, it was necessary to double a point of the Maitre Isle ; and this they had no sooner accomplished, than they came in sight of three chasse marées, which had been concealed behind the point. On the sudden appearance of the English boat, the men on board the chasse marées were thrown into some confusion, and Lieutenant Thomas determined to attack them before they had time to recover themselves. On communicating his intention to his boat's crew, they dashed forwards at once with a loud cheer, but had scarcely pulled a dozen strokes when a body of soldiers, who had been concealed behind some rocks on the Maitre Isle, poured in so severe a fire that Lieutenant Thomas, seeing the superiority of the French in point of numbers, thought it prudent to retreat. No sooner had he given orders to do so, than a shot struck him on the lower jaw and passed through his tongue, rendering him incapable of further exertion. A second volley of musketry riddled the boat, so that she began to fill with water, and finding that they had no alternative but to surrender, the English made a signal to that effect, which was either unobserved, or purposely disregarded, as the firing did not cease till the arrival of the officer in command of the French, when the little party were all made prisoners. Upon Lieutenant Thomas being carried on shore, he found that he had fallen into the hands of a Capitaine de Frigate, who commanded a detachment of fourteen boats and a hundred and sixty men. As soon as the captives were landed, a party of the French troops proceeded to the wreck of the Grappler, and made prisoners of the men who were on the adjacent rock, and after seizing all the stores and provisions, they blew up the remains of the brig.

When Lieutenant Thomas had partially recovered from the faintness and insensibility caused by his wound, he handed his pocket-book to the French officer. After reading the orders of Sir James Saumarez, which it contained, this officer expressed much regret that Lieutenant Thomas had been so seriously wounded, and alleged that the troops had fired without his orders. Such was the apology of the French commander, but it certainly does not tell well for the discipline of his troops, nor is it easy to understand how so large a body of men could be left without a commissioned officer even for a moment, much less how they could have kept up a continued fire, which this seems to have been. Perhaps, however, it is not fair to comment too severely upon the conduct of the French on this occasion ; the signal of surrender might not have been observed, and as the English had commenced the attack, the enemy may naturally have supposed that a larger force was shortly advancing to the support of their comrades. We should also bear in mind that the war had just broke out anew, after a short cessation of hostilities, and that national animosity was at its height.

Thus far we may attempt to palliate the conduct of the French, but it might naturally be supposed that upon learning from his papers the errand of mercy upon which Lieutenant Thomas had been engaged, the French officer would have done all in his power to alleviate the sufferings of his prisoner, and have shown him every mark of courtesy and attention. However this may be, no sooner were all arrangements completed, than the prisoners were marched to the boats, and Lieutenant Thomas was handed over to the care of two grenadiers, with directions that every attention should be paid to him ; but the officer's back was scarcely turned, when these grenadiers, assisted by some of their comrades, stripped poor Thomas of all his clothes, broke open his trunk, which had been restored to him, and appropriated to themselves every article of value that he possessed. Having secured their plunder, they dragged their unfortunate victim to the beach, regardless of his wound and sufferings, and after gagging him with a pocket-handkerchief, threw him on the deck of one of their boats.

The wind blowing fresh on their passage to Granville,

which was three leagues from Chaussey, the greater part
of the soldiers were prostrated by sea-sickness, whilst the
seamen were in such a state of intoxication, that had
Lieutenant Thomas been able to rise, or to communicate
with his fellow-prisoners, he might easily have overpowered the French, and gained possession of the vessel.
If such an idea flashed across his mind, it was but for a
moment : he could neither speak nor move, and lay for
many hours exposed to the insulting jeers of the French,
and the inclemency of the weather.   It was late at night
when they landed at Granville, but the naval and
military staff waited upon Mr. Thomas the next morning,
and told him that it was the intention of the authorities
to send him back to England, in consideration of his
kindness to the French prisoners.   The expectation raised
in the English officer's breast by these promises were, to
the disgrace of the French government of that day, never
realized.   He was thrown into prison, and treated with
the utmost severity ; in vain did he protest against this
injustice—in vain did he represent that he was engaged
on no hostile expedition at the time of his capture,
which, moreover, was not through the fortune of war, but
through the violence of the elements.   He was kept in
close confinement at Verdun for ten years, and when he
was at last released, liberty was scarcely a boon to him.
The damp of his prison, and the sufferings attendant on
his wound, had impaired his eyesight, and otherwise so
injured his constitution, that he was no longer fit for active
service.   He was, however, promoted to the rank of commander immediately on his return to England : this
rank he still holds, but the best years of his life had
been spent in captivity, and his hopes of promotion were
not realized till too late for the enjoyment of its honours,
or for the service of his country.

THE APOLLO.

THE following account of the loss of the Apollo is taken almost verbatim from the narrative of Mr. Lewis, clerk of the ship, an eye-witness of the occurrence. His narrative is too graphic to be suppressed :—
'On Monday, the 26th of March, 1804, His Majesty's ship Apollo sailed from the Cove of Cork in company with the Carysfort, and sixty-nine sail of merchantmen under convoy, for the West Indies. On the 27th, we were out of sight of land, with a fair wind blowing fresh from the west-south-west. At eight o'clock on the evening of Sunday, the 1st of April, the wind shifted from south-west to south-east. At ten o'clock, we up mainsail and set mainstay-sail. At a quarter past ten, the mainstay-sail split by the sheet giving way. All hands were called upon deck. It blew strong and squally; we took in the foretop-sail and set the foresail. At half-past eleven the maintop-sail split; furled it and the mainsail. The ship was now under her foresails, the wind blowing hard, with a heavy sea.
'At about half-past three on Monday morning, April 2nd, the ship struck the ground, to the astonishment of every one on board, and by the last reckoning, we conjectured we were upon an unknown shoal.
'The vessel struck very heavily several times, by which her bottom was materially injured, and she made a great deal of water. The chain pumps were rigged with the utmost despatch, and the men began to pump, but in about ten minutes she beat and drove over the shoal, and on endeavouring to steer her, they found her rudder was carried away. The ship was then got before the

wind, the pumps were kept going, but from the quantity
of water shipped, there was every probability of her
soon foundering, as she was filling and sinking very fast.

' After running about five minutes, the ship struck the
ground again with such violent shocks, that we feared
she would go to pieces instantly; however, she kept
striking and driving further on the sands, the sea washing completely over her. Orders were given to cut away
the lanyards of the main and mizen rigging, when the
masts fell with a tremendous crash over the larboard-
side: the foremast followed immediately after. The ship
then fell on her starboard-side, with the gunwale under
water. The violence with which she struck the ground
and the weight of the guns (those on the quarter-deck
tearing away the bulwarks) soon made the ship a perfect
wreck abaft, and only four or five guns could possibly be
fired to alarm the convoy and give notice of danger.

' On her drifting a second time, most pitiful cries were
heard everywhere between decks; many of the men
giving themselves up to inevitable death. I was told
that I might as well stay below, as there was an equal
likelihood of perishing if I got upon deck. I was, however, determined to go—and attempted, in the first place,
to enter my cabin, but I was in danger of having my
legs broken by the chests floating about, and the bulk-
heads giving way.

' I therefore desisted and endeavoured to get upon deck,
which I effected after being several times washed down
the hatchway by the immense body of water incessantly
pouring down. As the ship still beat the ground very heavily,
it was necessary to cling fast to some part of the wreck to
save oneself from being washed away by the surges, or
hurled overboard by the concussions. The people held
on by the larboard bulwark of the quarter-deck and in

the main chains. The good captain stood naked upon
the cabin skylight grating, making use of every soothing
expression that suggested itself—to encourage men in
such a perilous situation. Most of the officers and men
were entirely naked, not having had time to slip on even
a pair of trousers.

'Our horrible situation became every moment more
dreadful, until at daybreak, about half-past four o'clock,
we discerned land at two cables' distance, a long sandy
beach reaching to Cape Mondego, three leagues to the
southward of us. On daylight clearing up, we could
perceive between twenty and thirty sail of the convoy
ashore, both to northward and southward, and several of
them perfect wrecks. We were now certain of being on
the coast of Portugal, from seeing the cape mentioned
above,—though I am sorry to say no person in the ship
had the least idea of being so near the coast. It was
blowing very hard, and the sea was running mountains
high, so that there was little hope of being saved. About
eight o'clock, the ship seemed likely to go to pieces, and
the after part lying lowest, Captain Dixon ordered every
one forward,—a command it was difficult to comply
with, from the motion of the mainmast working on the
larboard gunwale, there being no other way to get forward. Mr. Cook, the boatswain, had his thigh broken
in endeavouring to get a boat over the side. Of six
boats not one was saved, all being stoved, and washed
overboard with the booms, &c.

'Soon after the people got forward, the ship parted at
the gangways. The crew were now obliged to stow
themselves in the fore-channels, and from thence to
the bowsprit end, to the number of 220,—for, out of
the 240 persons on board when the ship first struck, I
suppose twenty to have previously perished between

decks and otherwise. Mr. Lawton, the gunner, the first
who attempted to swim ashore, was drowned; afterwards,
Lieutenant Witson, Mr. Runice, surgeon, Mr. McCabe,
surgeon's mate, Mr. Staudley, master's mate, and several
men, were also drowned (though they were excellent
swimmers), by the sea breaking over them in enormous
surges. About thirty persons had the good fortune to
reach the shore upon planks and spars, amongst whom
were Lieutenant Harvey and Mr. Callam, master's mate.
On Monday night, our situation was truly horrible; the
old men and boys were dying from hunger and fatigue;
Messrs. Proby and Hayes, midshipmen, died also. Captain
Dixon remained all night upon the bowsprit.

'Tuesday morning presented no better prospect of
relief from the jaws of death. The wind blew stronger,
and the sea was much more turbulent. About noon, our
drooping spirits were somewhat revived by seeing Lieutenant Harvey and Mr. Callam hoisting out a boat from
one of the merchant ships to come to our assistance.
They attempted several times to launch her through the
surf; but she was a very heavy boat, and the sea on the
beach acted so powerfully against them, they could not
effect their purpose, though they were assisted by nearly
one hundred of the merchant sailors and Portuguese
peasants. This day, several men went upon rafts made
from pieces of the wreck; but not one reached the
shore: the wind having shifted, and the current setting
out, they were all driven to sea, and amongst them our
captain and three sailors. Anxious to save the remainder
of the ship's company, and too sanguine of getting safe
on shore, he had ventured upon the spar, saying, as he
jumped into the sea, ' My lads, I'll save you all.' In a
few seconds, he lost his hold of the spar, which he could
not regain : he drifted to sea, and perished: and such

was also the fate of the three brave volunteers who shared his fortune.

'The loss of our captain, who had hitherto animated the almost lifeless crew, and the failure of Lieutenant Harvey and Mr. Callam, in their noble exertions to launch the boat, extinguished every gleam of hope, and we looked forward to certain death on the ensuing night, not only from cold, hunger, and fatigue, but from the expectation that the remaining part of the wreck might go to pieces at any moment. Had not the Apollo been a new and well-built ship, that small portion of her could not have resisted the waves, and held so well together, when all the after-part from the chess-tree was gone, the starboard bow under water, and the forecastle deck nearly perpendicular. The weight of the guns hanging to the larboard bulwark on the inside, and on the outside the bower and spare anchors, which it was not prudent to cut away, as they afforded a resting-place to a considerable number of men, added to the danger. It had become impossible to remain any longer in the head, or upon the bowsprit, the breakers washing continually over those places, so that one hundred and fifty men were stowed in the fore-channels and cat's-head, where alone it was possible to live.

'The night drawing on, the wind increasing, with frequent showers of rain, the sea washing over us, and the expectation becoming every instant more certain, that the forecastle would give way and that we must all perish together, afforded a spectacle truly deplorable, and the bare recollection of which makes me shudder. The piercing cries of the people, this dismal night, as the sea washed over them every two minutes, were pitiful in the extreme. The water running from the head down over the body kept us continually wet. On that fearful night

every man's strength was exerted for his own individual
safety. From crowding so close together in so narrow a
compass, and having nothing to moisten their mouths,
several poor wretches were suffocated, like those in the
black hole,—with this only difference, that we were confined by water instead of strong walls; and the least
movement or relaxation of our hold would have plunged
us into eternity.

' Some unfortunate men drank salt water, several endeavoured to quench their raging thirst by a still more
unnatural means; some chewed leather, myself and
many others thought we experienced great relief by
chewing lead, as it produced saliva.

' In less than an hour after the ship had struck the
ground, all the provisions were under water, and the ship
a wreck, so that we were entirely without food. After
a night of most intense suffering, daylight enabled us to
see Lieutenant Harvey and Mr. Callam again endeavouring to launch the boat. Several attempts were made
without success, and a number of men belonging to the
merchant ships were much bruised and injured in their
efforts to assist. Alternate hopes and fears possessed
our wretched minds.

' Fifteen men got safe on shore, this morning, on pieces
of the wreck. About three, P.M., of Wednesday, the 4th,
we had the inexpressible happiness of seeing the boat
launched through the surf, by the indefatigable exertions
of the two officers, assisted by the masters of the merchant
ships, and a number of Portuguese peasants, who were
encouraged by Mr. Whitney, the British Consul from
Figuera.

' All the crew then remaining on the wreck were
brought safe on shore, praising God for this happy
deliverance, from a shipwreck which never yet had its
parallel.

'As soon as I slipt out of the boat, I found several persons whose humanity prompted them to offer me refreshment, though imprudently, in the form of spirits, which I avoided as much as possible.

'Our weak state may be conceived when it is remembered that we had tasted no nourishment from Sunday to Wednesday afternoon, and had been exposed all that time to the fury of the elements. After eating and drinking a little, I found myself weaker than before, owing, I imagine, to having been so long without food. Some men died soon after getting on shore, from taking too large a quantity of spirits. The whole of the crew were in a very weak and exhausted state, and the greater part of them were also severely bruised and wounded.'

Such is Mr. Lewis's account of the wreck of the Apollo, one of our finest frigates, and the loss of sixty of her men.

The cause of this catastrophe seems to have been an error in the reckoning. At twelve o'clock on Sunday, the land was supposed to be thirty or forty leagues distant, nor were they aware of their true position when the vessel struck at three o'clock the following morning, on what was supposed to be an unknown shoal. Never, perhaps, in the annals of maritime disaster, was there a scene more rife with horror than that upon which the daylight broke on the morning of the 2nd of April.

The frigate, which but a few hours before had been careering on her way with her gallant company full of life and energy, now lay a hapless wreck—her timbers crashing beneath the fury of the waves. The merchant vessels around were stranded in all directions, and the air resounded with the despairing shrieks of those on board. The destruction of the Apollo seemed inevitable; but in this hour of trial, the captain was firm and resolute, sustaining by words and example the courage of his crew; and when no other means of escape presented themselves, he sacrificed his own life in the endeavour to obtain rescue for those under his charge.

The narrator of this sad tale has touchingly described in no exaggerated terms the sufferings of the wretched crowd who were exposed for nearly three days and nights to the worst of physical and mental evils—hunger, thirst, cold, and nakedness—in their most aggravated form, rendered still more painful by the almost utter hopelessness of their condition, while they watched the repeated failures of Lieutenant Harvey and Mr. Callam in their attempts to send a boat to their relief. We need not therefore dwell on this subject further than to observe that, under Providence, it was by the undaunted courage and perseverance of those two officers that the remainder of the crew of the Apollo were saved from destruction—for no one else had been found bold enough to attempt their rescue, although the Consul of Figuera had offered 100 guineas to any man that would take a boat to the wreck.

No less than forty merchantmen were wrecked at the same time. Several sunk with all their crew, and the remainder lost from two to twelve men each. Yet Mr. Lewis describes the situation of these ships as not so dangerous as that of the frigate, because the merchantmen, drawing less water, were driven closer in to shore, and the men were enabled to land after the first morning.

The Apollo's company received every mark of kindness and attention when they got on shore, from the masters of the merchant vessels, who had erected tents on the beach, and who shared with the sufferers whatever provisions they had saved from the wrecks.

Dead bodies floated on shore for many days after, and pieces of wreck covered the beach, marking the scene of

this sad calamity. Fortunately, the Carysfort, with part
of the convoy, escaped the fate of her consort by wearing,
and arrived safely at Barbadoes. The surviving officers
and crew of the Apollo marched to Figuera, a distance
of eighteen miles, from whence they were conveyed in a
schooner to Lisbon, and brought by the Orpheus frigate
to Portsmouth.

On their arrival in England, they were tried by a
court martial; and it is satisfactory to know that they
were all fully acquitted.

It is a principal object in this work to draw attention
to the advantages of firm and steady discipline in all
cases of emergency. We cannot, therefore, omit to show
than when a spirit of insubordination breaks out under
circumstances of danger, how surely it is attended with
fatal results.

In the course of the evidence adduced before the court
of inquiry upon the loss of the Apollo, it was proved
that about twenty of her men had broken into the spirit
room; disorder, of course, ensued; and Lieutenant Harvey
gave it as his opinion, that, if these men had remained
sober, many lives might have been spared. There is so
much cause for regret in the whole catastrophe, that we
will not harshly impute blame to one party or another.
We may see some palliation for the misconduct of the
men in the awful situation in which they were placed—
their fears, perhaps, made them forgetful alike of their
duty to their king, their country, and themselves; but it
is cheering to know that such cases are rare in the British
Navy, and we are happy in having very few such to
record: they are alluded to only in the hope that our
seamen may learn from them to value that strict discipline and order, which, in a moment of danger, is their
greatest safeguard.

Lieutenant, now Rear Admiral, Harvey subsequently served in the Amethyst, Amaranthe, and Intrepid. His promotion to the rank of commander took place in 1808, when he was appointed to the Cephalus, in the Mediterranean, and there he captured four of the enemy's privateers, and several merchant vessels. His post commission bears date April 18, 1811, and he was employed off Corfu till the month of December following. His last ship was the Implacable, which he paid off in 1814. He obtained his flag as rear-admiral in December, 1847. This officer now holds the appointment of Admiral Superintendent of Malta Dockyard.

THE HINDOSTAN.

IN the year 1804, the Government sent out the Hindostan, of 1100 tons, laden with supplies for Lord Nelson, then commander-in-chief of the Mediterranean fleet. This ship was commanded by Captain Le Gros, with 259 persons on board, including passengers, women, and children.

She arrived at Gibraltar in the month of March, and sailed again from thence in company with the Phœbe frigate, to join Lord Nelson off Toulon, but she was separated from her consort during a heavy gale of wind, in the Gulf of Lyons.

On the 2nd of April, at about seven o'clock in the morning, the ship being then thirteen leagues to the south-east of Cape St. Sebastian, a thick smoke was observed to issue from the fore and main hatchways.

Lieutenant Tailour, who was on the quarter-deck, heard the cry of " fire," and saw the people rushing up the

hatchway in the midst of volumes of smoke, coming from
the orlop deck. He instantly called for the drummer
and the mate of the watch, and desired the former to
beat to quarters, and the latter to inform Captain Le
Gros of what had occurred, whilst he himself would go
below, and endeavour to ascertain the cause and the
place of the fire.

Lieutenant Tailour then went down into the orlop
gratings, and penetrated some distance into each tier ;
the smoke was very thick in both, particularly forward.
He next went to the sail room, where there was no
appearance of either fire or smoke. He was then joined
by Lieutenant Banks and several other officers, and they
proceeded together to the hold. Here the smoke was
very dense, and it affected the throat like that from hot
tar. The officers were satisfied, upon inquiry, that there
had not been either light or tar in the hold. They then
tried to re-enter the tiers, but were driven back by the
suffocating smoke. The absence of heat, however, convinced them that the fire was not in that part of the
ship. A cry was heard that the fire was down forward,
—but we will use Lieutenant Tailour's own words to
describe the scene. He says,—

' When I reached the fore-ladder, none being able to
tell me where the fire was, I went down to examine,
when at the orlop, I put my head over the spars which
were stowed in the starboard side, then behind the ladder
in the larboard side; the smoke came thickest in the
starboard side from aft ; feeling nothing like fire heat, I
attempted to go down to the cockpit, but ere I reached
the third or fourth step on the ladder, I felt myself
overpowered, and called for help. Several men had
passed me upwards on my way down, none I believe
were below me. By the time I came up to the orlop
ladder, some one came and helped me ; when I reached

the lower deck, I fell, but not, as many did that day, lifeless.'

When Lieutenant Tailour recovered, he made strict inquiries whether any fire had been discovered in the cockpit or storerooms, and being assured that there had not, he ordered the lower deck to be scuttled.

So energetic was this officer, that eight or ten minutes only had elapsed since the first alarm had been given, before the hammocks were all got on deck, and the ports opened, to give light and room below, until the place of fire could be discovered, and better means obtained for drawing water. Mr. Tailour did not recover from the suffocation so fast as he expected, and was obliged to go upon deck for air. There he found Captain Le Gros in consultation with the master, who, being of opinion that the fire was on the larboard side, gave orders to wear the ship, so as to allow the water which had been hove in to flow over her. Mr. Tailour differed from them, and said he was convinced that the fire was on the orlop starboard side. In a few minutes he again went below and assisted in working the engine, and giving directions for scuttling on the larboard side, where the smoke appeared most dense.

The engine, however, proved of little avail, for the smoke increased to such a degree as to prevent the people working on the orlop deck ; the hatches were, therefore, laid over, the ports lowered, everything covered up, and all means used to prevent the circulation of air. Having taken these precautions, Lieutenant Tailour reported to Captain Le Gros what had been done, and at the same time advised that the boats should be got out without loss of time. The captain seems to have objected to this, on the plea that if the boats were got out, the people would all crowd into them, and abandon the ship without an effort to save her. To this objection Mr. Tailour replied, that to save human life must be their first consideration, and that every moment's delay was fraught with peril and death. ' If we wait,' said he, ' till the last moment, it may not be possible to save any ; we can get the marines under arms.' Captain Le Gros yielded the point ; he directed the sergeant of marines to get his men under arms, with orders to load with ball, and to shoot without hesitation the first man who should attempt to go into the boats without permission. All hands were then turned up, and the command given to ' out boats.'

The order was promptly executed, and as soon as the boats were out and secure for towing, the ship's head was pointed to the north-west, with the view of nearing the land, and in hopes that she might fall in with the Juno.

In the meantime, a party was employed in getting the booms overboard for a raft, the fore and main gratings were laid up and covered over, and Lieutenant Banks was sent down to get the powder out of the magazine, and stow it away in the stern gallery. He could only partially accomplish this; for the smoke increased upon them so much that the men were obliged to desist. The powder they had got up was thrown overboard, and water was poured down to drown that which remained ; but the task of filling the magazine was hopeless, and therefore abandoned. Many of the men were drawn up apparently lifeless, amongst whom were Lieutenant Banks and the gunner. Lieutenant Tailour then went below to ascertain how matters were going on ; he found only the boatswain's mate in the cockpit, who was almost stupified by the smoke. Mr. Tailour assisted him to reach the deck, and then the gallant officer was preparing to return to the magazine, taking a rope with him by way of precaution, when Lieutenant Banks, with noble generosity, darted past him, also with a rope in his hand, and descended on the dangerous service ; but in a

short time he was drawn up in a state of insensibility.
All hope of doing anything with the magazine was then
given up ; but although the smoke was so powerful
below, it had not yet got possession of the after part of
the lower deck.

It was therefore proposed, and the proposition was immediately acted on, to cut scuttles through the starboard
foremost cabin in the ward-room, and one under it in the
gun-room, into the magazine. This was found more practicable than was at first supposed, as the cabins kept out
the smoke. When they were cutting these scuttles, the
smoke came up in such dense volumes through the after-
hatchway, that it was necessary to shut it closely up, and
the scuttle in the after-part of the captain's cabin was
opened for a passage to the ward-room, and they began
to haul up the powder, and heave it overboard out of
the gallery windows. The ward-room doors, and every
other passage for the smoke were carefully closed, and
thus it was kept tolerably well under ; yet many of the
men employed in the duty were taken up to all appearance dead. Amongst them we again find Lieutenant
Banks, and Mr. Pearce, the gunner. We cannot proceed
without expressing the admiration we feel for the heroism
and self-devotion displayed by officers and men. This is
the third time we have seen Lieutenant Banks risk his
life in the performance of his duty, and it was not the
last of such efforts to save the vessel and the lives of his
fellow-sufferers.

For the present, we will again adopt the language of
Lieutenant Tailour :—'About noon,' said he, ' I went
aft upon the poop, where many were collected, but the
marines were drawn up on duty upon the poop above.
Francis Burke, the purser's steward, was lying dead on
one of the arm chests, said to have been suffocated by
the smoke below. Soon after this, my attention was

drawn forward, where a vast body of smoke issued from
the hatchway, gallery doors, funnels, and scuttles, which
I soon saw were blown off; I rushed forward and got
them secured again, and in coming aft found the hatches
had all been blown off; the two foremost main-gratings
had gone down the hatchway. The after one I assisted
to replace, also the tarpaulin, which was excessively hot,
and left the carpenter to get it secured on. I next
thought of the magazine, where I dreaded some accident.
On my way aft, I met some people again bringing Mr.
Banks up in their arms. On reaching the ward-room, I
saw through the windows the stern ladders filled with
people; I broke a pane of glass, and ordered them on
the poop, threatening instant death to any one who dared
disobey. On their beginning to move up, I just took
time to summons the men from the magazine, and went
up to the poop to see every one was once more under
the eye of the marines. This done, the smoke having in
a great measure subsided, the maintop-sail was filled, and
top-gallant sails set.'

About two o'clock in the afternoon, when they had
been seven hours contending with the fire and smoke,
land was discerned through the haze, on the weather-bow,
and it was supposed to be above Cape Creux.

Captain Le Gros, fearing the signals might fall into
the enemy's hands, hove them all overboard. The sight
of land gave a turn to the men's thoughts, and spurred
them on to greater exertion. The fire rapidly increased;
but the efforts of the captain and his noble crew increased
with the danger.

Again they attempted to clear the magazine; but the
smoke again drove the men from below, and rendered
them powerless. Their courage was, indeed, kept up by
the sight of land, though still five leagues distant; but
there was still much to be done—many perils yet

surrounded them—and it was awful to feel that fire
and water were contending for the mastery, and that
they must be the victims of one of these elements, unless
by the mercy of God the progress of the conflagration
was stayed, and time allowed them to reach the distant
shore. The fire was increasing fearfully; so much so,
that Lieutenant Tailour describes the lower deck 'burning like the flame in an oven.' All communication was
cut off from the fore-part of the ship. The flames flew
up the fore and main hatchways as high as the lower
yards, but still the brave crew remained firm to their
duty; and by keeping tarpaulins over the hatchways,
and pouring down water, they managed for a time to
keep the fire from taking serious hold abaft.

But the crisis was fast approaching when human skill
and human fortitude could be of no avail. In defiance
of all their exertions and precautions, the devouring element pursued its course. Every moment it was gaining
aft; and had not officers and men been true to themselves and to each other, they must all have perished.
The mizenmast was on fire in the captain's cabin, and
the flames were bursting from all the lee-ports. It was
now a quarter past five o'clock, and they were entering
the Bay of Rosas. Could they venture to hold on their
way, and still remain in the ship? A moment's glance
around him sufficed for Captain Le Gros to decide the
question. The now triumphant element was no longer
smouldering and creeping stealthily onwards amidst
smoke and darkness, but with a lurid glare, and a
sullen roar, the flames rolled on. The word was given
to launch the raft; it was obeyed, and in a few minutes
more the vessel struck, about a mile from the beach,
between the Fort of Ampurius and the Church of St.
Pierre. She was now on fire both fore and aft. Self-
preservation is the law of nature, it is said; but there

is a stronger law governing the actions of the British seaman. Officers and men were of one mind. They all united in putting first the women and children, then the sick and the foreigners, into the launch. The two yawls and the jolly-boat took as many as they could carry from the stern, and put them on board some Spanish boats from La Escada, which had been sent to their assistance, but which neither threats nor entreaties could avail to bring near to the ship.

The remainder of the people were then ordered on to the raft, and by the time it was covered, the flames came aft so thick, that it was necessary to send it off from the stern. All now had left the ill-fated vessel, except the gallant Captain Le Gros, Lieutenant Tailour, and the master. When they saw all the rest clear away, and not till then, did they descend by the stern ladders into one of the yauls and pulled towards the shore, which they had scarcely reached when she blew up.

The value of this ship was estimated at 100,000*l.*, and the loss to Lord Nelson must have been incalculable. Yet it is said that he was much more distressed by the loss of the despatches, which were taken by the enemy, about the same time, in the Swift cutter.

In a letter to Lord St. Vincent, dated the 19th of April, Admiral Nelson says, speaking of Captain Le Gros,—"If his account be correct (he was then upon his trial), he had great merit for the order in which the ship was kept. The fire must have originated from medicine chests breaking, or from wet getting down, which caused the things to heat. The preservation of the crew seems little short of a miracle. I never read such a journal of exertions in my whole life.'*

---

* Clark and McArthur, vol. ii. p. 361.

The captain, officers, and ship's company were most honourably acquitted by the sentence of court-martial.

Brenton, in his *Naval History*, remarks, ' In support of the reasonable conjectures of the Admiral (Lord Nelson), as to the origin of the fire, we might adduce many instances of ships in the cotton trade having been on fire in the hold during a great part of their voyage from China, owing to the cargo having been wet when compressed into the ship. Hemp has been known to ignite from the same cause ; and the dockyard of Brest was set on fire by this means in 1757. New painted canvas or tarpaulin, laid by before it is completely dry, will take fire ; and two Russian frigates were nearly burnt by the accidental combination of a small quantity of soot, of burnt fir wood, hemp, and oil, tied up with some matting.'

Mr. Thomas Banks, acting-lieutenant of the Hindostan, was recommended to Lord Nelson for promotion, by the members of the court-martial, in consequence of his conduct on this occasion; and he was advanced to the rank of lieutenant on the 23rd of June, 1804. This gallant officer died in 1811. Lieutenant George Tailour was appointed to the Tigre in 1808, and was promoted for his gallant conduct in cutting out a convoy of transports which had taken refuge in this same Bay of Rosas, where, five years before, he had equally distinguished himself, under even more trying circumstances.

THE ROMNEY.

' IN the month of November, 1804,' writes Brenton, in his *Naval History*, 'the severity of blockading the Ports of the Texel was practically experienced in the loss of the Romney, of fifty guns, commanded by Captain the Hon. John Colville.'

The Romney sailed from Yarmouth on the 18th of November, under orders to join Rear-Admiral Russel, off the Texel; but on the 19th she went aground on the south-west part of the sand-bank off the Haaks. Regular soundings had been made during the run from Yarmouth; and a few minutes before the ship struck, the pilots were confident they were on the edge of the Broad Fourteens. They then sounded, and the pilots proposed standing in under double-reefed topsails, and foretopmast stay-sail, with the wind S.S.W., until they should be in ten or eleven fathoms. To this Captain Colville objected, as from the unsettled appearance of the weather, and the thickness of the fog, he deemed it would be imprudent to approach the shore. They were accordingly in the act of wearing, when they perceived, through the fog, a large ship bearing east by north. They stood towards her to make her out more plainly, and in four or five minutes they discovered that she was a large merchant vessel on shore.* Upon this, the pilots were anxious to haul off on the larboard tack; but before the ship could be brought to the wind, she struck. The wind was increasing, the fog very great, and a heavy sea rolling in. In spite of every exertion, the water

---

* She proved to be an American, and she went to pieces during the night.

gained upon the vessel so fast, that all hope of saving her was soon at an end ; and had she been in deep water, she must have sunk immediately. The pilots supposed that the Romney would be dry at low water, the topmasts were therefore struck, and every preparation made to shore her up.

The captain having done all in his power to save his ship, next turned his attention to the preservation of his officers and men, determined to use every possible means for their safety. Minute guns were fired, in the hope that they might attract the notice of some of our cruisers, and procure assistance.

At this time it blew a gale from the south-west, and the sea ran so high, as to endanger the boats which were lowered in order to lighten the ship.

The two cutters were sent to a galliot and a schuyt, that were in sight near the land, to ask for help, but they failed in obtaining it; and one of them in returning to the Romney was upset in the breakers, and a master's mate with her crew perished. Lieutenant Baker, who commanded the other cutter, finding it impossible to reach the ship again, bore up to the Texel, in hopes of being more successful in obtaining assistance there than he had been with the schuyt.

On board the ship, in the meantime, the minute guns were fired, and officers and men looked anxiously for a responsive signal that would tell them of approaching succour—but they waited in vain ; no help was at hand. The people were therefore set to work to make rafts, and three were soon finished. Between two and three o'clock in the afternoon the ship struck again, with such violence, that the rudder broke away, and she seemed likely to go to pieces immediately. The captain seized the first moment of the weather-tide slacking to order the masts to be cut away, which was promptly done, and fortunately without causing any injury in their fall. After this, the ship became more easy, although the sea still made a clean breach over her. Captain Colville saw that the slightest alteration in her position would be attended with imminent danger, and he therefore ordered the bower anchors to be let go—her head then swung to the wind, and this enabled her to settle gradually on the sand, where she lay comparatively easy. Darkness was fast gathering around, and the hearts of the crew were becoming dreary and hopeless.

> Nor sail nor shore appeared in sight,
> Nought but the heavy sea and coming night.

When the tide flowed, no part of the ship below the quarter-deck was accessible. To add to the misery of their situation, out of the four bags of bread which had been put for safety into the cabin, one only could be got upon deck, and that one was so soaked in salt water, that the bread could scarcely be eaten. This, with two cheeses, and a few gallons of wine, composed the whole of their stock of provisions, and during the day they had had no leisure to take refreshment of any kind.

Such was the condition of the crew of the Romney, who passed that awful night on the quarter-deck, the starboard side of which was under water at high tide. The wind blew in violent gusts; sleet and rain were falling, and the sea dashed over the vessel every instant. Although the men were shivering with cold and hunger, not a murmur escaped their lips, not a whisper of complaint; but they patiently awaited the break of day. At length the morning dawned, and with it hope dawned upon the hearts of those patient sufferers, for the wind and the waves subsided, the clouds gradually dispersed, and the sun shone forth with glorious and invigorating light and warmth.

E 2

All eyes were turned to the offing, but still no assistance appeared. Captain Colville then resolved to hoist the white flag on the stump of the mizen mast, in hopes that it might be seen from the shore, and that he might preserve the lives of his crew by surrendering to the enemy.

This step was necessary, as it was the only means of rescue that remained to them. The barge had been swamped along side, soon after the masts were cut away, and three of the crew had been drowned. The launch, also, which was lying to leeward, had parted from her grapnel, and had been obliged to bear up for the Texel.

At 11 o'clock A.M., Captain Colville asked the carpenter if he thought they could remain another night upon the wreck: the carpenter assured him that he considered it almost impossible to do so, and that the attempt would be attended with the greatest risk to all on board. The ship had already parted amid-ships, the main beam and several others being broken.

Five rafts had been carefully constructed, each fitted with a mast and sail; and at the earnest entreaty of the crew, Captain Colville, on hearing the carpenter's report, allowed a part of the men to leave the wreck on these rafts.

About noon, as the fifth and last raft was about to leave the ship, seven boats (one bearing a flag of truce) were seen coming towards them from the shore. The captain ordered the people to throw the quarter-deck guns, and all the arms and warlike stores overboard, which they did.

When the boats arrived alongside, an officer hailed the wreck, and said that if Captain Colville was willing to secure the preservation of his officers and crew, by surrendering as prisoners of war, the whole company should be conducted in safety to the Helder. Captain

Colville felt himself obliged to submit to the imperious dictates of necessity, and he accordingly accepted the proffered conditions, and surrendered himself to the Dutch, with all the ship's company that remained on the wreck.

Before nightfall they were all landed. Only those who have been placed in similar circumstances can judge of the feelings of men so rescued from the awful contemplation of immediate and certain death. How happy now did they feel in occupying a position, which two days before they would have shrunk from with horror, and have shed their life's blood to avoid. But 'there is no virtue like necessity.'

> All places that the eye of heaven visits,
> Are to a wise man ports and happy havens.
>
> RICHARD II.

And the Romney's company were wise enough to rejoice, under the circumstances of their hard case, in finding themselves safely landed in an enemy's country as prisoners of war.

Nine seamen had been drowned; thirteen others, who had left the wreck upon a raft of timber, were afterwards picked up and taken on board the Eagle; the others who had been saved by the boats and rafts joined Captain Colville at the Helder. The following extracts from Captain Colville's dispatches show the high estimation in which he held the services of his officers and crew :— ' That every possible exertion was made to lessen the calamity, after having struck, I trust will appear from the minutes.' .... ' Under the uneasiness of mind which the loss of the ship I had the honour to command, naturally occasioned, I feel some alleviation in reflecting upon the zealous, active, and orderly conduct of my officers and crew in circumstances the most trying, and under which they endured the severest hardships with cheerfulness, and in perfect reliance on Divine Providence, whose interposition in our behalf was strongly evident.'

Nothing could exceed the kindness and consideration shown by the Dutch admiral towards the crew of the Romney. Captain Colville, in a letter addressed to the Secretary of the Admiralty, does ample justice to a generous foe:—

'We have experienced,' he says, 'from the Dutch Admiral Kirkhurt, every attention that our distressed situation made so necessary, and which his disposition seems incapable of withholding, even from an enemy. But the wants of my fellow-sufferers are great, for not an article of clothing or anything else was saved by any one from the general wreck. I hope the Dutch government will be disposed to alleviate, in some degree, their wants,—in clothing, particularly. And I have solicited the assistance of Rear-Admiral Russel in obtaining these necessaries.' .... 'I have reason to believe we shall be sent to Amsterdam, until exchanged.'

Subsequently, the Dutch admiral, with noble generosity, sent Captain Colville, with eight of his officers, to Rear-Admiral Russel. It is always delightful to record such traits of magnanimity and kindness, and we feel that British sailors can well afford to do honour to those virtues in others, for which they have ever been so distinguished themselves.

Admiral Russel handsomely acknowledged his obligation to the Dutch government in the following letter to Admiral Kirkhurt:—

H. B. M. Ship Eagle, Dec. 2, 1804.

'Sir—I have this moment received your flag of truce, conveying to me the Honourable Captain Colville, late of his Majesty's ship, the Romney, (wrecked upon your coast,) with eight of his officers, whom you have first humanely saved from impending destruction, and whom

your government, with its ancient magnanimity, has
released and restored to their country and their friends,
on their *parole d'honneur.* They are all, Sir, most
sensibly affected with heartfelt gratitude to the Batavian
government for their emancipation from captivity; to
Admiral Kirkhurt for their preservation from the jaws of
death, and to all the Dutch officers and inhabitants of
the Texel, for their kindness and most humane attention.

' This, Sir, is nobly alleviating the rigours of war, as
the Christian heroes of your country and mine were wont
to do in these seas, before a considerable portion of
European intellect was corrupted by false philosophy.
Captain Colville will communicate to the Right Honourable the Lords Commissioners of the Admiralty, your
proposal for an exchange of prisoners. Accept my
sincere thanks, and the assurance that I am, &c. &c.

' (Signed)   T. M. RUSSEL.'

On the 31st of December, Captain Colville, the officers
and ship's company of H.M. (late) ship Romney were
tried by a court-martial on board the Africaine at Sheerness, for the loss of their ship off the Tezel on the 19th of
November.

It appeared to the court, that the loss of the ship had
been occasioned by the thickness of the fog and the
ignorance of the pilots; that the utmost exertions had
been used by the captain, officers, and crew, to save the
vessel after she struck, and to prevent the ship's company
becoming prisoners of war. The sentence of the court
was to this effect: that the captain, officers and crew
were fully acquitted of all blame, but that the pilots
should forfeit all their pay, and be rendered henceforth
incapable of taking charge of any of his Majesty's ships
or vessels of war, and that they should be imprisoned in
the Marshalsea—one for the space of twelve, and the
other, of six months.

In 1805, Captain Colville was appointed to the Sea
Fencibles, at Margate. In 1807, he obtained the command of L'Hercule, a 74-gun ship, on the coast of
Portugal, and subsequently commanded the Queen on
the North Sea Station.

He succeeded to his title (Lord Colville) on the death
of his father in 1811, and was advanced to the rank of
rear-admiral in 1819. On the 10th of November, 1821,
he hoisted his flag on board the Semiramis, as commander-in-chief on the Irish station. Lord Colville died
an Admiral of the White, in 1849.

We are aware that the foregoing narrative may appear
deficient in novel and striking incidents, but we have
introduced it for the sake of exhibiting some of the best
and noblest attributes of the true-hearted sailor—courage,
patience, and perfect obedience under the most trying
circumstances, and generous kindness towards an unfortunate enemy. It is well to think of these things, and
the more we read of the details of naval life—its sufferings, dangers, and trials, the more fully shall we be persuaded that *true* courage is ever generous and unselfish.
In the words of the quaint old song—

> Says the captain, says he, (I shall never forget it,)
> 'If of courage you'd know, lads, the true from the sham,
> 'Tis a furious lion in battle, so let it,
> But, duty appeased, 'tis in mercy a lamb.'

> That my friend, Jack or Tom, I should rescue from danger,
> Or lay down my life for each lad in the mess,
> Is nothing at all,—'tis the poor wounded stranger,
> And the poorer the more I shall succour distress:
>   In me let the foe feel the paw of the lion,
>   But, the battle once ended, the heart of a lamb.

VENERABLE.

ON Saturday, the 24th of November, 1804, the fleet under the command of Admiral the Hon. W. Cornwallis, lay at anchor in Torbay. As it was late in the year, and the night dark and stormy, orders were given for the fleet to put to sea.

Unfortunately, in fishing the anchor of the Venerable, 74-gun ship, the fish-hook gave way, and a man was precipitated into the sea. The alarm was immediately given, and one of the cutters was ordered to be lowered. Numbers of the crew rushed aft to carry the orders into effect, but in the confusion, one of the falls was suddenly let go, the boat fell by the run, filled, and a midshipman and two of the crew were drowned. In a few minutes another boat was lowered, which fortunately succeeded in picking up the man who first fell overboard.

Owing to this delay, the Venerable fell off considerably towards Brixham, and getting sternway, was unable to weather the Berry Head. Every effort was made to stay her, but the ship refused ; and, not having room to wear, she drove on shore, at the north part of the bay, on a spot called Roundem Head, near Paington.

Orders were given to cut away the masts, in the hopes of their falling between the ship and the shore. This was found impracticable, as the ship, from her position on the declivity of the rock on which she struck, heeled to such an extent, as to render the falling of the masts in the desired direction quite impossible.

Her commander, Captain John Hunter, however, with undaunted fortitude, continued to animate the crew with hope, and encouraged them to acts of further perseverance, with the same calmness and self-possession as if

he were simply conducting the ordinary duties of his
ship. From the moment the ship struck, not the least
alteration took place in his looks, words, or manner;
and everything that the most able and experienced
seaman could suggest was done, but in vain. On signals
of distress being made, H.M. cutter Frisk, Lieutenant
Nicholson, immediately stood towards her, and hailing to
know in what manner she could be useful, was requested
to anchor as near as possible to receive the crew, with
which her commander immediately complied, assisted
by the boats of the Goliath and Impetueux.

All hope of saving the Venerable being now abandoned, the only object that remained was to preserve the
lives of the crew, who were told to provide for their own
safety on board the boats which had been sent to their
assistance, the captain and officers declaring their intention of remaining on board till all the men had
quitted the wreck.

At this time the sea ran tremendously high, and the
men lowered themselves into the boats from the
stern, this being the only accessible part of the ship.
Most anxious was the situation of the officers and
men who were left, during the absence of the boats.
Many gave up all hopes of rescue, for every time
the boats approached the ship, the attempt became
more and more dangerous. The night still continued
dark and foggy, with driving sleet and violent gusts of
wind, which seemed to freshen every hour. In this
forlorn and dismal state, the officers continued on the
outside of the ship (for she was nearly on her beam
ends), encouraging the men, and affording every assistance for their escape on board the boats.

The Venerable was now a complete wreck, beating
against the rocks, and was expected to go to pieces at

every surge; yet all this time was she so near the shore that those on board were able to converse with the people, whom the report of the guns had brought in great numbers to the rocks. With much difficulty, they at last contrived to fling a line on shore, which, being secured there, some of the crew attempted to land themselves by it. The surf, however, broke with such violence between them and the shore, although they were scarcely twenty yards distant, that the poor fellows who made the attempt were either drowned or dashed to pieces.

It was now past five o'clock on Sunday morning, the weather still growing worse. The crew, with the exception of seventeen, had succeeded in quitting the ship, and these nobly declared that they would remain to share the fate of their officers. The situation of the whole was indeed appalling, and sufficient to quail the boldest heart; the sea breaking over them, the fore part of the ship under water, and the rest expected momentarily to go to pieces. Under these circumstances, the officers, feeling that they could be of no further use on board, deemed it their duty to represent to the captain the necessity of endeavouring to save their lives, they having one and all resolved on sharing his fate.

This point being arranged, the hopes of life began to revive; but a further difficulty presented itself, which seemed to render their safety more problematical than ever. This was, who was to lead the way. The pause had well nigh been fatal to them all. At length a junior lieutenant, long known on board, and celebrated for his courage, agreed to lead the way, the rest solemnly promising to follow. One after another they descended from the stern by a single rope, wet, cold, and benumbed; and in this condition they gained the boats,

which were in perilous attendance below. About six
o'clock they reached the Impetueux, where they were
treated with every attention and kindness which their
unfortunate position so loudly called for. They quitted
the ship in a most critical time, for in a little more than
an hour after they had left her, she parted amidships—
that part on which they had been standing for the last
five or six hours capsized and was buried in the surf.
In sixteen hours from the time she first struck, the whole
vessel had disappeared, under the action of a raging surf,
lashed into fury by the violence of the gale.

The conduct of the people on shore was most inhuman;
not the slightest assistance was offered; not a single
boat from Brixham or Torquay having put out to their
assistance during the whole of this dreadful night. To
add to this disgraceful conduct, the cowardly wretches
were observed, when daylight broke, plundering everything of value as it floated ashore.

The following is the tribute of praise which Captain
Hunter so justly pays to Captain Martin and the officers
and crew of the Impetueux:—

'To Captain Martin, of the Impetueux, whose feelings
as a man, as well as his zeal as an officer, were on this
distressing occasion so conspicuous.—It is the desire of
the officers and crew of the Venerable in this place to
express the high sense they have of the obligations they
are under to his personal exertions, as well as those of
the officers and boats' crews whom he employed in this
difficult and dangerous service,—for it is to their exertions they owe the life they now enjoy."

Captain Hunter also speaks of the conduct of his own
ship's company in the highest terms. Their steadiness
throughout was most remarkable, and to this, in a great
measure, may be attributed the preservation of their own
lives.

One solitary instance of neglect of duty occurred; and when we consider the circumstances in which the men were placed, and the temptations which never fail to present themselves on such occasions, the highest praise is not only due to the crew, but also to the captain and officers, who, by their previous conduct, had gained the respect and confidence of those under them. It is in such moments of severe trial that the character of a ship's company is put to the test; and the good behaviour of the men who remained with their officers proves that, in order to maintain a proper degree of discipline, no undue severity need be practised.

To a comparatively recent period, the captain of a man-of-war had the power of inflicting corporal punishment to an unlimited extent. This practice has of late years much diminished; owing, in a great measure, to the increased good feeling of naval officers, as also to the Admiralty discountenancing such strong measures, unless in most urgent cases. A captain of a man-of-war has, notwithstanding, and very properly so, an almost absolute power, and corporal punishment rests with him alone; but the humane officer, like Captain Hunter, punishes one man to save many others, and shares with the delinquent the pain which, for the sake of example, he is obliged to inflict. The discipline of a ship of course depends almost entirely upon the conduct of the captain; to him the officers look for guidance and example; and whilst they see that the men do their duty properly, they also learn from him to treat them with due consideration, having their happiness and comfort in view. As in the case of the Venerable, when the hour of danger arrives, each cheerfully performs the duties allotted to him, relying with confidence on those who, from their clemency, combined with firmness, they have been accustomed to look up to with respect.

An additional interest belongs to the fate of this
vessel, when we bear in mind that her crew, whilst
serving under Lord Duncan, in 1797, remained untainted
during the celebrated mutiny at the Nore.* She also
bore a conspicuous part in Lord Duncan's action with
the Dutch fleet, in October of the same year, engaging
the Vryheid, the flag-ship of the Dutch admiral. ·

The account of this great battle, however, is too well
recorded in the page of history to need repetition. It
is sufficient to add, that the Vryheid, after a noble
resistance, was ultimately obliged to strike, under the
destructive fire of the Venerable, Triumph, Ardent, and
Director.

THE SHEERNESS.

ON the afternoon of the 7th of January, 1805, His
Majesty's ship Sheerness, of 44 guns, was lying
at anchor in the Colombo Roads, Ceylon.

It was one of those days of extreme stillness which
often precede the frightful hurricanes that sweep the
eastern seas. Not a breath of air stirred, not a cloud
was to be seen; the ship lay motionless on the calm and
glassy water. The ensign drooped in heavy folds from
the stern, and many of the crew lay stretched on the
decks in listless apathy, little anticipating the terrible
convulsion of the elements which was so soon to arouse
them in fear. The monotony on board was broken for a
moment by the voice of the captain, Lord George Stuart,

---

* Captain Hunter died in 1807.

who ordered his gig to be manned that he might go on shore with his first lieutenant, Mr. Swan, and some other officers, whom he had invited to dine with him under a tent. The bustle of their departure from the ship was soon over, and again all was still. The captain and officers had scarcely landed and seated themselves at table, when a roaring sound was heard, at first distant, but becoming louder and louder every moment, and before they could conjecture the cause, the canvass of the tent was almost torn from its fastenings by the sudden violence of the wind.

Every one thought first of the Sheerness, and rushing from the tent a scene presented itself to their gaze little calculated to diminish their alarm for the ship.

The sea, which a few minutes before had been smooth as a polished mirror, now displayed a picture of terrific grandeur; the waves, crested with foam, rolled and tossed over one another in wild confusion, whilst the roaring of the winds, and the torrents of rain, added to the awful sublimity of the scene. Lord George, though aware of the imminent danger to which he exposed himself, determined at all risks to get on board his ship. Without a moment's delay he collected the crew of the gig, and pushed from the shore towards the vessel—himself steering the boat, whilst Lieutenant Swan pulled the bow oar. The wind had now increased to such a hurricane as is only known in tropical climates, and the waves threatened every instant to engulf the frail bark. As they advanced, the danger became more and more urgent; the sea broke over them continually; nevertheless, they persevered, and strained every nerve to effect their object.

The stunning roar of the hurricane prevented any communication except by signs, and several times the wind caught the oars with such force that the men could scarcely retain their seats. In vain were all their efforts :—

> The winds arise,
> The thunder rolls, the forky lightning flies ;
> In vain the master issues out commands,
> In vain the trembling sailors ply their hands,
> The tempest, unforeseen, prevents their care,
> And from the first they labour in despair.
>
> DRYDEN.

The boat filled with water three times, and became so nearly unmanageable, that they saw it would be impossible to gain the ship, and they bore up to the west part of York Island, from whence they waded to the shore, but so exhausted from the fatigue they had undergone, that they could never have reached the land, had they not been assisted by some workmen who were on the spot.

When they arrived, they found Mr. Warner, a midshipman, had just landed from the Sheerness, with a message to the effect that the ship had parted an anchor, but that she was riding in safety with two others. Mr. Warner had been sent in the launch, but in nearing the shore, she had been upset, and two of her crew were drowned ; there was little hope, therefore, of any boat weathering the storm in an attempt to reach the ship.

Lord George, however, would not give up the attempt, and he expressed so much anxiety to join his vessel, that it was proposed to go to the weathermost part of the bay. Thither they accordingly struggled on foot, with the utmost difficulty making head against the wind, and suffering acutely from the sand driving into their eyes. In addition to their personal sufferings, the spectacle around was one of such desolation and horror as no man can witness without pain. The shore, as far as the eye could reach, was covered with wrecks, and with the bodies of the dying and the dead, while the roaring of the surf, and the howling of the tempest, mingled with the piercing cries of those on board the stranded vessels, who were yet struggling with their fate, added to the awfulness of the scene.

At half-past six in the evening, exhausted with fatigue and suffering, they arrived at the head of the bay; but here they were again doomed to disappointment, for they found no one to assist them in launching the boat, although the crew of the launch had been directed to join them for that purpose.

The ship was still in sight, but they found it would be impossible to reach her, and they therefore proceeded to the neighbouring town of Ostenberg, where they directed a soldier whom they met, to hasten to his commanding officer, and request that a party of soldiers with torches should be ordered out ready to save the crew of the Sheerness, in case of her driving on shore.

Lord George and his companions then went to the master attendant's house, where they passed the night; but although they were worn out in mind and body, sleep never closed their eyes that night—they passed it in listening to the reports of the signal guns from the Sheerness, and in watching the rockets which from time to time illuminated the darkness, telling of distress and danger which they could not alleviate.

When morning broke, they assembled all the workmen they could muster, and manning a cutter with the crew of the launch, they went off to the Sheerness, which had been driven on shore to the west of York Island.

There a most distressing sight presented itself; two vessels had been driven on shore, one of which was totally lost. The Sheerness had parted her cables during the night, and for a time her situation was exceedingly perilous, it was impossible to stand upon deck till the main and mizen masts had been cut away. The water

rose above the orlop deck till it became level with the
surface of the sea.

Not a barrack-house or tree escaped the ravages of the
storm; many were levelled with the ground, others ex-
tensively damaged, and the hospital was completely
unroofed, which rendered the situation of the sick most
deplorable. One of the patients was killed by the falling
beams. Several Europeans fell a sacrifice to the storm,
many of them being exposed to the torrents of rain
without any place of shelter within reach.

Lord George Stuart, the officers and crew of the Sheerness were acquitted of all blame respecting the loss of
that vessel, it being the opinion of the court, that
' Every exertion was made for the preservation of the
ship by the captain, officers, and crew upon that trying
occasion ; and that, owing to the violence of the hurricane,
the loss of the ship was inevitable ; and every subsequent
attempt to get her afloat proved ineffectual, in consequence of the damage she had sustained in grounding
when driven on shore, from the impossibility of keeping
her free by means of the pumps.'

Lord George Stuart entered the navy in the year 1793
as a midshipman on board the Providence, in which ship
he had the misfortune to be wrecked in the year 1797.

He received his post rank in 1804, and was almost
constantly employed from that time until 1809, when he
assumed the command of a light squadron at the mouth
of the Elbe.

Here he performed an important service in taking the
town of Gessendorf, situated on the banks of the Weser,
and in driving from the fortress a body of French troops
who had made frequent predatory and piratical excursions
in the neighbourhood of Cuxhaven.

A few days after the defeat of the French, the gallant
Duke of Brunswick also arrived on the opposite banks of

the Weser, after having almost succeeded in effecting his retreat through the heart of Germany. By the previous dispersion of the enemy and the destruction of the fortress, he succeeded in crossing the river and escaping his pursuers, who would otherwise, in all probability, have captured or destroyed the whole of his detachment.

His Lordship was next appointed to the Horatio, a 38-gun frigate. Whilst cruizing on the morning of the 7th December, 1813, off the Island of Zealand, he received a letter from a gentleman who had been in the British service, requesting his aid to drive the French from Zierick-Zee, the capital of Schowen. He at once complied with this request, and directed a detachment of seamen and marines to storm the batteries as soon as the tide would answer for the boats to leave the ship, which could not be done until nine P.M. In the meantime, a deputation arrived on board from the principal citizens, bearing a flag of truce from the French general, and requesting, that in order to save the effusion of blood, and to prevent the disorders which would in all probability arise, as the city was then in a state of insurrection, terms of capitulation should be granted, by which the French should be allowed to withdraw with their baggage to Bergen-op-Zoom. To this, Lord George Stuart gave a peremptory refusal, and summoned the French to surrender unconditionally. After a short delay, the signal of surrender was made, and thus, by the promptitude and decision displayed by the British officer, the French were compelled to evacuate the Island of Schowen without bloodshed, and the ancient magistrates of Zierick-Zee resumed their former functions.

Lord George Stuart subsequently commanded the Newcastle, and was employed in the last American war. In 1815, he received the Order of the Companion of the Bath, and died as rear-admiral in 1841.

ATHENIENNE.

THE Athenienne, of 64 guns, commanded by Captain Robert Raynsford, with a crew of 470 men, sailed from Gibraltar on the 16th of October, 1806, and at noon on the 20th, the Island of Sardinia was seen in the distance. The ship continued under a press of sail with a fair wind, and sped on her course towards Malta. At eight o'clock of the evening of the 20th, the first watch had been stationed, and the officer on duty had reported the ship's progress at nine knots an hour. The labours of the day were over, and all, save the few whom duty or inclination kept on deck, had gone below. Another hour passed away; the majority of the crew had retired to their berths to seek repose after the toils of the day, and to gain fresh strength for the morrow—that morrow which many of them were destined never to behold.

One there was on board the Athenienne, to whose care the safety of the vessel and the lives of her crew had been entrusted, who appeared to have misgivings as to the course she was steering. The captain was seated in his cabin, looking over the chart with one of his officers, when he exclaimed, ' If the Esquerques do exist, we are now on them.' Scarcely were the words out of his mouth when the ship struck.

For the information of our readers, we must state that the Esquerques, or Shirki, are a reef of sunken rocks lying about eighty miles west from Sicily, and about forty-eight from Cape Bon, on the coast of Africa. In 1806, the charts were not as accurate as they are in the present day, and the reef was not laid down in all of them; the very existence, indeed, of these rocks was

positively denied by some navigators, though it was as
positively asserted by others.

It would be vain to attempt to describe the scene that
followed the first shock, on the vessel's striking the rock.
Upon the captain's hastening on deck, he found the
crew rushing up from their berths, many of them in a
state of nudity, and so stupified as to be utterly incapable
of making the least effort for their own preservation.
Some went below, and for the moment resigned themselves to despair, while others rushed to the poop for
safety.

In a few minutes, the officers had gathered round their
captain. It needed no words to point out to them the
imminence of their danger, and the necessity of their
setting an example of steadiness and intrepidity to the
men. They suffered no signs of dismay to appear in
their demeanour, but immediately proceeded to consider
what were the best steps to be taken to meet the impending danger. The calmness and courage thus displayed
by the captain and his officers could not fail of having
the desired effect upon the ship's company, who recovered
from their panic, and seeing the necessity for instant
exertion, held themselves in readiness to execute each
order as it was issued.

In order to prevent the ship falling on her broadside,
the masts were cut away; but she continued to beat so
violently upon the rocks, that in less than half-an-hour
she filled with water up to the lower deck ports, and
then fell over to larboard on her beam ends. Captain
Raynsford, foreseeing the inevitable loss of his vessel, had
ordered the boats to be hoisted out, with the idea that
they would be useful in towing a raft, which he had
caused to be constructed to leeward. This raft would
probably have been the means of preserving a great

many lives, had not the men in charge of the two jolly-boats pushed off, and left their unhappy comrades to their fate. Unfortunately, both the cutter and the barge, in hoisting out, were stove, and immediately swamped, no less than thirty men perishing with them. Several of the crew had been killed by the falling of the masts, and others were severely injured. Two midshipmen were crushed to death between the spanker boom and the bulwarks.

Brenton has thus described the horrible scene on board : —' Nothing was to be heard but the shrieks of the drowning and the wailings of despair. The man who would courageously meet death at the cannon's mouth, or at the point of the bayonet, is frequently unnerved in such a scene as this, where there is no other enemy to contend with than the inexorable waves, and no hope of safety or relief but what may be afforded by a floating plank or mast. The tremendous shocks as the ship rose with the sea, and fell again on the rocks, deprived the people of the power of exertion ; while at every crash portions of the shattered hull, loosened and disjointed, were scattered in dreadful havoc among the breakers. Imagination can scarcely picture to itself anything more appalling than the frantic screams of the women and children, the darkness of the night, the irresistible fury of the waves, which, at every moment, snatched away a victim, while the tolling of the bell, occasioned by the violent motion of the wreck, added a funereal solemnity to the horrors of the scene.'

The fate of the hapless crew seemed fast approaching to a termination. When the vessel first struck, signal guns had been fired, in the hope that some aid might be within reach, but none appeared ; the guns were soon rendered useless, and when the ship fell on her beam ends, the wreck, with the exception of the poop, was

entirely under water. Here were collected all that
remained of the ship's company, whose haggard countenances and shivering forms were revealed to each other,
from time to time, by the glare of the blue lights, and
by the fitful moonbeams which streamed from beneath
the dark clouds, and threw their pale light upon the
despairing group.

> The sea-breached vessel can no longer bear
> The floods that o'er her burst in dread career;
> The labouring hull already seems half filled
> With water, through an hundred leeks distilled;
> Thus drenched by every wave, her even deck,
> Stripped and defenceless, floats a naked wreck.
>
> FALCONER.

Two boats only remained, one of which was useless, her
side having been knocked in by the falling of the masts;
and the other, the launch, was therefore the sole means
of preservation left. She was already filled with men,
but it was found impossible to remove her from her
position on the booms; and even if she had floated, she
could not have contained above one-fourth of the crew.
For about half an hour she continued in the same
position, (the men who were in her expecting every
moment that her bottom would be knocked out by the
waves dashing against the spars on which she rested,)
when suddenly a heavy sea lifted her off the bows clear
of the ship. Three loud cheers greeted her release, and
the oars being ready, the men immediately pulled from
the wreck, with difficulty escaping the many dangers
they had to encounter from the floating spars and broken
masts.

These gallant fellows, however, would not desert their
companions in misfortune, and although their boat
already contained more than a hundred, they pulled
towards the stern of the frigate; but so great was the

anxiety of the poor creatures upon the poop to jump into the boat, that in self-defence they were obliged to keep at a certain distance from the wreck, or the launch would have been instantly swamped. They were therefore reduced to the terrible alternative, either of leaving their comrades to perish, or of throwing away their own lives. Nine of the men who had jumped overboard were picked up, but to have attempted to save any more would have been to sacrifice all. One of the officers left on board the wreck endeavoured by every argument to persuade Captain Raynsford to save himself by swimming to the launch, but all in vain. This intrepid man declared that he was perfectly resigned to his fate, and was determined not to quit his ship whilst a man remained on board. Finding that all entreaties were useless, the officer himself jumped overboard from the stern gallery into the sea, and swimming through the surf, gained the launch and was taken on board.

The general cry in the boat was, 'Pull off!' and at twelve o'clock, as the moon sunk below the horizon, her crew took their last look of the Athenienne. The situation of the launch was of itself imminently perilous: she had neither sail, bread, nor water on board. Fortunately there was a compass, and for a sail the officers made use of their shirts and the frocks of the seamen. On the following morning they fell in with a Danish brig, which relieved, in some degree, their urgent necessities. Lieutenant John Little, a passenger in the Athenienne, with a party of seamen, went on board the brig, for the purpose of prevailing on her master to return with them to the wreck, in hopes of rescuing any of the crew who might be still alive; but this generous purpose was frustrated by violent and adverse winds.

On the 21st, at four o'clock in the afternoon, the party reached Maritimo, having been sixteen hours in the open boat, and the next day they proceeded to Trepani, in Sicily. On the 24th, they arrived at Palermo; the news of the sad event had already been conveyed thither to Sir Sidney Smith, by a letter which had been written from Maritimo. The Eagle, of 74 guns, was instantly ordered to the Esquerques, but returned with the intelligence, that all who were left upon the wreck had perished, with the exception of two men, who had been picked up on a raft by some fishermen. They related that the poop had separated about eleven o'clock on the morning after the launch left them, and that they, together with ten others, clung to it, but all had either been washed off or died except themselves. There were also two other rafts, on one of which were three warrant officers, and on the other Captain Raynsford and Lieutenants Swinburne and Salter; but it was found impossible to disengage the rafts from the rigging to which they were attached, and the unfortunate men all perished.

The existence of the Esquerques, as we have already stated, had been doubted, but from Captain Raynsford's exclamation, previous to the ship striking, we may infer that he himself was not sceptical on the subject. From whatever cause this fine frigate may have been lost, the gallantry, at least, and self-devotion of her commander, from the time the vessel first struck, will rescue his memory from reproach.

There's a prayer and a tear o'er the lowliest grave;
But thousands lament o'er the fall of the brave;
And thou, whose rare valour and fate we bemoan,—
In the suff'rings of others forgetting thy own,—
O'er thy dust, though no trophies nor columns we rear,
Though the storm was thy requiem, the wild wave thy bier;
Yet thy spirit still speaks from its home on the flood,
Still speaks to the gen'rous, the brave, and the good;
Still points to our children the path which you trod,
Who lived for your country, and died in your God.

J. H. J.

F

Three hundred and fifty of the crew perished, while one hundred and forty-one men, with two women, were all who were saved.

THE NAUTILUS.

ONLY a few weeks after the loss of the Athenienne, and of so many of her crew, a shipwreck occurred in another part of the Mediterranean, attended by circumstances of most painful interest.

His Majesty's sloop, Nautilus, commanded by Captain Palmer, left the squadron of Sir Thomas Louis in the Hellespont, on the morning of the 3rd of January, 1807, bearing dispatches of the utmost importance for England.

The wind blowing fresh from the north-east, the sloop continued her course through the Archipelago without danger or mischance, until the evening of the 4th, when she was off Anti Milo; the pilot then gave up his charge, professing himself ignorant of the coast they were now approaching. As the dispatches confided to Captain Palmer were of great moment, he determined to run every hazard rather than retard their delivery. He therefore sailed from Anti Milo at sunset, and shaped his course to Cerigotto. At midnight, the wind had risen to a gale; the night was dark and gloomy; torrents of rain were falling, accompanied by loud and incessant peals of thunder, whilst vivid flashes of lightning ever and anon illuminated for an instant the murky sky, and left all in obscurity more dismal than before.

At two o'clock A.M., the tempest and the darkness having increased, the captain gave orders to close-reef topsails, and prepare for bringing-to until day-break. A little after three o'clock, a bright flash of lightning discovered to them the Island of Cerigotto right ahead, and about a mile distant. The captain considered his course to be now clear, and therefore directed all possible sail to be kept on the vessel without endangering the masts, at the same time he congratulated Lieutenant Nesbitt upon their escape from the threatened dangers of the Archipelago.

He then went below, and was engaged with the pilot in examining the chart, when a cry was heard of ' Breakers a-head !' Lieutenant Nesbitt, who was on deck, ordered the helm a-lee ; it was scarcely done, when the vessel struck. The shock was so violent, that the men below were thrown out of their hammocks, and they had difficulty in getting upon deck, for every sea lifted up the ship and then again dashed her upon the rocks with such force that they could not keep their feet. All was confusion and alarm. Every one felt his own utter helplessness.

' Oh ! my Lord,' writes Lieutenant Nesbitt to Lord Collingwood, ' it draws tears from my eyes when I reflect on the complicated miseries of the scene ! Heaven, now our only resource, was piteously invoked ; and happy am I to say, our gallant crew left nothing untried which we imagined could save us—all cheerfully obeying the orders of the officers. An instant had hardly elapsed ere our main-deck was burst in, and a few minutes after the lee bulwark was entirely overwhelmed. A heavy sea broke entirely over us, and none could see the smallest aperture through which hope might enter, and enliven the chill and dreary prospect before us.'

The only chance of escape for the crew was by the boats, and one only, a small whale-boat, got clear of the ship in safety, the others were all either stove or washed off the booms and dashed to pieces on the rocks by the raging surf. The boat that escaped was manned by the coxswain, George Smith, and nine others. When they got clear of the wreck, they lay on their oars, and those who had clothing shared it with others who were nearly naked. They then pulled towards the Island of Pauri, seeing that it was impossible for them to render any assistance to their wretched comrades, as the boat already carried as many as she could possibly stow.

After the departure of the whale-boat, the ship continued to strike every two or three minutes, but as she was thrown higher on the rock, the men perceived that a part of it was above water ; and as they expected the vessel to go to pieces at every shock, that lonely rock offered a safer refuge from the waves than the frail timbers to which they were clinging. The mercy of Providence soon provided them with the means of exchanging their perilous situation for one of less certain and instant danger. The mainmast fell over the side about twenty minutes after the vessel struck, and the mizen and foremasts followed. These all served as gangways by which the people passed through the surf from the wreck to the platform of the coral reef, and thus for the time were rescued from the certain death that awaited them if they remained on board.

The rock, which they reached with difficulty, was scarcely above water ; it was between three and four hundred yards long, and two hundred wide ; and upon this spot, in the midst of the deep, nearly a hundred men were thrown together, without food, almost without clothing, and with very little hope that they should ever escape from the perils that surrounded them. They had only left the wreck in time to hear her dashed to pieces against the rocks ; her timbers quivering, rending, and groaning, as they were riven asunder by the remorseless waves.

When day dawned upon the cheerless group, its light only revealed new horrors: the sea on all sides was strewed with fragments of the wreck; not a sail was visible on the waters, and many of their comrades were seen clinging to spars and planks, tossed hither and thither by the waves. The situation of the survivors was truly distressing; they were at least twelve miles from the nearest island, and their only chance of relief was in the possibility of a ship passing near enough to see the signal which they hoisted on a long pole fixed to the rocks.

The day was bitterly cold, and with much difficulty the unfortunate men contrived to kindle a fire, by means of a knife and flint that were happily in the pocket of one of the sailors, and a small barrel of damp powder that had been washed on to the rock. They next constructed a tent with pieces of canvas, boards, and parts of the wreck, and so they were enabled to dry the few clothes they had upon them. And now they had to pass a long and dreary night, exposed to hunger, cold, and wet; but they kept the fire burning, hoping that it might be visible in the darkness, and be taken for a signal of distress. And so it proved; for the coxswain and crew of the whale boat, who were on the Island of Pauri, observed the fire in the middle of the night, and the next morning the coxswain and pilot, with four of the men, pulled to the rocks, in hopes that some of their comrades might be still living.

They were beyond measure astonished to find so many survivors from the wreck, when they had scarcely dared to hope that any could have been saved except themselves. They had no food or water in their boat; for they had found nothing on the Island of Pauri (which was only a mile in circumference) but a few sheep and goats, kept there by the inhabitants of Cerigo, and a

little rain-water that was preserved in a hole of the rock.
The coxswain attempted to persuade Captain Palmer to
come into the boat, but the intrepid officer refused.
'Never mind me,' was his noble reply; 'save your unfortunate shipmates.'

After some consultation, the Captain ordered the coxswain to take ten of the people from the rock and make
the best of his way to Cerigotto, and return as soon as
possible with assistance.

Soon after the departure of the boat, the wind increased
to a gale, the waves dashed over the rock and extinguished the fire, and some of the men were compelled
to cling to the highest part of the rock, and others to
hold on by a rope fastened round a projecting point, in
order to save themselves from being washed away by the
surf; and thus a second night was passed, even more
wretched than the first. Many of the people became
delirious from the fatigue, hunger, thirst, and cold, which
they had suffered, and several died during the night;
some, apparently, from the effect of the intense cold
upon their exhausted frames. Terrible was the scene
which daylight presented: indiscriminately crowded
together on a small spot, were the living, the dying, and
the dead; and the wretched survivors unable to give any
help to those whose sufferings might shortly be their
own.

There was nothing to be done, but to wait in hope
for the return of the whale-boat, when, to the indescrib-
able joy of all, a ship, with all sail set, hove in sight:
she was coming down before the wind, and steering
directly for the rock.

This cheering sight infused vigour into the weakest
and most desponding. Signals of distress were instantly
made, and at last they were perceived by the vessel,
which brought to, and then hoisted out her boat. Great

was the joy of all the famishing creatures on the rock, to see their deliverance at hand; the strongest began to fasten spars and planks together to form rafts, on which they might get to the ship; the boat came within pistol-shot. She was full of men, who rested on their oars for a few minutes, as if to examine the persons whom they were approaching: the man at the helm waved his hat, and then the boat's head was put round and they pulled back again to the ship, and left the crew of the Nautilus to their fate.

The transition from hope to despair was terrible,—all that day they watched in vain for the return of their own boat from Cerigotto; but hour after hour passed away, and they began, at length, to fear that she had been lost in the gale of the preceding night.

Death, in its most horrible forms, now stared them in the face; the pangs of hunger and thirst were almost insupportable. There was—

> Water, water everywhere,
> Yet not a drop to drink.—COLERIDGE.

Some, indeed, of the poor sufferers were desperate enough to allay their raging thirst with salt water, in spite of the entreaties and warnings of those who knew how terrible are its effects. In a few hours those who had drunk it were seized with violent hysteria and raving madness, which in many ended in death.

Another night drew on, and they made their sad preparations for it by huddling together as closely as they could, to keep alive the little warmth that remained in their bodies, and covering themselves with the few ragged garments that were left. Happily the weather was more moderate, and they hoped to be able to get through the night ; but worn out as they were, the ravings of some of their companions banished sleep from the eyes of the rest. In the middle of the night they were unexpectedly hailed by the crew of the whale-boat.

The first cry from the rock was—' water! water!' but water they had none. They had found it impossible to procure anything but earthen vessels, and these could not be carried through the surf. The coxswain, however, informed them that next morning a large vessel would come to their relief; and in this hope of a speedy deliverance they were encouraged to further endurance. The morning broke at last, but no boat appeared; then came a reaction, and the heart-sickness of hope deferred. The scenes that occurred on that day were too dreadful to relate—it was the fourth on which they had not tasted food.

> . . . . . . Savagely
> They glared upon each other;
>
> . . . .
> . . . . and you might have seen
> The longings of the cannibal arise ·
> (Although they spoke not) in their wolfish eyes.—Byron.

They must now either taste human flesh or perish—there was no alternative.

A young man who had died the previous night was selected to be food for the rest.* Most of them had not power to masticate or to swallow—

> For every tongue, through utter drought,
> Was withered at the root.
> Coleridge (*Ancient Mariner*).

---

* 'I well remember,' says a naval surgeon, 'the above melancholy event, and particularly from one of the survivors being drafted on board the ship to which I belonged, (the Thunderer, then in the Dardanelles.) The poor fellow became my patient; he complained of no pain but that which arose from the horrible recollection of his having tasted human flesh to preserve his life. This preyed so deeply on his mind, that it rendered him incapable of performing any duty, and when I saw him sinking under the heavy load, I felt it to be my duty to order him to the hospital, that he might be invalided and sent home.'

Before evening death had made fearful ravages, and had numbered amongst its victims Captain Palmer and the first lieutenant.

Another night came on ; long and anxiously had they gazed upon the horizon—in vain had they strained their blood-shot eyes to see some vessel coming to their relief. The shades of night closed round them, and sadly they awaited the dawn of another day, resolving that if they lived to see it they would construct a raft and commit themselves to the waves, rather than remain to die of hunger and thirst. Accordingly, at day-light they began to put their plan into execution by fastening some of the larger spars together, and in a few hours the raft was completed. The eventful moment for launching it arrived, when with bitter grief and disappointment they beheld the work of their hands, which it had cost them so much labour to achieve, dashed to pieces in a few seconds and scattered adrift upon the waves. Some of the men, rendered desperate by seeing their last chance of escape thus snatched from them, rushed into the sea, grasping at such parts of the wreck as came within their reach ; but they were all swept away by the current, and their unhappy comrades saw them no more.

In the afternoon, the coxswain arrived in the whale-boat, but he came without bringing them any food or means of escape—for all his entreaties had been unavailing to persuade the Greek fishermen to put to sea whilst the gale continued. They had, however, promised to come to the relief of the sufferers the next day if the weather should be more favourable.

This was the fifth day that these wretched men had passed without food of any kind except the disgusting morsel they had attempted to swallow. Many who were completely exhausted, stretched their weary limbs on the hard rocks and expired, and before night the greater

F 3

part of the survivors were in a state of complete insensibility.

On the sixth morning they were scarcely able to raise
themselves from the rock to look once more upon the
sea, when one less feeble than the rest exclaimed, 'the
boats are coming.' And most welcome was the sight of
four fishing vessels, and the whale-boat steering towards
them. Such joy was theirs as can only be understood by
those who have experienced a similar deliverance from
the jaws of death. The boats reached the rocks ; they
contained a supply of water and food, which were distributed in moderation among the perishing seamen, who,
when they were a little renovated, were taken on board
the boats, and in a few hours landed on Cerigotto.

The poor but hospitable inhabitants of the island
received the strangers most kindly, and tended them with
the utmost care. Out of one hundred and twenty-two,
sixty-four only survived. And when we think of the
complicated miseries they had so long endured, we may
wonder that so many were spared.

After remaining eleven days at Cerigotto, the remnant
of the crew of the Nautilus went to Cerigo, and from
thence they sailed to Malta.

Lieutenant Nesbitt and the survivors were tried by a
court-martial at Cadiz for the loss of the Nautilus.

The court gave it as their opinion, ' That the loss of
that sloop was occasioned by the captain's zeal to forward
the public dispatches, which induced him to run in a
dark, tempestuous night for the passage between the
Island of Cerigotto and Candia ; but that the sloop
passed between Cerigotto and Pauri, and was lost on a
rock, on the south-west part of that passage, which rock
does not appear to be laid down in Heather's Chart, by
which the said sloop was navigated.

' That no blame attaches to the conduct of Lieutenant

Nesbitt, or such of the surviving crew of the Nautilus, but that it appears that Lieutenant Nesbitt and the officers and crew did use every exertion that circumstances could admit.'

Lieutenant Nesbitt died in 1824.

THE FLORA.

EARLY in January, 1807, H.M. ship Flora, of 36 guns, under the command of Captain Otway Bland, had been cruizing off the Texel, for the purpose of reconnoitring the ships of the enemy. This object having been effected, they shaped a course towards Harlingen, the captain ordering the pilots not to run the slightest risk, but to give the sands of the island sufficient berth, so as not to endanger the Flora; and so often did he reiterate these instructions, that the pilots appeared hurt that their nautical skill and knowledge of the track should be doubted. However, to the astonishment of all on board, and to the dismay of the pilots, the ship took the ground, and struck on the Shelling Reef, about noon on the 18th of January. It was only just past high water when she struck, and there was therefore no chance of getting her off till the next tide. In the meantime all weight was removed from aloft, and the topmasts were lowered over the side, to shore her up. Towards evening the wind increased to a gale, and a heavy swell came on, which prevented their getting out a bower anchor, although a raft was made for the purpose; but the night became so dark, and the sea so rough, they were obliged to relinquish the attempt, and resolved to wait with patience for high water, lightening the vessel as much as possible, by starting the water, and heaving most of the shot and other heavy articles overboard. All hands took their turn at the pumps, and worked vigorously; yet the water gained rapidly upon the vessel: this was partly attributable to her having struck amidships, and having a hole through her bottom, instead of her side, to supply the cistern. At about nine o'clock P.M., she began to heave, but as the tide made, the wind freshened, the sea rose, and she brought home the stream anchor, backed by the kedge, and forged on the sand. At half-past nine o'clock, a last effort was made to get her off, by letting go a bower anchor with a spring abaft, which brought her head round. They then made all sail and forced her over the reef. The ship once more floated in deep water: but this object was not attained without a most serious loss. The rudder had been carried away, and with it the launch and the jolly-boat, so that only one anchor and the worst boat were left for service. After those moments of breathless anxiety, and after giving utterance to a short but fervent expression of thankfulness that they had got clear of the reef, the men, almost worn out as they were, by so many hours of continued labour, again betook themselves to the pumps, in hopes of keeping the water under until they could reach an English port. But in spite of every exertion, in spite of continued bailing and pumping, and though a thrumbed sail was under the ship's bottom, the water gained to eight feet. As the danger increased, so did the vigour of the men. All was order, energy, and steady obedience throughout. The captain perceiving that it would be impossible to keep the vessel much longer afloat, gave orders to wear ship, and run her on the enemy's shore; nor could even this be done without much difficulty and danger, as it was necessary to let go their last anchor. Most of the guns were now thrown overboard, and everything done to lighten the ship; and about half-past six A.M., on the 19th, her head was brought round, and, steered by the sails and a cable veered astern, towards the islands. The weather was becoming more gloomy and threatening, and before ten o'clock A.M. the vessel was so terribly shaken, that it became absolutely necessary to cut away the main and mizen masts, leaving the foremast standing, with sail set, to force the ship on as much as possible, and also to prevent her drifting off with the ebb, or with a change of wind. Although the dangerous situation of the Flora was clearly perceived by the people on shore, no boat put out to her assistance, the authorities having forbidden them to render such aid on pain of death.

Captain Bland, during his cruize on these seas, had allowed the fishing-boats of the enemy to range unmolested, and had given strict orders that not a fish should be taken from them without payment; but even these boats now came near the labouring ship and passed on, leaving her and her crew to perish. About four o'clock in the afternoon when she seemed to be sinking, she took the ground and there remained, surrounded by breakers, the crew in vain firing guns, and making other signals of distress, which were totally disregarded. All hands that could be spared from the pumps had been employed in making rafts, and these were now launched into the surf, and about one hundred and thirty of the crew got upon them, and were fortunate enough to gain the high land.

Captain Bland, with a few officers and men, pushed off in the barge, the only boat that was left, and after rowing for eighteen hours without any sustenance, they reached the Island of Amoland, where they were made prisoners.

The rest of the crew, who had chosen to stay by the

ship, remained on board for four days and nights, and,
excepting nine, who perished from the severity of the
weather, they all got safe on shore. The above is a plain,
unvarnished account, taken from the narrative of Captain
Bland : it is a true tale, and needs not the aid of romance
to give it interest. For more than twenty-four hours
the crew suffered the horrors of uncertainty ; their vessel
thrown upon a hostile shore, whose inhabitants were forbidden on pain of death to assist them, whilst of all
their boats one only remained. Yet, even during this
time of trial and danger, discipline was not for a moment
abandoned ; no man's heart appeared to fail him ; each
one performed his duty with cheerfulness and alacrity ;
and nobly did they all earn the praise bestowed on them
by their commander.

  ' I cannot help paying here,' said Captain Bland, 'the
last tribute of praise to my crew ; they behaved with
order, respect, and perfect coolness to the last moment ;
nor would they quit the ship's side in the barge, though
at the risk of her being dashed to pieces, till I took the
place they had reserved for me.'

  The gallantry and seamanship displayed by Captain
Otway Bland, when in command of the Espoir, 14-gun
brig, in his attack and subsequent capture of a Genoese
pirate, well deserve a place in these pages.

  On the 7th of August, 1798, the Espoir was sailing
near Gibraltar in charge of part of a convoy, when a
large vessel, which appeared to be a man-of-war, was
seen steering apparently with the intention of cutting off
some of the convoy. Captain Bland, notwithstanding the
superiority of the force with which he had to contend,
determined upon attacking the stranger, which proved to
be the Liguria, mounted with 26 guns of various calibres.

  On approaching within hail, an officer on board the
Liguria ordered the commander of the Espoir to sur-

render, or he would sink his ship, enforcing the demand
by one shot, and afterwards by a whole broadside. The
fire was returned in a spirited manner by the Espoir,
and was kept up on both sides by the great guns and
musketry for upwards of three hours, when the captain
of the Liguria hailed the Espoir, begging her captain not
to fire any more, as he was a Genoese. Upon this,
Captain Bland desired him to lower his sails, and come
on board. As no attention was paid to this demand,
and the Genoese appeared to be attempting some
manœuvre, the Espoir poured in another broadside,
which the Liguria returned ; but on the Espoir tacking
to fire her opposite broadside, her opponent surrendered.

The crew of the Liguria consisted of one hundred and
twenty men of all nations, whilst that of the Espoir was
but eighty men, of which the master was killed, and six
men wounded.

Captain Bland died in 1810.

THE AJAX.

ON the evening of the 14th of February, 1807, H.M.
ship Ajax, 74 guns, commanded by Captain the
Hon. Sir Henry Blackwood, lay at anchor off the mouth
of the Dardanelles, in company with the squadron of
Vice-Admiral Sir John Duckworth. The wind, which
during the day had been boisterous, was partially lulled,
and in the clear moonlight every object was visible with
a distinctness almost equal to that of day.

The scene from the deck of the Ajax was one of sur-
passing beauty and interest. The bright moonbeams

rested on the waters, and left a silvery track upon the waves. Ahead and astern, the lofty masts of the squadron tapered darkly towards the sky, whilst the outline of every rope and spar was sharply defined against the clear blue vault of heaven. Every man in the ship, from the commander to the youngest boy, could feel and understand this natural beauty ; but there were many on board the squadron who had still higher enjoyment, as they gazed on those isles and shores which recalled the classic verse of Homer and of Virgil. For them every island, cape, river, and mountain was fraught with interest. There lay Tenedos, renowned of old ; there the mountain isle of Imbros stood out in bold relief from the snow-clad summits of Samothracia. In the distance appeared Mount Ida, and at its foot lay stretched the plains of Troy, o'er which the ' gulfy Simois' wanders still as it did of old. There is Cape Sigæum, and on it the tomb of Patroclus, round which Achilles dragged the godlike Hector's corpse ; there, too, the ashes of Achilles repose near those of his friend ; and a little further north, on the Rhœtian promontory, is the tomb of ' mighty Ajax.' Homer, Euripides, and Virgil have, it is true, a very small share in the studies of a youthful sailor, as they do not form an essential ingredient of a nautical education ; but an English gentleman, although his head be crammed with mathematics and equations, always contrives to pick up enough of classic lore to enable him thoroughly to enjoy such a scene as that we have attempted to describe. He is much to be pitied who cannot appreciate such enjoyment ; but in these days, when the schoolmaster is aboard, and when, by the wise liberality of the Government, our ships are furnished with useful and interesting books, none need of necessity be deprived of the exquisite pleasure which is to be derived from visiting scenes which have been 'dignified either by wisdom, bravery, or virtue.' We are constantly reminded that 'knowledge is power ;' but it might be well to impress upon youngsters, that '*knowledge* is enjoyment.' There is, indeed, no acquirement in literature or science that will not at some time or other be productive of real pleasure.

We have lingered on this subject longer than we should have done, for we must now relate how soon the tranquillity of that fair scene was disturbed—how for a time another light, redder and fiercer than that of the moon, shone on the blue waters of the Hellespont.

Soon after nine o'clock P.M., Captain Blackwood had received from his first lieutenant the report of the safety of the Ajax, and all, except the officers and men who were on duty, had retired to their berths. A very short time, however, had elapsed, before the stillness of the night was broken by the appalling cry of 'Fire!' It must be a fearful sound to hear—the cry of 'Fire!' as awful as the voice of him who

Drew Priam's curtain in the dead of night,
And would have told him half his Troy was burned.

The officer of the watch instantly informed Captain Blackwood of the alarm. He hastened upon deck, and found too surely that flames were bursting from the afterpart. He gave orders to beat to quarters—to fire the guns as signals of distress, and directed Lieutenant Wood and a midshipman to proceed in one of the boats to all the ships of the squadron to request assistance.

These orders were promptly given, and promptly obeyed ; but who can enter fully into the feelings of Captain Blackwood at that awfully critical moment. Here was his ship and six hundred men threatened with immediate destruction, and each one of that six hundred looked to him for direction and guidance.

In order to inspire others with courage and confidence, he must display decision in every look and gesture. Whatever others might do, his lip must not tremble, nor his eyelid quiver—no look of apprehension must be seen on his brow. He must stand forth calm and undaunted —the recollection of tender ties and loving hearts might wring his soul with agony, but these thoughts must be banished ; the safety of six hundred human beings depended, under God, on his firmness and exertion, and every eye was directed to him in anxious inquiry. When the ship's company had turned out, every man took his station calmly and in obedience to orders.

The captain, followed by several of his officers, went down to the cockpit, from whence issued clouds of smoke. Every effort was made to extinguish the flames in that part of the ship, but they increased so rapidly, it soon became impossible for any one to remain below. Several of the men who were throwing down water fell from suffocation with the buckets in their hands. To give more air to the men so employed, the lower-deck ports were hauled up; but this rather increasing than diminishing the density of the smoke, they were closed again, and the after-hatchway shut down. The carpenter's attempt to scuttle the afterpart of the ship was also ineffectual.

Ten or fifteen minutes only had elapsed after the first alarm had been given, before the flames raged with such fury, that it was impossible to hoist out the boats; the jolly-boat had fortunately been lowered in obedience to the captain's orders when he first went upon deck. As the flames burst up the main-hatchway, dividing the fore from the afterpart of the ship, the captain ordered all hands to the forecastle, and seeing that it was utterly beyond human power to prevent the destruction of the vessel, he desired every man to provide for his own safety.

The silent plague through the green timber eats,
And vomits out a tardy flame by fits;
Down to the keels, and upwards to the sails,
The fire descends, or mounts, but still prevails;
Nor buckets pour'd, nor strength of human hand,
Can the victorious element withstand.

DRYDEN'S *Æneid, Book V.*

The luckless ship was now wrapped in flames from amidships to taffrail, and the scene of horror is beyond the powers of description. Hundreds of human beings were assembled together on the forecastle, bowsprit, and sprit-sail-yard. No boat had yet come to their assistance. Their perilous situation had levelled all distinction of rank ; men and officers were huddled together, watching with despairing hearts the progress of the fiery element, which threatened to hurry them so quickly into eternity. Volumes of black smoke rose in huge pillars from all parts of the ship, whilst far above the hissing and crackling of the flames, as they licked the masts and rigging, rose the shrieks and death yells of the hapless men, who, unable to gain the forecastle, had sought safety aloft, where the flames had now reached them.

Some, rather than endure the horrible suspense, trusted themselves to the mercy of the waves, and by plunging overboard, ended their lives and sufferings in a watery grave. Many, in their agony, fell on their knees, imploring God for that help which they despaired of receiving from mortal agency. Perhaps these men would not have thought of prayer to heaven in face of a human foe, but now that the 'last enemy' glared upon them in so fearful a shape, they felt compelled to fly to Him who hath said, ' Call upon me in the day of trouble.'

The booming of the guns, as they exploded, echoed far and wide over the waters, and added to the horrors of that awful night.

In the midst of his people stood the captain, endeavour-

ing to sustain their sinking spirits, and exhorting them
to be firm and to depend upon the boats which were now
heaving in sight. He then bade them farewell, and
sprung into the sea ; he breasted the waves for a length
of time, but his strength was nearly exhausted, when,
happily, he was seen, and picked up by one of the boats
of the Canopus.

As the boats from the squadron neared the Ajax, the
agonizing fears of the sufferers were changed into wild
transports of joy ; so sudden was the transition from
despair to hope, that many of the crew lost all self-possession, and perished by jumping into the sea in their
impatience to reach the boats.

Such details as these, showing the effects of fear upon
untutored minds, make us thankful that a great change
for the better has been effected within the last forty
years with respect to the religious and moral instruction
of our sailors.

Every ship's company is exposed to casualties similar
to that which befel the crew of the Ajax,—to shipwreck,
fire, and sudden destruction,—and no man will deny that
in times of extreme peril, a calm and composed mind is
the greatest of blessings—the want of it, the greatest
misery. Few will be sceptical enough to deny, on the
other hand, that the best security for such composure,
in a moment of unforeseen danger, or of unlooked-for
deliverance, is a firm and sure trust that there is a God
above, who 'ruleth over all ;' whom the winds and the
sea obey, and who is 'mighty to save,' even in the hour
of man's direst extremity. To instil this knowledge and
trust into the hearts of our seamen, and by it to make
them both better men, and better sailors, should be the
chief object of every improvement in education.

Lieut. Willoughby, of the St. George, had hastened
in a cutter to assist the crew of the Ajax, and he very

soon rescued as many men as his boat could carry.
Numbers, however, were still surrounding him, who, for
the safety of those in the already overladen boat, were,
with much reluctance, left to their fate. Fortunately
some launches and a barge arrived in time to pick them
up, and convey them to. the different ships of the
squadron.

The Ajax all this time was drifting towards the island
of Tenedos, with her stern and broadside alternately presented to the wind. The humane exertions of Lieutenant
Willoughby had been twice crowned with success; his
boat was, for the third time, nearly filled with people,
when he observed the Ajax round to, and that several
men were hanging by ropes under her head. He
resolved, at all hazards, to rescue these poor fellows
before she again fell off. Dashing, therefore, towards
her, he succeeded in the first part of his object, but not
until the vessel was again before the wind, flames issuing
from every part of both hull and rigging, and with the
cutter across her hawse.

To extricate himself from this perilous situation was
almost impossible, for every moment increased the speed
with which the Ajax was surging through the water, and
the sea thrown up from her bows threatened his small
boat with instant destruction.

We will now take up the account as given by Marshall,
in his *Naval Biograghy :**

' Whilst the Ajax was propelling the cutter in the
above alarming manner, the flames reached the shank,
painter, and stopper, of her remaining bower anchor, and
it fell from her bows, nearly effecting the destruction of
the boat at its first plunge into the water. The cable
caught her outer gunwale, over which it ran, apparently

* *Life of Sir Nisbet Willoughby.*

one sheet of fire; orders, exertion, and presence of mind
were now of no avail. Death to all in the cutter appeared
inevitable. The sole alternative was either to be burned
or drowned, for they were all too much exhausted to be
able to save themselves by swimming.

'The boats at a distance saw that the cutter was
enveloped in flames, and therefore considered it impossible to assist her. All that Lieutenant Willoughby
and his companions could do while the cable was running
out and binding their boat more firmly to the ship, was
to keep the sparks and flames as much as possible from
the uncovered parts of their persons. Providentially,
however, although the inner portion of the cable had
been burnt through, the anchor took the ground, and
gave the ship's head a check to windward, before the
less consumed part had entirely left the tier; and thus
the very event which had seemed to seal the doom of the
cutter was in all respects ordained by the Almighty for
her preservation. The change in the ship's position
enabled the boat to get clear, but not before every
individual in her was more or less severely scorched, and
the heat was no longer endurable.'

The wreck drifted on shore on the north side of the
island of Tenedos, where, at five o'clock in the morning,
she blew up with an explosion which might be felt on
the adjacent shores of Europe and of Asia; and all that
remained of the Ajax were a few smoking spars, which
rose to the surface of the sea.

Such was the fate of this noble ship, destroyed by a
conflagration more rapid than had ever been known,
and of which the cause has never been clearly ascertained.
It appears, however, certain that, contrary to orders,
there had been a light in the bread-room; for when the
first lieutenant broke open the door of the surgeon's
cabin, the after bulk-head was already burnt down; and

as the purser's steward, his assistant, and the cooper, were among the missing, it is but reasonable to suppose that the fire had been occasioned by their negligence.

' I trust,' says Captain Blackwood, in his defence before the court of inquiry, ' that I shall be able to prove to the satisfaction of this court, that I had instituted a regulation, which obliged the first lieutenant, the warrant officers, and master at arms, in a body to visit all the quarters, store-rooms, wings, &c., and report to me at eight o'clock on their clearness and safety ; and that I had also received at nine o'clock the report of the marine officer of the guard.' .... ' I trust this court will consider that in ordering the first lieutenant and warrant officers to visit all parts of the ship, whose report, as well as that of the master at arms, I had received at a few minutes past eight o'clock, I had very fully provided for every want, and might with perfect confidence have considered my ship in a state of perfect safety with respect to fire.'

Captain Blackwood, his surviving officers and men, were all most honourably acquitted of any blame respecting the loss of the Ajax.

Out of six hundred men, three hundred and fifty were saved by the boats of the squadron ; but two hundred and fifty perished that night by fire or water.

Amongst the lost were Lieutenants Reeve and Sibthorpe ; Captain Boyd, Royal Marines ; Mr. Owen, surgeon ; Mr. Donaldson, master ; twenty-five midshipmen ; two merchants of Constantinople, and a Greek pilot.

The melancholy fate of the gunner must not be passed over unnoticed.

This poor man had two sons on board, whom he was bringing up to his own profession.

When the first alarm of fire was given, he had rushed below, and was soon seen emerging from the smoke with one of the boys in his arms.

He threw the lad into the sea and the jolly-boat picked him up; but on going down for the other, the unfortunate father fell a victim to his paternal affection, and either perished in the flames, or was suffocated.

Of three women who were on board, one saved herself by following her husband down a rope from the jib-boom, and was received into a boat.

Captain Blackwood served as a volunteer in the subsequent operations of the squadron in forcing the passage of the Dardanelles, and his services then were most highly spoken of in a letter from Sir J. Duckworth to Lord Collingwood. He had distinguished himself on many previous occasions. He was in the memorable action of 1st of June, 1794; and he commanded the Euryalus at the battle of Trafalgar.

When Sir Henry Blackwood bade farewell to Nelson, on leaving the Victory to repair on board his own ship, before the commencement of the action, Lord Nelson said, with prophetic meaning, 'God bless you, Blackwood; I shall never see you again.'

In 1810, he commanded the inshore squadron off Toulon, and for his gallant conduct on that station he received the thanks of the commander-in-chief, Sir Charles Cotton.

In 1814, Captain Blackwood was advanced to the rank of rear-admiral, and in 1819 he was appointed commander-in-chief in the East Indies.

He died a vice-admiral in 1832, and his name is enrolled among the first class of naval heroes who have fought under the British flag.

The memory of Blackwood is still held in veneration by the old weather-beaten tars of the Nelsonian school.

Lieutenant Willoughby, whom we have seen displaying so much gallantry in his efforts to save the crew of the Ajax, entered the service in the year 1790.

Before his promotion to the rank of lieutenant, in the year 1798, he distinguished himself on more than one occasion by that promptitude of action for which his after career was so remarkable.

In 1801, he served on board the Russel, at the battle of Copenhagen. The gallant manner in which he boarded the Provestein block ship, excited so much admiration, that the Russel's crew gave him three cheers upon his return to the ship. We next find this young officer performing a most important service when the French forces capitulated at Cape François, St. Domingo, in 1803.

He was at this period serving on board the Hercule, flag-ship to Sir John Duckworth. According to the terms agreed upon, the French men-of-war were to keep their colours hoisted until they got outside of the harbour, when they were each to discharge a broadside in return to a shot fired athwart their bows, by one of the British ships, and then to make the usual signals of submission.

The Clorinde frigate, in going out of the harbour, grounded under Fort St. Joseph, at the moment when the launch of the Hercule, commanded by Mr. Willoughby, was entering the harbour. When Mr. Willoughby saw the critical position of the Clorinde, and the danger which menaced all on board of her (for he knew that even if they succeeded in gaining the shore, which was doubtful, no quarter would be given them by the blacks), he pulled towards the frigate, and when he came alongside, he proposed terms to General La Poyne (who was on board of her) by which the safety of the crew would be secured.

Mr. Willoughby promised, that if the frigate would hoist English colours, he (Mr. Willoughby) would wait upon General Dessalines, and demand that the British flag should be respected ; and in the event of the Clorinde going to pieces during the night, the crew and passengers should be considered prisoners of war.

G

General La Poyne readily accepted the proposed terms, and accordingly, Mr. Willoughby proceeded to negotiate with General Dessalines, who promised compliance with his request.

The boats of the Hercule were sent to the assistance of the Clorinde, and they succeeded in heaving her off.

Thus by the timely exertions of this zealous young officer, some hundreds of lives were saved, and the British navy obtained a frigate which, for many years, was one of the finest of the 38-gun class.

At the attack on Curaçoa, in 1804, Mr. James relates, that for the sake of encouraging his men, Mr. Willoughby used to take his meals 'sitting in a chair upon the breast-work of a battery, while the earth was ploughed up all around; and one man, we believe, was killed on the spot; but still the table and chair, and the daring officer who sat there, remained untouched.

In the following year, the Hercule had captured a merchant schooner, and one of the prisoners gave notice that a Spanish corvette of twenty guns, was lying in St. Martha, South America. Mr. Willoughby thereupon volunteered to attack her; and on the 4th of July, he took the command of the prize, and parted company with his ship, accompanied by three midshipmen and thirty volunteers. On the 6th, they entered the harbour of St. Martha; Captain Samuel Roberts, then a midshipman, was at the helm, with a check shirt on, his head covered with a French kerchief, and his face blackened. The rest of the men were below, except a black, and a mulatto.

The schooner being well known, the deception was perfectly successful, and she passed the batteries without interruption; but, to the disappointment of all on board, no corvette was to be found.

Mortified in the extreme, they put about, but not in

time to escape detection. The enemy had found out the trick that had been played upon them; and the batteries from the island and harbour opened upon the schooner a volley of no very gentle reproaches. However, she luckily avoided the danger, and returned in safety to the Hercule, without receiving a single shot.

In 1807, Mr. Willoughby was appointed to the Royal George. We have already alluded to his humane exertions to save the crew of the Ajax, while the squadron was off the Dardanelles. He soon afterwards received a severe wound whilst he was taking more thought for others' safety than for his own. Upon the return of the squadron from Constantinople, an attack was made upon a large building on the island of Prota.

Lieutenant Willoughby perceiving that three men were very much exposed to the enemy's fire, called out to them, desiring them to stoop. At that moment, he was himself struck by two pistol balls; one entered his head, just above the right jaw, and took a slanting direction upwards—and has never been extracted; the other shot cut his left cheek in two; For some minutes he lay apparently lifeless, but fortunately the movement of an arm indicated enough of life to awaken hope in his companions; and they carried him on board the Royal George.

In 1808, he was promoted to the rank of commander, and appointed to the Otter sloop, then employed in cruizing off the Isle of France. Here he distinguished himself in cutting out some vessels under the protection of the batteries of the Black River; and for his services at the capture of St. Paul, he was appointed to the Nereide.

In 1810, he made an attack upon Jacotel: he thought this a somewhat dangerous enterprise; and, therefore, to inspire his men with more than usual courage and ardour, he headed them himself, in full uniform. After a desperate resistance on the part of the enemy, he succeeded in spiking the guns of the fort, and taking prisoner the commanding officer. For this service he was promoted to the rank of captain.

In the course of the same year, 1810, a musket burst in the hands of one of the men, so near to the place where Captain Willoughby stood, that his jaw was fractured, and the windpipe laid bare, so that his life was despaired of.

He had hardly recovered from this wound, before he was engaged in an attack upon Port Louis, Isle de France. The disasters which befel the squadron upon this occasion have now become a matter of history, and they need not be recounted here,—suffice it to say, that Captain Willouhgby continued to keep up an unequal conflict until nearly all on board the Nereide were either killed or wounded. Nor did he surrender, although he had entirely lost one of his eyes, and the other was much injured, 'until (to use the words of Vice-Admiral Bertie) after a glorious resistance, almost unparalleled even in the brilliant annals of the British navy.'

Upon his return to England, Captain Willoughby had a pension of 550l. per annum awarded to him in consideration of his wounds.

Having no immediate prospect of employment at home, he repaired to St. Petersburg, and offered his services to the Czar.

In his very first engagement in his new career, Captain Willoughby was taken prisoner by the French,—falling a victim to his own generosity. During the action, he saw two Prussian soldiers severely wounded,—dismounting himself, and desiring his servant to do the same, he placed the wounded men upon his own horses, and attended them on foot. They were quickly overtaken by some French cavalry, and Captain Willoughby was made prisoner. He was soon afterwards informed that if he would sign a paper, pledging himself to hasten to France by a certain route, he would be allowed to travel alone.

He gladly consented to this; but to his astonishment, after signing the required paper, he was ordered to march with the other prisoners. In vain he protested against this breach of faith—he was obliged to proceed. His sufferings from cold and hunger whilst crossing the deserts of Russia and Poland were intense. After witnessing the heartrending scenes of Moscow, he at length reached Mayence. Thence he was removed to Metz, and he had scarcely reached the town, before an order came for his confinement in the Chateau of Bouillon, where he remained a close prisoner for nine months. He was then taken to Peronne, and there he continued until the arrival of the Allies at Chalons, when he contrived to make his escape.

Soon after his arrival in England, Captain Willoughby received the Order of the Bath,—an honour scarcely commensurate with the many and valuable services he had performed for his country. It may safely be asserted that no officer living has been engaged in so many hard-fought actions, or has received so many dangerous wounds. From his first entrance into the service, to the end of the late war, all his energies were devoted to the service of his country; and now that his services are no longer required, with a constitution shattered by age and wounds, he is employing the remainder of his days in deeds of charity and kindness towards his fellow-creatures.

Captain Willoughby became admiral in 1847, and since the foregoing pages were written, death has closed his eventful life.

THE ANSON.

THE year 1807 was most disastrous to the British navy: during that period, we lost no less than twenty-nine ships of war, and, unhappily, the greater part of their crews. Some of these vessels foundered at sea, others were wrecked or accidentally burnt, and it was at the close of this eventful year that a calamity occurred which equalled, if it did not surpass, any previous disaster.

The Anson, of 40 guns, under the command of Captain Charles Lydiard, after completing her stores for a few months' cruise, sailed from Falmouth on the 24th of December, to resume her station off Brest. The wind was adverse, blowing very hard from the W.S.W., until the morning of the 28th, when Captain Lydiard made the Island of Bas, on the French coast. As the gale was increasing rather than subsiding, he determined to return to port, and accordingly shaped his course for the Lizard. At three o'clock P.M. land was discovered, apparently about five miles west of the Lizard, but owing to the thickness of the fog, there was a difference of opinion as to the land that was seen, and therefore the ship was wore to stand out to sea. She had not been long on this tack before land was descried right ahead.

It was now evident that their position was extremely dangerous,—the ship was completely embayed, and the wind raged with increasing fury. Every exertion was made to keep the Anson off shore, but without success, and it was not until she was fearfully near to the rocks that she could be brought to an anchor, in twenty-five fathoms, with the best bower anchor veered away to two cables' length. The top-gallant masts were lowered upon deck, and in this state she rode from five o'clock P.M., when she anchored, till four o'clock the next morning, when the cable suddenly parted. During the night, the gale was tremendous, and the sea ran mountains high; they had nothing now to depend upon for the safety of the ship but a small bower anchor, which was immediately let go, and this held until eight o'clock, when it also parted. The ship was no longer an object of consideration; Captain Lydiard felt that he had done his utmost to save her, but in vain, and that now every energy must be put forth for the preservation of human life. The tempest raged with such fury that no boat could possibly come to their aid, nor could the strongest swimmer hope to gain the shore. It appeared to Captain Lydiard that the only chance of escape for any of the crew was in running the ship as near the coast as possible. He gave the necessary orders, and the master run the vessel on the sand which forms the bar between the Loe Pool and the sea, about three miles from Helstone. The tide had been ebbing nearly an hour when she took the ground, and she broached to, leaving her broadside heeling over, and facing the beach.

The scene of horror and confusion which ensued on the Anson striking against the ground, was one which baffles all description. Many of the men were washed away by the tremendous sea which swept over the deck; many others were killed by the falling of the spars, the crashing sound of which, as they fell from aloft, mingled with the shrieks of the women on board, was heard even amidst the roar of the waters and the howling of the winds. The coast was lined with crowds of spectators, who watched with an intense and painful interest the gradual approach of the ill-fated vessel towards the shore, and witnessed the subsequent melancholy catastrophe.

Calm and undaunted amidst the terrors of the scene,
Captain Lydiard is described as displaying in a remarkable degree that self-possession and passive heroism,
which has been so often the proud characteristic of the
commander of a British ship of war under similar
harassing circumstances. Notwithstanding the confusion
of the scene, his voice was heard, and his orders were
obeyed with that habitual deference which, even in
danger and in death, an English seaman rarely fails to
accord to his commanding officer.

He was the first to restore order, to assist the wounded,
to encourage the timid, and to revive expiring hope.
Most providentially, when the vessel struck, the mainmast, in falling overboard, served to form a communication between the ship and the shore, and Captain
Lydiard was the first to point out this circumstance to
the crew. Clinging with his arm to the wheel of the
rudder, in order to prevent his being washed overboard
by the waves, he continued to encourage one after
another as they made the perilous attempt to reach the
shore. It was fated that this gallant officer should not
enjoy in this world the reward of his humanity and his
heroism. After watching with thankfulness the escape
of many of his men, and having seen with horror many
others washed off the mast, in their attempts to reach
the land, he was about to undertake the dangerous
passage himself, when he was attracted by the cries of a
person seemingly in an agony of terror. The brave man
did not hesitate for a moment, but turned and made his
way to the place whence the cries proceeded; there he
found a boy, a protégé of his own, whom he had entered
on board the Anson only a few months before, clinging
in despair to a part of the wreck, and without either
strength or courage to make the least effort for his own
preservation. Captain Lydiard's resolution was instantly

taken,—he would save the lad, if possible, though he might himself perish in the attempt. He threw one arm round the boy, whilst he cheered him by words of kind encouragement, with the other arm he clung to the spars and mast to support himself and his burthen. But the struggle did not last long; nature was exhausted by the mental and physical sufferings he had endured; he lost his hold, not of the boy, but of the mast, the wild waves swept over them, and they perished together.

It must not be supposed that the people on the shore were unconcerned spectators of the fearful tragedy that was enacted before their eyes. British fishermen are proverbial for their daring and intrepidity. Inured from childhood to the dangers and hardships attendant on their perilous calling, with very few exceptions our fishermen have always been ready to succour the wrecked and tempest-tossed mariner. There is not, we believe, a fishing village between the Land's End and the Orkneys, that cannot produce its true *heroes*—men who have risked, and are willing again to risk, their own lives to save others. Our fisheries are the best nurseries for our navy. Englishmen may be justly proud of the boatmen, from amongst whom spring those 'hearts of oak' which have so long rendered our fleets pre-eminent over those of every other country in the world. But, besides the generous disposition to assist any perishing fellow-creature, there were in this instance more powerful motives to exert every effort to save the crew of the Anson. This ship had been stationed for some time at or near Falmouth, so that acquaintances, friendships, and still dearer ties, had been formed between the inhabitants of the neighbouring towns and villages, and the people of the unfortunate vessel. But a few days before they had witnessed a far different scene, when she left their shores in all the pride of a well-ordered and well-dis-

ciplined man-of-war, amidst the shouts, and cheers, and
blessings of the multitude, who now beheld her lying
within a few fathoms of them a helpless wreck, her
masts gone, her bulwarks broken in, the waves sweeping
over her, and breaking up her timbers.

The surf ran so high, it was impossible that any boat
could reach the wreck. The life-boat, in 1807, had not
been brought to the state of perfection it has attained in
our day; and the many inventions which science and art
have since introduced for the preservation of life, were
for the most part unknown in the times of which we are
now writing.

Several men attempted to swim to the ship, but without success; they were all, one after another, cast back
exhausted upon the beach, and many of them without
sense or motion. At last, when there seemed no hope
left of affording aid to the sufferers, Mr. Roberts, of Helstone, seized hold of a rope, and boldly struck out in the
direction of the Anson. He was a powerful swimmer,
and his courageous efforts were watched from the shore
and from the wreck with intense interest, and many a
heartfelt prayer was breathed for his safety and success.
Tossed on the foaming waters, at one moment lost to
sight, and almost suffocated in the spray, and at another
rising on the top of a huge wave, he at last reached the
ship, and was hailed as a deliverer by those who were
still clinging to the spars and rigging. The rope which
Mr. Roberts had taken with him was made fast to the
wreck, and this formed a communication with the shore,
by which many a poor wretch was saved who must
otherwise have perished.

Another instance of heroic self-devotion was exhibited
by a Methodist preacher, a little later in the day, when,
as no one appeared on the ship's side, it was supposed

that every one had either come on shore, or had been
drowned ; but this brave and good man thought that
there might be some still left on board who were unable
to make an effort to save themselves, and, under this
impression, he ventured his life through the surf, followed by a few other daring spirits like himself. With
great difficulty they gained the wreck, where, as they
had anticipated, they found several persons lying below,
all too much exhausted to get upon deck. Some, in
terror and despair, called upon God for mercy ; others,
in hopeful trust, seemed resigned to their fate ; and
others were so weak as to be indifferent to the horrors
around them. Two women and two children were of
the number. The preacher and his gallant comrades
had the happiness of saving the women and some of
the men, but the children were lost.

Sixty men, amongst whom were Captain Lydiard and
his first-lieutenant, perished in the wreck of the Anson.
The survivors of the crew were conveyed to Helstone,
where they received every attention and kindness which
their unfortunate condition required. The body of
Captain Lydiard, which was washed on shore, was
interred at Falmouth with military honours.

We feel assured that the following particulars of the
life of Captain Lydiard will not be unacceptable to the
reader.

He entered the navy in the year 1780, in the flag-ship
of Admiral Darby, who then commanded the channel
fleet, and from that time served as a midshipman under
several commanders on various stations, both at home
and abroad, during thirteen years. In 1794, he was
appointed a lieutenant of the Captain, of 74 guns, in
which ship he served in two general engagements in the

Mediterranean. In July of the following year he removed to the Southampton frigate, commanded by Captain Shields, and afterwards by Captain Macnamara.

On the evening of the 9th of June, 1796, the Southampton was stationed with the fleet under Sir John Jervis, off Toulon, when a French cruizer was discovered working up to Hieres Bay. The commander-in-chief called the captain of the Southampton on board the Victory, and pointing out the ship, directed him to make a dash at her through the Grand Pas. Accordingly, the Southampton weighed, and, in order to delude the French into the supposition that the ship was either a neutral or a French frigate, hauled up under easy sail close to the batteries at the north-east of Porquerol. The stratagem succeeded; for before the enemy were aware of the approach of the Southampton, the ship was alongside of the French cruizer. Captain Macnamara cautioned her commander not to make a fruitless resistance; but he replied by snapping his pistol, and pouring in a broadside. In a moment, the English boarded, led on by Lieutenant Lydiard, with an impetuosity that nothing could withstand. After ten minutes' spirited resistance on the part of the French captain and a hundred of his men under arms, the 'Utile' surrendered, but not before the death of her gallant commander, who fell at the beginning of the onset.

Lydiard was instantly promoted, and appointed to the command of the ship he had so gallantly captured. In the year 1801, he was advanced to the rank of post-captain, and though frequently soliciting employment, did not succeed in obtaining a command until 1805, when he was appointed to the Anson.

These pages will not admit of our recounting the many instances in which this officer's gallantry was conspicuous. Before concluding, however, we cannot refrain

from laying before our readers the following account of
the last enterprise in which Captain Lydiard was engaged,
and which is related by his biographer in *The Naval
Chronicle.*[*]

'No sooner had the Anson been refitted, than she
was again selected, with three other frigates, under the
command of Captain Brisbane (as Commodore), of the
Arethusa, to reconnoitre, and, if possible, to sound the
minds of the inhabitants of Curaçoa upon the suggestion of an alliance with this country; but the gallant
Brisbane, and his equally gallant partner in this expedition, soon formed a plan for curtailing this mode of
proceeding, and determined, at all risks, by a *coup de
main*, either to capture the island, or to perish in the
attempt.

'With this resolution, having arranged their plan of
attack, they proceeded in their course for the island, and
they reached the entrance of the harbour just at the
dawn of day, on the 1st of January, 1807.

'In order to inform the reader, who may not be
acquainted with the amazing strength of Curaçoa on
the sea face, we will give some account of the difficulties
which they had to contend with; and, at the same time,
shall avail ourselves of such statements of the facts as
the different official and other communications upon the
subject will furnish us with.

'The harbour was defended by regular fortifications of
two tier of guns. Fort Amsterdam alone mounting sixty-
six pieces of cannon; the entrance only fifty yards wide,
and so circumstanced, that it is impossible for a ship to
return by the same wind that takes it in. Athwart the
entrance of the harbour was the Dutch frigate Kenaw
Hatslau, of 36 guns, and the Surinam, of 22 guns, with

---

* Vol. xix., p. 449.

two large schooners of war; a chain of forts was on
Mesleberg heights, and that almost impregnable fortress,
Fort Republique, within the distance of grape-shot,
enfilading the whole harbour.   The cool determined
bravery of British seamen perceives obstacles only to
surmount them; and with this determination the
squadron entered the harbour, the Arethusa, Captain
Brisbane, leading, followed in close line by the Latona,
Captain Wood; Anson, Captain Lydiard; and Fisguard,
Captain Bolton.

'When the headmost ship got round the point of the
harbour's mouth, the wind became so unfavourable that
she could not fetch in; but to return was impossible—it
was too late.   What a trying moment!   At that instant,
however, there came on a squall, in which the wind
shifted two points in their favour, and they proceeded
close together.

'The enemy were panic-struck at such unexpected
gallantry, and all was confusion.   A severe and destructive cannonade now commenced, and the Dutch frigate
was boarded by Captain Brisbane, when the Latona
instantly warped alongside and took possession, and
Captain Brisbane proceeded to the shore.   The Surinam
was boarded from the larboard bow of the Anson, while
her starboard guns were firing at the batteries; and
Captain Lydiard, upon securing the Surinam, went immediately on shore, and landed at the same moment
with Captain Brisbane.   Immediately debarking their
respective officers and ship's companies, they proceeded
to storm the forts, citadel, and town, which were by
seven o'clock completely in their possession, and at ten
o'clock the British flag was hoisted on Fort Republique.
Captains Brisbane and Lydiard were the first upon the
walls of Fort Amsterdam.   Indeed, too much cannot be
said in praise of the almost unparalleled bravery dis-

played by the officers and men of all the ships on this occasion. It may be truly said to be 'perfectly in union with everything glorious in the past, and an example of everything glorious to the future.''

The same year that opened so brilliantly upon the career of Captain Lydiard, witnessed, at its close, the total destruction of the Anson, and the untimely fate of her brave commander.

THE BOREAS.

IN the afternoon of the 21st of November, 1807, the Boreas, of 22 guns, Captain George Scott, proceeded in search of a pilot-boat, which had been blown off the coast of Guernsey in a gale of wind.

This boat was picked up and taken in tow, when about six o'clock P.M. it was discovered that the ship was near the Hannois rocks, about two miles to the south-west of Guernsey. Orders were immediately given by the pilot to put the helm down, but whilst in stays, the ship struck on the larboard bow; and although every exertion was made to get her off, it was found impossible to do so. The point of a rock was reported to be through the well, rendering the pumps useless. The ship then heeled on her larboard broadside, and the captain gave orders to cut away the masts.

The moment the ship struck, the pilots basely deserted her, and made off in their own boat, without even offering assistance to those who had encountered this danger and disaster in their service. Had the pilots returned to Rocquaine, only two miles distant, they might have procured aid for the Boreas, and preserved the lives of her crew. When Captain Scott was convinced that there was no chance of saving his ship, he ordered an allowance of spirits to be served round, and the gig, the launch, and cutter to be prepared for lowering.

The gig, with Lieutenant Bewick, a lieutenant of marines, and six men, was sent to give information, and obtain assistance. The launch, with the gunner, and some others, was ordered to take on board the sick, and land them at Hannois Point, and then to return to the ship; and the cutter, with the boatswain, and a few men, was despatched on the same service. Captain Scott, with noble intrepidity, remained to share the fate of his vessel.

The launch, under the orders of the gunner, succeeded in reaching the Hannois Rocks, as did also the cutter; but the greater part of the crew of the launch abandoned her as soon as they touched the land. In vain did the gunner use every persuasion to induce the men to return with him to the assistance of their comrades who were left on board the Boreas; they were deaf to his entreaties, and he was obliged to put off again with only four men. The wind and tide were so strong, and so much against them, that the utmost exertion was necessary to enable them to make their way towards the ship, and when they got within two hundred yards of the back of the rocks, the launch was half filled with water. They then tried to make the land again; but before they could reach it the boat was swamped, and the men were saved with difficulty by Mr. Simpson, the boatswain, in the cutter. There is little doubt that if the launch had not been deserted by the greater part of her crew, she might have reached the Boreas, and have saved many valuable lives. And here, in justice to the majority of the ship's company, we must observe, that those who manned the launch were chiefly smugglers and privateer's men lately impressed, and were not to be considered as part of the regular crew of the ship.

In addition to the boats we have already mentioned as having left the ship, was a small cutter, (containing two midshipmen, of the names of Luttrell and Hemmings, and two men,) which was lowered into the sea by order of the first lieutenant, whose humanity induced him to take this expedient for saving the lives of the two boys. The current was so strong that in a few moments the cutter drifted away from the ship, but the generous feelings of the boys forbade them to desert their comrades in distress, and with great exertion they pulled back to the vessel; they called for a rope, but were ordered to keep off, and again their little boat was carried away by the current. Once more they attempted to get back, but their strength was unequal to the task, and they were carried out into the open sea. Their situation was in many respects little better than that of the friends whom they had left upon the wreck,—the night was pitch dark, the boat had neither mast nor sail, and the sea ran so high that they could do nothing with the oars. Every now and then the flash of a gun, seen across the black distance, told them that the Boreas still held together, and that she was making signals of distress; but no sound reached their ears save the roar of the winds and the waves. Even the booming of the guns was lost in that dismal roar.

The little party scarcely expected to survive the night; they were drenched to the skin, and suffering intensely from the cold; the waves broke over the bows of their frail boat, and threatened each minute to overwhelm it; but their brave hearts did not sink in utter despair; they did their utmost to keep themselves afloat, by incessantly baling out the water with their hats and hands. They thought the night would never end,

and that they should never see the morrow; but day
dawned upon them at last, and then with what
anxious eyes did they sweep the horizon. But in vain
they looked; not a sail was to be seen. An hour
passed away; they shipped such a quantity of water that
their imperfect attempts to bale it out were almost useless. The boat sank deeper and deeper, and their hearts
sank too. Suddenly a ship hove in sight, and she seemed
to be bearing towards them. Hope and fear struggled
for the mastery in their breasts; hope urged them to
renewed efforts to keep themselves from sinking, whilst,
in breathless anxiety, they watched the vessel. She
came nearer and nearer; the watchers felt sure they
were perceived; then a boat was lowered, and they
thanked God for their deliverance. In a few minutes
they were received on board H.M. ship Thalia, more dead
than alive, after so many hours' endurance of cold,
hunger, and dismay.

We must now return to Captain Scott and his companions on the wreck. The men were mustered by the
officers on the quarter-deck; they numbered ninety-five,
or ninety-seven, and they had been all actively employed
in making rafts, and lashing together spars and other
materials, by which they hoped to save themselves, in
the event of the ship going to pieces before assistance
should arrive. Hour after hour passed away, and no
help came; by the noise of the vessel grinding against
the rocks they knew that she could not hold together
much longer. Captain Scott continued to issue his
commands with coolness and decision, and they were
promptly obeyed by both officers and men. About
four o'clock in the morning, the quarter-deck being no
longer tenable, all the crew were obliged to betake
themselves to the main and mizen chains. They had

already suffered severely from the cold, but they had now to endure it in greater intensity. In their exposed situation the waves frequently washed entirely over them, and their limbs were so benumbed with cold that it was with the utmost difficulty they could hold on to the wreck, so as to save themselves from being swept into the abyss of waters that seemed yawning to receive them. By degrees, even the cries and the complaints of the sufferers became hushed: not a word was spoken; in awful silence they listened to the groaning of the timbers, and the sullen roar of the waves dashing against the rocks.

In this state they had remained another hour, when a hollow sound was heard below them; still they spoke not a word, for from the captain to the youngest boy, every one knew what that sound foretold, and that the last struggle was at hand,—for many, the last hour of existence. Then a universal tremor was felt through the wreck, and the boldest heart responded to that shudder. The very timbers seemed to dread their impending doom: with a mighty crash they yielded to the force of the waves; for a moment the ship righted, and then sank beneath the foaming waters.

The pen is powerless when we attempt to describe an event like this, for we cannot penetrate into the secret recesses of the heart, nor can we delineate the agonies of conscience which too often increase the anguish of such scenes, when the near approach of death unveils to men, truths they have been unwilling to learn or to believe. Many a cry for pardon and mercy is raised in the hour of shipwreck, from lips that never prayed before. The best and bravest then bow their heads in awe, however well they may be prepared for the dangers that are incident to their profession; and though from childhood ' these men see the works of the Lord, and His wonders in the

deep,' yet it must be an appalling moment when the
plank they have been wont to tread in calm security, is
torn from beneath their feet, and they are left as helpless
as infants, to be the sport of the wild billows !

The moment the vessel sunk, many of the men struck
out for the plank nearest to them; a few of the strongest
and best swimmers gained the raft, but others who were
benumbed with cold, or otherwise unable to swim,
perished immediately. The quarter-master was one of
those who reached the raft, and he found the captain,
the doctor, and some others, already upon it. Captain
Scott was so much exhausted by the mental and bodily
sufferings he had endured, that the doctor and the
quarter-master were obliged to support him on the raft.
He became gradually weaker, and lingered but a short
time ere he expired in their arms; and a few minutes
afterwards a huge wave swept over the raft, and bore
with it the body of the lamented commander of the
Boreas. About eight o'clock in the morning, a number
of boats put out from Guernsey to the relief of the
survivors, and carried them safely on shore.

We have already mentioned the cowardly and inhuman
conduct of the pilots in deserting the Boreas, and it is
also a matter of surprise, that although twenty guns were
fired as signals, and several rockets and blue lights
burned, no help of any kind was sent from the shore
till the next morning. One of the witnesses on the
court-martial affirmed, that a pilot on shore had heard
the guns firing, and had inquired of a soldier on guard
whether it was an English or French man-of-war! On
the soldier replying that he thought it was an English
vessel, the man refused to put to sea, saying, by way of
excuse, that 'it blew too hard.'

Through the exertions of Lieut. Colonel Sir Thomas
Saumarez, about thirty seamen and marines were taken

off the rocks of the Hannois at daylight, making the entire number saved about sixty-eight; whilst the loss amounted to one hundred and twenty-seven.

The following is an extract from the dispatch of Vice-Admiral Sir James Saumarez:—' The greatest praise appears due to Captain Scott and his officers and men, under such perilous circumstances—in a dark and tempestuous night, in the midst of the most dangerous rocks that can be conceived, and I have most sincerely to lament the loss of so many brave officers and men, who have perished on this melancholy occasion.

' Captain Scott has been long upon this station, and has always shown the greatest zeal and attachment to his Majesty's service, and in him particularly his country meets a great loss, being a most valuable and deserving officer.'

THE HIRONDELLE.

THE Hirondelle, a 14-gun brig, had been originally a French privateer. She was taken by the boats of the Tartar in the year 1804, when attempting to escape from that vessel through a narrow and intricate channel between the islands of Saona and St. Domingo. ' The Tartar finding from the depth of the water that she could not come up with the schooner, despatched three of her boats under the command of Lieutenant Henry Muller, assisted by Lieutenant Nicholas Lockyer and several midshipmen, all volunteers, to endeavour to bring her out. The instant the boats put off, the Hirondelle hoisted her colours, fired a gun, and warped

her broadside towards them. As they advanced, the
privateer opened a fire from her great guns, and as they
drew nearer, from her small arms also.   In spite of this,
and of a strong breeze directly on the bows of the boats,
Lieutenant Muller intrepidly pulled up to the privateer,
and after a short but obstinate resistance, he boarded
and carried her, with the loss only of one seaman, and
one marine wounded.'*

Such was the first introduction of the Hirondelle into
the British navy.   Her career in it was of short duration,
and its conclusion fearfully sudden and disastrous, as the
following account, given by the survivors, will show.

On the 22nd of February, 1808, the Hirondelle,
commanded by Lieutenant Joseph Kidd, sailed from
Malta, bound to Tunis, with dispatches on board.   On
Wednesday evening they steered a course towards Cape
Bon, but unfortunately they got within the action of the
strong current that sets eastward along the Barbary
Coast, so that, instead of making the Cape as she
intended, the brig fell some few leagues short of it to
the eastward, and run aground.   As soon as the alarm
was given, all hands were turned up ; the night was so
dark it was impossible to ascertain the exact position of
the ship, but they distinctly heard the breakers on the
shore.   Every effort was made to bring the vessel up, by
endeavouring to anchor, but without effect ; while this
was going on, the cutter had been manned with ten or
twelve men, and she might have been the means of
saving many lives, but she was no sooner lowered, than
the people rushed into her in such numbers that she was
almost immediately swamped, and all who were on board
her perished, except one man, who regained the deck of
the Hirondelle.   The commander now saw that the loss

---

* James's *Naval History.*

of his ship was inevitable, and he therefore desired his crew to provide for their own safety. The order was scarcely uttered, no one had had time to act upon it, when suddenly the brig gave a lurch and went down; the sea washed over her, and of all her men, four only were left to tell the sad tale. Happily for them they were clinging to the wreck, and so escaped the fate of their companions who were swept overboard; and by aid of some of the spars they succeeded in gaining the shore.

This account is necessarily brief: so short a time elapsed between the unexpected striking of the ship and her going to pieces, that there is no incident to relate. The commander and officers of the Hirondelle seem to have done all in their power to extricate her from her unfortunate position; indeed, it would appear that had they attended less anxiously to the preservation of the ship, many lives might have been saved.

BANTERER.

HIS Majesty's ship Banterer, of 22 guns, under the command of Captain Alexander Shephard, was lost on the 29th October, 1808, between Port Neuf and Point Mille Vache, in the River St. Lawrence, whilst in the execution of orders, which Captain Shephard had received from Sir John Borlase Warren, directing him to proceed to Quebec, with all possible despatch, to take a convoy to England.

The following is the account of this disastrous affair, as given by Captain Shephard :—

' Being as 'far as the Island of Bie in pursuance of
orders, through rather an intricate navigation, with foul
winds the greater part of the time, where the charge of
the ship devolved upon myself, and the only chart I
could procure of the navigation in question being on a
very small scale, I felt myself relieved from much anxiety
by receiving a branch pilot on board on the 28th October
last, on which night at eight P.M. we passed between
that island and the south shore, with the wind north by
west, and very fine weather ; at nine, the wind coming
more round to the westward, we tacked for the north
shore, in order, as the pilot said, not only to be ready to
avail himself of the prevailing northerly winds in the
morning, but because the current was there more in our
favour.   At midnight we tacked to the southward, and
at two A.M. again laid her head to the northward ; and
at four A.M. the pilot having expressed a wish to go
about, the helm was accordingly put down, and on rising
tacks and sheet, it was discovered that the ship was
aground.   As we had then a light breeze at west, the
sails were all laid aback, the land being in sight from the
starboard-beam, apparently at some distance, I immediately ordered the master to sound round the ship, and
finding that the shoal lay on the starboard quarter and
astern, ordered the sails to be furled, the boats hoisted
out, the stream anchor and cable to be got into the
launch, and the boats to tow her out two cables' length
south-west from the ship, where we found the deepest
water ; but by this time the wind had suddenly increased
to such a degree that the boats could not row a-head,
and latterly having lost our ground, we were obliged to
let the anchor go in fifteen fathoms, about a cable's length
W.S.W. from the ship, on which, having got the end of
the cable on board, we hove occasionally as the flood
made, and in the meantime got our spare topmasts over

the side, with the intention of making a raft to carry out
a bower anchor should it moderate ; but the intense cold,
and the still increasing gale rendered it impossible.

' About half-past eleven A.M. the stream cable being
then taut ahead, the wind W.S.W., with a very heavy
sea, the ship canted suddenly with her head to the southward, where we had deep water; we immediately set
our courses, jib and driver, and for some time had the
most sanguine hopes of getting her off, but were unfortunately disappointed, and as the ebb made we were
obliged again to furl sails.

' As the ship was then striking very hard, with a heavy
sea breaking over her in a body, we cut away the topmasts, not only to ease her, but to prevent their falling
upon deck; we also endeavoured to shore up the ship,
but the motion was so violent that four and six parts of
a five-inch hawser were repeatedly snapped, with which
we were lashing the topmasts as shores, through the main-
deck ports. At about eight P.M., fearing the inevitable
loss of the ship, as the water was then gaining on the
pumps, I availed myself of the first favourable moment
to land the sick, and a party of marines and boys with
some provisions,—this could only be effected at a certain
time of tide, even with the wind off shore,—and employed
those on board in getting upon deck what bread and
other provisions could be come at.

' Though the water was still gaining on the pumps as
the flood made, the wind coming more round to the
northward, we again set our foresail, but without the
desired effect. As the stream anchor had, however,
come home, the wind was too doubtful to attempt to
lighten the ship.

' On the morning of the 30th, it being moderate, with
the wind off shore, we hove our guns, shot, and everything that could lighten the ship, overboard, reserving

H

two on the forecastle for signals. As the flood made,
we again set what sail we could, and hove on the stream
cable,—though, with all hands at the pumps, we found
the water increase in the hold as it flowed alongside;
and it was the prevailing opinion that the ship would
have foundered if got off. Being now convinced, from
concurring circumstances, as well as the repeated repre-
sentations of the carpenter, that the ship could not swim,
the water having flowed above the orlop deck, and much
sand coming up with the pumps, we desisted from further
attempts to get her off the shoal, and continued getting
such stores and provisions as we could upon deck.

'Towards the afternoon, the wind again increasing
from the W.S.W., and the water being on the lower deck,
I judged it proper to send some provisions, with such
men as could be best spared, on shore, that, in the event
of the ship going to pieces, which was expected, the
boats might be the better able to save those remaining
on board; and on the morning of the 31st, conceiving
every further effort for the preservation of the ship
unavailing, it then blowing strong, with every appearance
of increasing, I felt myself called on, by humanity as
well as duty to my country, to use every effort in saving
the lives of the people intrusted to my care, and accordingly directed the boats to land as many of them as
possible, keeping the senior lieutenant and a few others
on board with me.

'The whole of this day there was little prospect of
saving those who remained with the wreck, as the surf
was so great that the boats could not return to us;
several guns were fired, to point to those on shore our
hopeless situation, and stimulate them to use every
possible effort to come to our relief; but they could not
effect it, notwithstanding every exertion on their part,
which we were most anxiously observing. As the only

means which then occurred to me of saving the people
on board, I directed a raft to be made with the spars left
on the booms, which was accomplished, with much difficulty, in about six hours; the sea then breaking over the
ship with great violence, and freezing as it fell with such
severity, that even the alternative adopted presented little
prospect of saving any one left on the wreck. During
this state of awful suspense, we had every reason to think
that the ship was completely bilged, and were appre-
hensive, from the steepness of the bank, that she would
fall with her decks to the lee, as the ebb made, in which
case all on board must have inevitably perished.

'About half-past eleven P.M., the barge came off; and as
the lives of the people were now the primary consideration,
I sent as many of them on shore by her as possible, as well
as by the launch, when she was able to come off; and
at two A.M., on the 1st November, having previously
succeeded in sending every other person on shore, I left
the ship with regret, in the jolly boat, and landed, with
some difficulty, through the surf. About eight A.M., the
same morning, I attempted to go off in the barge to save
as much provisions and stores as possible, but found it
impracticable, as the boat was nearly swamped. All
this and the succeeding day, the gale continuing, we
could not launch the boats, and were employed carrying
such provisions and stores as were saved, to some empty
houses which were discovered about six miles to the eastward of where we landed. Finding that with all our
exertions we had only been able to save three days' bread,
the officers and crew were put upon half allowances,
with the melancholy prospect of starving in the woods.

'On Thursday, the 3rd November, the weather mode-
rating, we launched the boats before daylight, and dispatched the jolly boat, with the purser, to a village

H 2

called Trois Pistoles, about forty-five miles distant, on
the opposite side of the river, that he might find his way
to Quebec, to procure us assistance and relief, there being
no possibility of communicating with any inhabited
quarter from where we were but by water.

'During our stay near the wreck, we had repeated
gales of wind, both to the eastward and westward; and
so violent, and with so much sea, that the mizen-mast
was thrown overboard, all the upper deck beams broken,
and the ship's bottom beaten out.

'We embraced every intervening opportunity of going
off to save stores by scuttling the decks, which were
covered with ice, the ship on her broadside, and the
water flowing over the quarter-deck. On these occasions
we were generally away ten or twelve hours, exposed to
the wet and cold, without nourishment; from which, and
fatigue, I had to lament seeing the people every day
become more sickly, and many of them frost-bitten from
the severity of the weather. By the indefatigable exertions of the officers and crew, we succeeded in saving
all our spare sails, cables, and stores, to a considerable
amount; though the cables were frozen so hard, that we
were obliged to cut and saw them as junk.

'On the 7th, I again sent a boat with the second lieutenant, to Trois Pistoles, in the hope of procuring, if
possible, some temporary supplies; but the wind increasing to a violent gale from the eastward, with a heavy
fall of snow, they got frozen up on the opposite shore, and
did not return till the 12th, having then only procured
three hundred weight of flour, a few potatoes, and some
beef—two men having deserted from the boat.

'At this period, I had a respectful request made me
from the people, to be allowed to go to Trois Pistoles,
that they might shift for themselves whilst the weather

would admit of it, dreading the consequences of remaining longer where we were; but out boats would not have carried above one-third, and I conceived the public service would have suffered from allowing them to separate. We had, also, several desertions—in consequence, I believe, of hunger, and the melancholy prospect before them; two of the deserters were brought back, and one returned delirious, after five days' absence, with his feet in a state of gangrene, having had only one small cake to eat during that time. Those still missing must have perished in the woods, from the accounts of the men who were brought back.

'On Sunday, the 20th November, we were relieved from the most painful state of anxiety by the arrival of a small schooner, with a fortnight's provisions, from Quebec, and information that a transport had been procured, and was equipping for us, which nothing but the ice setting in would prevent coming down; and on the 24th I had the satisfaction of receiving a letter by the government schooner, announcing a further supply of provisions, with some blankets for the people; it, however, then blew so hard, with a heavy fall of snow, that she was obliged to take shelter under Bie. On the 25th the schooner returned, when we embarked, and were carried to the opposite side of the river, where the transport was expected,—the pilot conceiving it unsafe to bring the ship nearer to us at that season of the year.'

'Captain Shephard concludes his narrative in paying the following tribute to the discipline and good conduct of his crew :—

In justice to the officers and crew, it now becomes my duty, and a very pleasing part thereof, to bear testimony to the particular perseverance with which they bore the cold, hunger, and fatigue, whilst endeavouring to save the ship ; and when that idea was given up, in

saving the stores with the dire prospect before them of
being cut off from all supplies had the winter set in, the
ice rendering all communication impracticable during
that season of the year.'

The sufferings and privations endured by the officers
and crew of the Banterer, during such trying circumstances, have been ably described in the above narrative
of Captain Shephard. From the 29th of October, to the
24th of November, a period of twenty-seven days, these
men, with little hopes of succour, had borne, with almost
unexampled fortitude, not only hunger and cold, but, to
use the words of the surgeon, 'a considerable number of
the crew were affected with inflammation of the extre-
mities, which in nearly twenty cases produced partial
mortification, and one extensive gangrene on both feet,
attended with delirium and other dangerous symptoms.'

Captain Shephard died, as rear-admiral, in 1841.

THE CRESCENT.

H IS Majesty's Ship Crescent, of 36 guns, Captain
John Temple, sailed from Yarmouth about
four o'clock in the afternoon of the 29th of November,
1808, for Gottenburg. When she left Yarmouth, the
wind blew fresh from the south-west, and it continued
favourable till the following afternoon, when the weather
became overcast, and the wind increased to a gale. The
vessel proceeded on her course for some days, and at
daylight, on the 5th of December, the coast of Norway
was discernible from the deck. At one o'clock, P.M.,
they sounded in twenty-five fathoms, on the coast of
Jutland ; an hour later they sounded in eighteen fathoms,

and at three o'clock they were in thirteen fathoms. The
pilots in charge of the Crescent requested the master to
inform Captain Temple that they desired that the ship
should be hove to, with her head to the southward, and
the topsails close reefed. The advice of the pilots was
immediately acted upon, and they at the same time
assured the captain that they were well acquainted with
the soundings, and they had no doubt the ship would
drift with safety. Suddenly she did drift into ten
fathoms, and remained in that depth until eight
o'clock, P.M.

Captain Temple felt anxious for the safety of his ship
and her crew, and he inquired of the pilots if any alteration could be made with advantage. They replied that
none was necessary; but that the Crescent should be
kept on the same tack till daylight. The vessel drifted
till ten o'clock, P.M. when she struck. A boat was immediately lowered to sound. The men reported the current
setting to eastward at the rate of two and a-half or three
miles an hour.

As the sails were now only forcing the ship further on
the shoal, orders were given to furl, and to hoist out all
the boats except the jolly-boat and gig—both of these
orders were promptly obeyed. At this time, the current
was taking the ship on the larboard bow, and canting
her round. In order to draw her off, the sails were
loosed; but this, instead of having the desired effect,
hove her round into a worse position than before. The
sails were again furled, and an anchor and cable were
got into the launch. The boats then took the launch in
tow, and endeavoured to pull her out; but the force and
rapidity of the current rendered it impossible to do so.
The situation of the Crescent became every instant
more perilous; the gale had increased, and the wind,
which had veered round to the north-west, blew direct

on shore, forcing the vessel further on the shoal. As a last attempt to save the ship, the captain directed that the bower anchor should be let go, and the ship lightened by heaving the guns, shot, balls, &c., overboard. Little good resulted from this step ; and then the water was started and the provisions thrown overboard out of the fore and aft holds. Pumping now became useless, as the water had risen to the hatches ; and when at last the cable parted, all hopes of saving the vessel were abandoned, and at half-past six in the morning of the 6th of December the masts were cut away by the captain's orders, and she lay a helpless wreck. The boats which, until this time, had been lying off in tow, broke their hawsers ; and when the people on board found it impossible to regain the ship, from the force of the current, they made for the shore, and fortunately all succeeded in reaching it, with the exception of one of the cutters, which was lost with all her crew. Lieutenant Henry Stokes, who was in one of the other boats, fearing that she would be capsized, jumped overboard, and attempted to swim on shore, but had not strength to buffet with the waves, and was drowned. The storm continued to increase as the day advanced, and the men on board the wreck being completely exhausted, they piped to breakfast, and a dram was served round. At one o'clock, P.M., a raft was commenced, and in about an hour it was completed and launched, and placed under the charge of Lieutenant John Weaver, of the Marines, Mr. Thomas Mason, clerk, and Mr. James Lavender, midshipman. The crew of the raft was composed chiefly of the sick, or those least capable of exerting themselves for their own preservation. When the raft left the ship, the captain and gallant crew of the Crescent gave three hearty cheers to their companions, whom they were never likely to behold again. It is hard to say which of

the parties was in greatest peril, or nearest to destruction;
but in all such cases, those who are obliged to wait for
the awful moment, are subjected to more intense mental
suffering than those who act, and are enabled to take
any measures, however perilous, for saving their lives.
The people upon the raft returned the farewell cheer, and
as each wave dashed over them, and they again floated on
the surface, they announced their safety with another
and another shout. They had little hope indeed of
reaching the shore alive; they were standing up to
their middle in water, and every billow that rolled
over them carried away one or more of their number.
Happily some of those who were washed off the raft,
succeeded in regaining it; but seven of them perished,
the rest were safely landed, and to the constant exertions
of the officers to keep up the spirits of the men, they
were greatly indebted for their preservation.

A second raft was begun on board the Crescent, but it
was never completed; the sea made a clear breach over
her; the quarter-deck became filled with water, and it
was therefore necessary to launch the jolly-boat in order
to save as many lives as possible, though she could
scarcely be expected to live in such a sea. Once more,
Captain Temple and above two hundred men and officers
said farewell to the companions of their toils and dangers
—once more they bade God speed to the frail bark—
their own last chance of escape—and watched it as it was
now borne aloft on the crested wave, now buried in the
briny furrow. For a time they forgot their own danger
in anxiety for the others; but they were soon recalled to
what was passing around them—the groaning of the
timbers, as every sea struck the wreck with an increasing
shock, forewarned them that she could not long resist
that mighty force. There were two hundred and twenty
human beings entirely helpless to save themselves,

None may know the agonies of that hour, when even hope itself had fled—when nothing intervened between the soul and the unseen world. The Crescent went to pieces a short time after the departure of the jolly-boat, and every one left on board perished, to the number of two hundred and twenty, out of a crew of two hundred and eighty. Amongst the lost were the captain, three lieutenants, a lieutenant of marines, nine midshipmen, the surgeon, purser, carpenter, and gunner; two pilots, one passenger, six women, and a child.

The surviving officers and crew of the Crescent were tried by a court martial, at Sheerness, for the loss of the vessel, when the court was of opinion that ' the loss of the Crescent proceeded from the ignorance and neglect of the pilots, and that the master was blameable, inasmuch that he did not recommend to the captain or pilots either coming to an anchor, or standing on the other tack, for the better security of H.M. late ship Crescent.'

' The court was further of opinion that every exertion was made on the part of the remaining officers and crew for the safety of the Crescent.'

THE MINOTAUR.

HIS Majesty's Ship Minotaur, of 74 guns, Captain John Barrett, was ordered by Admiral Sir James Saumarez to protect the last Baltic fleet, in the year 1810.

After seeing the convoy through the Belt, the ship sailed from Gottenburg about the 15th December, and, with a strong breeze from the east, shaped her course alone for the Downs.

At eight o'clock, in the evening of the 22nd, Lieutenant Robert Snell took charge of the watch; the wind was then blowing hard from the south-east, the weather thick and hazy, and the ship, under close-reefed topsails, and courses, was going at the rate of four knots an hour.

At nine o'clock, the captain gave orders that soundings should be taken every hour, under the immediate direction of the pilot of the watch. At midnight, the pilot desired that the vessel might be put on the other tack, and all hands were instantly turned up to carry out his directions, and Lieutenant Snell was in the act of informing the captain of what was going on, when the ship struck.

The helm was ordered to be put up, but the first shock had carried away the tiller; fruitless attempts were then made to back the ship off, but she had struck with such force upon the sand that it was impossible to move her. The carpenter now reported fifteen feet water in the hold; and it increased so rapidly that in a few minutes it rose above the orlop deck. The officers and the whole of the ship's company were assembled upon deck, and the universal question passed from mouth to mouth— 'On what coast have we struck?'

The pilot of the watch maintained that they were on some shoal in the English coast; the other pilot, however, was of opinion that they were upon the North Haacks, and this proved to be actually the case.

For a few minutes after the ship first struck there was some degree of confusion on board; but this soon subsided; order and tranquillity were restored, and the men all exerted themselves to the utmost, although she struck the ground so heavily, it was almost impossible for them to keep their feet.

The masts were cut away, and other means taken to lighten the ship; and guns were fired as signals of distress, but no aid was afforded to them during that long and dismal night. The darkness was so intense, it was impossible to see beyond a few yards, and they could only judge of their proximity to land, by the sullen roar of the breakers as they dashed upon the shore. In this state of uncertainty and dread, the night passed away; and daylight at last discovered to the crew of the Minotaur the horrors of their situation. The ship was firmly imbedded in sand, and had gradually sunk till the water covered the forecastle. All the boats excepting the launch and two yauls were destroyed, either by the falling of the masts, or the waves breaking over them.

At eight o'clock, A.M., the Minotaur parted amid-ships, and the sea made a clear breach over her. The gunner, seeing that she could not hold together much longer, volunteered to go off in the yaul, and endeavour to obtain assistance from the shore. Captain Barrett at first refused the offer, as he thought it impossible the boat could live in such a sea; but upon further consideration, he gave his consent; and the gunner, with thirty-one of the crew, succeeded in launching the yaul, and getting clear of the wreck.

The ship now presented a most distressing scene—portions of her timbers and spars were floating about in all directions, with casks of spirits and provisions which had been washed up from the hold. Crowded together on the poop and the quarter-deck were officers and men watching with eager anxiety the progress of the boat. After two hours of breathless suspense they saw her reach the shore. Their comrades' success was hailed with joy by the shipwrecked crew as a happy omen for themselves—it inspired them with hope and confidence, and some of them immediately attempted to lift the launch into the sea. They fortunately succeeded in getting her afloat, and numbers then rushed to get into her, amongst whom was Lieutenant Snell. He failed in his first attempt, and then swam to the foretop, near which he knew the launch must pass, to enable her to clear the wreck. He watched his opportunity, and when the boat approached, jumped into the sea, and was taken on board.

In the course of an hour, the launch gained the shore, where, instead of receiving the assistance they expected, and the kindness their unfortunate circumstances demanded, the crew were met by a party of French soldiers, and immediately made prisoners. In vain, they implored the Dutch officers, who were also on the beach, to send boats to the aid of their unhappy comrades on the wreck, their earnest entreaties were met by a cold refusal.

During the morning, Captain Barrett, and about a hundred men, attempted to reach the shore in the second yaul, but she was swamped and all were lost. At two o'clock in the afternoon, the after-part of the ship turned bottom up, and the remainder of the crew perished.

The fate of Lieutenant Salsford was distinguished by a singular circumstance. A large tame wolf, caught at Aspro, and brought up from a cub by the ship's company, and exceedingly docile, continued to the last an object of general solicitude. Sensible of its danger, its howls were peculiarly distressing. It had always been a particular favourite of the lieutenant, who was also greatly attached to the animal, and through the whole of their sufferings kept close to his master. On the breaking up of the ship both got upon the mast. At times they were washed off, but by each other's assistance regained it. The lieutenant at last became exhausted by continual exertions, and benumbed with cold. The wolf was equally fatigued, and both held occasionally by the other to retain his situation. When within a short distance of

the land, Lieutenant Salsford, affected by the attachment
of the animal, and totally unable any longer to support
himself, turned towards him from the mast, the beast
clapped his fore paws round his neck, while the lieutenant
clasped him in his arms, and they sank together.*

Such was the fate of the Minotaur, her captain, and
four hundred of her crew. There is not the slightest
doubt but that, had the Dutch sent assistance, the greater
part of the ship's company would have been saved ; and
it would appear by the following extract from a letter,
written on the subject by Lieutenant Snell, that the risk
attending such a humane attempt, on the part of the
Dutch, would not have been great. Lieutenant Snell
says :—

'The launch which had brought on shore eighty-five
men, was of the smallest description of 74 launches, with
one gunwale entirely broken in, and without a rudder.
This will better prove than anything I can say how easy
it would have been for the Dutch admiral in the Texel
to have saved, or to have shown some wish to have saved,
the remaining part of the crew.'

On the other hand, we have the report from the chief
officer of the marine district of the North coast, addressed
to the Minister of Marine, in which he states, that ' Captain Musquetie, commander in the Texel Roads, sent,
at daylight on the 23rd, two boats to reconnoitre the
Minotaur, but the wind and sea prevented them approaching the vessel.'

It is to be hoped, for the honour of the Dutch officers,
that they *did* really put out to the relief of the Minotaur,
and that they considered the attempt an impossibility,
which a British sailor deemed one of little risk. It is
evident that there must have been considerable danger

---

* *Naval Chronicle*, vol. xxxvii. p. 183.

for boats, from the fact of the second yaul being lost, and Captain Barrett's hesitation before he allowed the gunner to leave the ship in the first yaul; and in charity we must give the Dutch the benefit of this evidence. At the same time, we have the equally conclusive testimony of the safe landing of two boats from the Minotaur, that it was not 'impossible' for even a somewhat crazy boat to live on such a sea. At daylight, on the 24th, the survivors of the Minotaur's crew were marched off as prisoners to Valenciennes. From which place, the gunner, Mr. Bones, contrived to make his escape on the 3rd of February. After suffering the greatest privations, concealing himself in barns and stables by day, and travelling by night, on the 17th of March he got on board a smuggling lugger, about a mile from Ostend, the Master of which agreed to land him in England for the sum of £50.

NOTE BY A NAVAL FRIEND.

The loss of the Minotaur may be attributed to their not knowing their position; the pilot's desire to put the ship on the starboard tack at twelve o'clock at night, with the wind from the south-east, showed that he thought himself on the English coast. This fatal error in the navigation of the ship is not easily accounted for; it arises in a great measure from the dread of approaching the dangerous shoals on our own coast, many of them far off the land, such as the Leman, and Ower, Smith's Knowl, the Ridge, and others further in shore. Great fear of these shoals is felt by all hands, and no doubt the man at the helm would be cautioned not to bring the ship to the westward of her course, and he would therefore be apt to err on the other side—currents also may have carried her to the eastward. I am tempted to offer this opinion from having experienced a similar danger. In the year of the Battle of Copenhagen, I was in the Lynx sloop of war on her return from the Baltic, and when we supposed ourselves in mid-channel, between Yarmouth and the Texel, about two o'clock, in the middle watch, we touched the ground in broken water; happily the weather was moderate, and, by hauling to the westward we soon got into deep water again. The following morning, about ten · o'clock, we spoke a lugger, and were informed that we were seven or eight leagues from the coast of Holland. The distance run from the time we struck, told us that we must have been on the Haacks. A happy escape !

THE PALLAS AND THE NYMPH.

IN the month of December, 1810, the Pallas, a 32-gun frigate, commanded by Captain Paris Monke, was returning, in company with the Nymph, Captain Edward Sneyd Clay, from a month's cruise on the coast of Norway, and was steering for Leith, with a prize in tow. She had not got far to the southward, when, on Tuesday morning, the 18th, between nine and ten o'clock, land was discovered, but the weather was so thick, it could not be clearly defined. The pilot, however, gave it as his opinion that they were north of the Red-head. Towards the middle of the day they fell in with some fishing-boats, and Captain Monke having requested one of the fishermen to come on board the frigate, he learnt from this man that the ship was at that time off Stone-hive and the Tod Head. At four o'clock, P.M., the usual

order to pipe to supper was given ; the wind was blowing
from the north-west, and the vessel going at the rate of
four knots an hour.   Supper being over, the drum beat
to quarters, and the captain, having received the usual
reports, ordered the watch to be called.   At six o'clock,
in compliance with the wish of the pilot, the course was
altered from south-west to south-south-west.   For the
last quarter of an hour the ship had been increasing her
rate of sailing from five and a half to six knots an hour ;
the topgallant scudding sails were therefore taken in,
and the royal and topgallant stay sails hauled down, as
also the jib and the spanker.   Soon after this the pilot,
pointing towards the coast, said to the captain, ' There's
Lunan Bay ;' and shortly afterwards he said, ' There's
the Red Head ;' but it was too dark, then, to see the
land, much less could the outline of the coast be distinguished.   The captain inquired if they should not soon
see the Bell Rock Light, and he was answered in the
affirmative.   He then ordered the officer of the watch
to hail the forecastle, and direct the men to keep a
vigilant look-out for the Bell Rock Light.

Ere many minutes had elapsed after the order was
given, a light was perceived before the starboard beam,
which the pilot declared to be a signal hoisted on the
pier at Arbroath to show that there was water enough
for vessels to enter the harbour.   The captain then went
below to consult the book of sailing directions, and when
he returned upon deck, he said to the pilot, ' If that
light be on Arbroath pier, as you suppose, we ought most
certainly to be in sight of the light on the Bell Rock.'
The pilot replied, ' We shall soon see it ;' and Captain
Monke repeated to the officer of the watch his order to
keep a sharp look out.

As the light on the Bell Rock did not appear, the
captain became exceedingly anxious ; the more so, as he

was convinced, by reckoning the distances from the Tod
Head to the Red Head, and from the Red Head to the
Bell Rock, and comparing their sum with the run from
four o'clock, that the ship had run as many miles to the
southward as would bring her up to the Bell Rock. To
ascertain exactly the position of the ship, he desired the
master to work off the run by the log up to eight o'clock,
P.M., and in a short time the master reported that by his
calculation the light which they saw was no other than
the floating light of the Bell Rock, and that they had
now only to bear up and shape a course for the Isle of
May.

The captain had been upon deck for more than five
hours, and was so much fatigued that he went down to
the gun-room to get some refreshment, at a little after
ten o'clock, leaving positive orders with the officer of the
watch and the master to be most attentive to the ship's
course; and he was so anxious for her safety, that he
had scarcely sat down in the gun-room before he sent
for the pilot-book of sailing directions, that he might
ascertain more exactly the position of the Bell Rock,
and the course and distance from thence to the Isle of
May. In a few minutes, the officer of the watch went
down to report that the May light was in sight, and
Captain Monke was in the act of going upon deck, when
the vessel struck the ground. He instantly rushed upon
deck, and inquired of the master where he supposed the
ship had grounded. The reply was a startling one:—' I
am afraid,' said he, ' that we are on the Bell Rock, and
not a soul will be saved, unless we can forge her over it.'
How they could possibly be upon the Bell Rock, when
the master had himself so confidently declared they
were running from it for some hours, appeared a mystery:
but this was no time for arguing the matter. Captain
Monke saw the danger both to the ship and all on board:

he ordered the drum to beat to quarters, and the men were soon on deck and each at his post. Having assured himself that the rudder was not damaged, the captain ordered the foretack to be hauled on board, and the yards to be braced with the larboard brace, which was done without loss of time. The lead was cast, to ascertain the depth of water, which the quarter-master reported to be twelve feet. The ship, which at first had taken the ground easily, now began to strike with great violence; and when they found that she did not forge ahead, the yards were braced aback, but to no better purpose, for she remained hard and fast as before.

Land was now seen to leeward, and the master changed his opinion, and imagined that the frigate had struck on the Isle of May; but the pilot thought they were on shore in St. Andrew's Bay, and blamed the master for having hauled too soon. As the tide was falling, there was little hope of getting the ship afloat, although this was so far fortunate, that it afforded a better chance of escape for the crew.

Orders were given to man the pumps, and the people obeyed with alacrity, and worked by turns throughout the night with the utmost vigour. The ship seemed to come up easier for a time, and the carpenter reported twelve feet water in the hold. When the moon rose, the position of the frigate with regard to the land was discovered; and as the tide ebbed, her larboard bow appeared to be but a short distance from the nearest rocks. From the time of the ship's striking, guns had been fired as signals of distress, to arouse the attention of the inhabitants of the coast, and these signals were soon answered by lights displayed along the shore, and large fires kindled on the beach. The glare of the torches moving to and fro on the shore denoted the inclination of the people to render assistance to the

unfortunate vessel. Voices were heard hailing the ship,
but it was impossible to distinguish the words. The
boatswain and carpenter, and some others, declared that
the men said, ' You are in St. Andrew's Bay—come on
shore.' Upon this, the boatswain and gunner volunteered
to land with two men in a small prize skiff, for the
purpose of reconnoitring the beach. This proposition
was immediately rejected by the captain, who assembled
the principal officers on the forecastle and declared to
them his determination not to suffer a single boat to be
lowered during the night—but that they should all stick
to the ship until daylight, as the only chance of preserving
their lives.

Happily the captain's orders were obeyed, though
doubtless many would feel tempted to risk a landing.
The Pallas became more and more uneasy—her rudder
was carried away, and the sea broke completely over her.
The men were each served with a dram, and were still
kept at the pumps until three o'clock A.M., when the
main beam broke and the others began to give way in
succession. In order to lighten the vessel, the mainmast
was cut away. At first, this did not appear to have the
desired effect—but in all probability it would have fallen
of itself and have done injury to the people ; it now hung
over the side, and promised to serve as a raft in case of
necessity. The foremast was then cut away, and the
mizenmast was doomed to follow—but the axe and
tomahawk, which had been carried forward, were lost, or
washed away. The ship by this time had fallen upon
her beam ends, and the sea was making breaches over
her, so that every individual had enough to do to keep
himself from being washed overboard.

About four o'clock in the morning, the spirits of the
crew were revived by seeing a boat appear between the
wreck and a large fire that had been kept burning imme-

diately opposite. This was a welcome sight, and it was hailed by three loud and hearty cheers from the Pallas.

Many of the men by this time were suffering much from cold, hunger, and fatigue, and those who were able, got into the weather chains for safety and shelter. Daylight discovered to them the real position of the ship; the light which had been supposed to be on the Isle of May was that of a lime-kiln on the main land, and as the Bass and North Berwick Law were plainly visible, it was evident from their bearings that the frigate was on shore near to Dunbar. She was now a total wreck—the bottom had separated to some extent amidships from her upper works; a considerable portion of her floor timber was lying about ten yards to windward of the rest of the hull, and the iron ballast within this frame of timber was thus open to view. It was now time for every man to provide as far as possible for his own safety. A Portuguese sailor, an excellent swimmer, was the first to quit the wreck and swim on shore; several men attempted to follow his example, but five of them perished. The life-boat from Dunbar, which had been launched with great difficulty on account of the heavy surf beating on the rocks, reached the ship at ten o'clock in the morning of the 19th, and she took off a boat-load from the wreck and landed them in safety.

This success encouraged the people to try to employ the boats of the Pallas, but they were all found to be stove, or otherwise rendered useless, with the exception of a sixteen-oared cutter. The cutter was launched without material injury, and fortunately reached the land with as many as she could carry. The life-boat again neared the ship, and made a second successful landing with a number of officers and men; and a third time she touched the wreck, and was again crowded with people, but unfortunately the rope which she carried as a

hauling line was too short to reach between the ship and
the shore, and this time she had scarcely put off from
the quarter before she filled and upset. By this accident,
six of the crew of the Pallas were drowned, and one of
the bravest fellows belonging to the life-boat. The other
thirteen men who manned the boat, and several people
from the wreck, were saved with great difficulty; a
small fishing-boat, which had been opportunely launched
through the surf, picked them up. Amongst others so
rescued from a watery grave were Captain Monke, and
Mr. Walker, the first lieutenant. The crew of the
fishing-boat persevered with great courage and good
judgment in their efforts to save the rest of the crew.
They procured a small tow-line, which being held by
one end on the beach, they made fast to the mizen
chains of the ship. The boat was then hauled to and
fro until, in eight or ten trips, she had cleared the
wreck of all the people; and, with the exception of
Mr. Tomlinson, the boatswain, and ten or twelve others
who perished, the whole of the ship's company were
saved.

The kindness and hospitality exercised by the inhabitants of Dunbar and the surrounding country were
beyond all praise. The sufferers, many of whom were
insensible when carried on shore, and unconscious of the
manner in which their lives had been preserved, were
lodged, fed, and clothed. Captain Monke, who was
much bruised, was carried by Captain Maitland to the
house of his father, Lord Lauderdale, at Dunbar. The first
lieutenant, Mr. Walker, who was picked up apparently
lifeless, was conveyed to Broxmouth, the seat of the
Duchess of Roxburgh, where he was, under Providence,
indebted for his restoration to the unremitting attentions
of the duchess and her husband, Mr. Manners.

The humblest of the crew were equally well cared for.

The duchess went from room to room, ministering to the wants of the sufferers, and seeing that every comfort was provided for them.

It is gratifying to record that a handsome pecuniary reward was given by government to the fishermen and other inhabitants of Dunbar who so nobly risked their lives for the sake of their fellow-countrymen; and the widow of the man who was lost in the life-boat had a pension of £25 per annum settled upon her.

'I am persuaded,' writes Captain Monke, in his narrative, 'that this court will participate in my feelings, and would think me most forgetful, if I did not here publicly express my grateful sense I shall ever retain of the humane and liberal conduct of the Duchess of Roxburgh and Mr. Manners, who in their hospitable mansion at Broxmouth administered every sort of comfort and medical relief to the far greater part of the suffering officers and people of the Pallas, many of whose lives were thereby preserved to their country. In justice to my own feelings, I cannot close my narrative without declaring to this honourable court that no men under similar circumstances could behave better than did the crew of the Pallas. So far from being dismayed by their perilous situation, they manifested equal firmness and subordination; and, in fact, from the first moment of the ship striking the ground, to the time when necessity compelled every individual to consult his own safety, they obeyed all the orders with as much alacrity as cheerfulness, and (what is more) without either noise or confusion. Hence, sir, I consider myself justified in asserting that, notwithstanding the number victualled on board at the time was reduced to one hundred and sixty, if any human exertion could, in the first instance, have got the Pallas afloat, she would not have been irrecoverably lost to the service. I must also beg leave to •

add, that the officers set every example ; and that from
Mr. Walker, the first-lieutenant, I derived, throughout
this trying scene, the most effectual support and assistance.'

The Nymph, which we have mentioned as being in
company with the Pallas, got on shore the same night, on
a rock called the Devil's Ark, near Skethard, misled by
some irregularity in the lights on the Bell Rock and
Isle of May.

The crew of the Nymph were all saved, but the fine
frigate was lost.

ST. GEORGE AND DEFENCE.

AMONG the many services in which the fleets of
Great Britain were engaged during the last war,
none was more rife with perils and hardships than that
on which the Baltic Fleet was employed. During the
long winter nights the crews were continually exposed to
intense cold, and the ships were often enveloped in such
impenetrable fogs, that sometimes even the pilots were
deceived as to their true position, and those lamentable
consequences ensued of which the loss of the Minotaur
was an example, (see page 154), her officers conceiving
they were on the coast of England, when they were
actually stranded on the opposite shore.

We will briefly mention two instances, which may
give the reader some idea of the severity of the climate
in the Northern Seas.

On the 23rd of December, 1808, the Fama (which
had sailed from Carlscrona the previous day, in consort
with some other men-of-war, and a convoy of merchant-
.men,) struck upon the Island of Bornholm, in the midst

of such dense darkness, and so blinding a fall of snow, that it was impossible to discern any of the surrounding objects. The moment the ship struck, Lieutenant Topping, her commander, sprung from his berth and rushed upon deck, without giving himself time to put on his clothes. In his anxiety for the safety of his ship, and of those who were on board, he continued to give his orders, without any other protection from the piercing blast and driving snow than a blanket, which one of his men had thrown over his shoulders; ' *in fifteen minutes from the time the vessel first struck, he fell upon the deck a corpse.*' One man and a woman shared the same fate, the rest of the crew survived the night, and were next morning saved by the Danes.

The circumstances attending the loss of the Pandora were still more horrible. She struck on the Scaw Reef, a shoal on the coast of Jutland, on the night of the 13th of February, 1811, and in three hours her rudder was carried away, and the hold nearly filled with water. The wind was bitterly cold, and, as the men were unable to get below, they were in danger of being either washed overboard, or frozen to death, before morning. In this dreadful state they remained until daybreak, when it was discovered that several of them had perished from the inclemency of the weather. The survivors contrived to cut a hole in the side of the deck which was above water, through which they crept below, one by one, to seek protection from the cold. During the day, some boats attempted to put out to their assistance, but the sea ran so high that it was impossible to approach the wreck. The unhappy crew, disappointed in their hopes of relief, endeavoured to launch the boats; but these were so encased in ice, that they resembled large blocks of marble, and it was impossible to move them. In the course of the night the wind and sea abated, and the

I

Danes succeeded in rescuing the people of the Pandora
from their perilous situation, but not before twenty-nine
had perished from the intense cold.

The month of November, 1811, was most disastrous
to the Baltic Fleet. The British ships of war had already
suffered so severely from attempting the dangerous navigation of the Northern Seas too late in the year, that the
commander-in-chief on the station received orders on no
account to delay the departure of the last homeward-
bound convoy beyond the 1st of November. In
obedience to these instructions, Rear-Admiral Reynolds
sailed with a convoy from Hano on that day, having
hoisted his broad pendant on board the St. George, of
98 guns, Captain Daniel Oliver Guion ; but owing to
severe gales he was compelled to put back on three
several occasions, and the weather did not permit him
finally to leave the anchorage until the 12th of the
month. On the 15th the St. George and convoy arrived
off the Island of Zealand, where they anchored to wait
for a favourable wind, having met with very rough
weather in their passage from Hano, and several of the
convoy having foundered, without its being possible for
the others to render them the least assistance. In the
course of the night of the 15th the wind increased to a
hurricane, and all hands on board the St. George were
summoned to give the ship cable. Before this could be
accomplished the sea poured through the hawse-holes,
carried everything away, and rendered it impossible for
many of the men to stand to their duty. They were
still in the act of veering away the cable, when a large
merchant vessel, which had been seen looming through
the darkness, drifted down upon them, its hull coming
violently in collision with the bows of the St. George,
and severing her cables ;—one piercing shriek followed,
—the merchantman gave a lurch, and the next instant
was engulfed in the raging billows.

However appalling the sight of this fearful tragedy might have been to the crew of the St. George, their own danger was too imminent to allow them much time for reflection, for on heaving the lead they found only fourteen fathoms, though they had anchored in twenty. The best bower anchor was at once let go, as the ship appeared to be fast drifting towards the shore; but such was the force of the wind and sea, that its massive ring broke off as if it had been only a piece of wire. Upon this it was resolved to wear her off the land, and the jib and foretopmast staysail were loosed, but before they could be set the sails were wrenched from the bolt-ropes, and borne away by the blast. The lead being cast again, eight fathoms were reported; the sheet anchor was let go, in hopes that it would hold, but, like the other anchor, it made no impression on the ship, and broke short off. As a last resource, the men began to cut away the masts, when, just as they fell, a heavy sea lifted the vessel and hurled her with violence upon a sand bank, where she remained fast, the masts having by good fortune fallen clear of her sides.

There was but little hope now of saving the ship, yet the crew behaved with the most admirable steadiness, and obeyed with cheerful alacrity when they were ordered to man the pumps. Towards daybreak the rudder was torn from its fastenings, and it was only the discovery that the water did not gain on the ship that sustained the drooping spirits of the seamen, exhausted as they were with their arduous exertions and long exposure to the biting cold and constant fall of sleet and snow. At half-past six the long-wished-for dawn appeared, when, to their dismay, they found themselves on a sand bank, four miles from the shore. As the wind and sea gradually abated, the rest of the squadron attempted to render them assistance, but did not venture

to approach too close to the shoal. The St. George continued to strike heavily until twelve that night, when
her head swung round to the land, and, contrary to all
expectations, the water was found to have risen three feet
since eight o'clock in the evening.   By ten the next
morning (Sunday, the 17th of November) she was clear
of all danger, and having fitted up jury-masts, with a
rudder supplied from the Cressy, she arrived in safety at
Gottenburg, about the 2nd of December.

Having partially repaired damages, Admiral Reynolds
weighed anchor on the 17th December, and proceeded,
in consort with the Defence and Cressy, to convoy a
homeward-bound fleet of merchantmen.

On the 23rd, another north-westerly gale was encountered, on the coast of Jutland.   At midnight, signals
were made to wear, but owing to the disabled state of
the St. George, this was found impossible.   In the hope
of bringing her head round to the wind, an anchor was
let go, but the hawser, catching under her keel, tore
away the temporary rudder, and snapped itself with the
strain, and again the ship fell off.   The captain gave
orders to strike the lower yards and topmasts, and to
lighten the vessel.   Between five and six in the morning
of the 24th, the report of a gun was heard from the
Defence, which was supposed to have got on shore about
two miles and a half off.   A short time after, the St.
George struck, and drifted towards the shore, and from
this moment all hope of saving the ship vanished.

Upon examining the well, the carpenter reported ten
feet water in the hold; and this rose so rapidly, that in
the space of half an hour it reached the lower deck,
driving the people to the main deck.   Admiral Reynolds
and the captain used every effort to encourage the men
to remain steady to their duty, as the only chance of
preserving their lives.   At ten o'clock, the sea swept the

main deck, so that all hands were obliged to seek refuge on the poop. All the boats, except the yawl, had either been stove or washed overboard. As an instance of the obedience and discipline of the crew of the St. George, three or four men came forward, and asked permission to attempt to reach the shore in the yawl: this request was at first granted, but as they were about to lower her into the sea, it was considered impossible that the boat could live, and the men were directed to return to their posts. Without a murmur, they instantly obeyed; and as if Providence had rewarded this implicit obedience and reliance upon their officers, two of these men were of the few that were saved.

It is impossible to describe the suffering of the helpless crew. Their numbers, originally about seven hundred and fifty, had been terribly thinned by the severity of the weather, and the surging of the waves, which every instant burst over them. At eight o'clock in the evening of the 24th, fourteen men took the boat and attempted to pull from the wreck, but they had not gone many yards when she upset, and her crew perished. The mizen-mast still stood, and orders were given for its being cut away, but as no axes could be found, the men were obliged to use their knives to cut the lanyards of the rigging; at this moment, a sea struck the mast, carrying away the poop, and the men who were upon it. As the poop was swept away from the wreck, it bore not only the living but the dead. The latter far outnumbered the former, and it became necessary for the general preservation to cast overboard the bodies of their dead comrades. But their strength, already weakened by previous suffering, was unequal to the performance of this painful duty; and while thus employed, a sea swept over the poop, scattering the men upon the foaming billows. Five regained it, but were again washed off, and again succeeded in reaching their former position. Of these, two died, and the other three were washed on shore.

The scene on board was one of the most harrowing description. Mingled together were the living, the dying, and the dead. The bodies were piled up by the survivors in rows one above another, as a shelter from the violence of the waves, which broke incessantly over them.

In the fourth row lay the admiral and his friend Captain Guion; whilst the groans of the dying, mingling with the roar of the tempest, unnerved the hearts of those who had hitherto shown an unappalled front to the perils surrounding them.

There still remained about two hundred men, who were employed in constructing a raft, as the last chance of saving their lives. After considerable labour, this was effected, by lashing together a topsail yard and a cross-jack yard, the only spars that remained.

Upon this, ten men left the wreck, but the timbers being improperly secured, they broke adrift, and the first sea that came washed five men off; the others gained the shore, one of whom died.

According to all accounts, even the few who survived would have perished, had it not been for the humane conduct of the Danes who came to their assistance; these, at the risk of their own lives, succeeded in rescuing from the raft the seven exhausted sufferers who survived, out of the crew of seven hundred and fifty men.

The St. George, as has been already mentioned, was in company with both the Cressy and Defence. Captain Pater, who commanded the former, seeing the impossibility of rendering any assistance to the St. George, and the imminent risk to his own ship if he remained longer on the starboard tack, wore, and escaped the danger.

The master of the Defence reported to Captain Atkins that the St. George had gone on shore, and that the

Cressy had veered and was standing to the southward, —at the same time pointing out the great danger the ship was in, and recommending that he should follow the example of the Cressy. The captain inquired whether the admiral had made the signal to part company; upon being answered in the negative, he replied, ' I will never desert my admiral in the hour of danger and distress.'·

At about six o'clock A.M., the hands were turned up to wear ship, but before this could be accomplished she struck, the sea made a breach over her, and washed several men overboard.

The captain gave orders to fire minute guns, and cut away the masts. Five or six guns only had been fired, before they broke adrift, so that it was impossible to fire any more; but providentially these had been heard by the look-out men on shore, to whose assistance may be attributed the preservation of the few lives that were saved.

The waves swept over the vessel, forcing numbers of the crew down the hatchways, the guns and other heavy articles had broken loose, killing some, breaking the arms and legs of others, whose agonizing cries served only to add to the horrors of a scene scarcely within the power of description.

The captain at this time stood on the poop, holding on only by a howitzer that was lashed before the mizen-mast, the officers and crew clinging to other parts of the wreck. The boats were all stove, except the pinnace, in which about twenty men had collected, when a sea, breaking over the wreck, washed her overboard, capsized her, and all perished.

Another sea struck the Defence with such excessive violence as to lift a spare anchor from its berth, throw it up on end, killing in its fall upon the forecastle about thirty men. The booms were washed away, and with them nearly one hundred men, who were clinging to the different spars.

The following account of the escape of one of her crew is so interesting, that it has been thought better to leave it as nearly as possible in his own words, than to alter it for the sake of brevity :—

' I got on one side of the booms that were floating among the rest of the wreck. At that time every man, except two, John Platt and Ralph Teasel, two of the men who were saved, were washed off. Myself and several more were at the same time swept off the mizen-top. I then made the best of my way from one spar to another, until I got on one side of the booms. At this time about forty men regained their position upon the booms, when another sea washed all off except four. I got on the booms a second time, and spoke to John Brown, and told him I thought we were approaching the shore. There were then about twenty men on them, but when we reached the shore there were only six left.

' Two Danes on the beach came to our assistance ; my foot got jammed in amongst the small spars, and my comrades, seeing that I was unable to get off the raft, were coming to my help, when the Danes made signs to them to be quiet. One Dane made three attempts before he succeeded in reaching the raft, and the third time he was nearly exhausted ; he managed to get hold of my foot, and wrenched it out, and carried me on shore. I was then taken up to a shed to wait for some carts which were coming for us, most of us being unable to walk. In about ten minutes a number of gentlemen arrived on horseback, and some carts came down upon the beach. We were then placed in them, and driven to a small village called Shelton. On the road the man who drove the cart spoke to a woman, and asked her if she had any liquor. She replied by drawing a bottle from her pocket, and made each of us take a dram, which I believe was in a great measure the saving of our lives.

'We soon arrived at the houses in the village, where we were stripped and put to bed, and treated by the inhabitants with the greatest hospitality and kindness. When I awoke, I found another seaman had been placed in the same bed with me ; he had come on shore some time after myself upon a piéce of wreck. He said, just as he reached the shore the poop and forecastle were capsized, and not a man to be seen, except a few upon pieces of wreck. In the evening, a gentleman who spoke English came to our bedside, and told us that an officer had been brought up to the house. He also told us that there was another ship on shore to the southward of us, which appeared to be a three-decker, lying with her stern on shore. We knew directly it could be no other than the St. George.

'He inquired if we were able to get up, and go and look at the body of the officer, and see if we knew him. We answered yes, and, with the assistance of the people, went into the barn, and recognised our captain. We then returned to bed again, being too exhausted to stand. The gentleman told us that medical assistance could not be procured that night, but that we should have every nourishment the house could afford. He then took his leave, promising that he would return in the morning, when we might be better able to speak to him.

'He accordingly came in the morning, and inquired what force our ship was.

'We told him a 74-gun ship, with a company of 600 men. Upon our inquiring if any more of our shipmates had reached the shore, he answered no ; and we returned most hearty thanks to the Almighty for our deliverance !

'On Sunday, the 29th, we put our captain into a coffin, and buried him in Shelton Churchyard, with two seamen alongside of him.

' It was some time, through the bitterness of the cold and the bruises we had received, before we were able to walk about. As soon as we had gained sufficient strength, we went down to the beach, where we saw, scattered for about two miles along the beach, the wreck of the Defence, but not a corpse was to be seen. We supposed they had drifted away to the southward and westward, a strong current setting that way. This opinion was in a great measure confirmed by seeing our officers' things sold, and other articles belonging to the ship, six miles to the southward of where we were cast away, when we went to join the few who were saved from the St. George. On the 13th January, our captain was taken up again, and carried to Rinkum Church, and placed in a vault with the honours of war.'

Such was the unhappy fate of the St. George and Defence ; only six men from the latter ship being saved, out of a crew of 600. Two days afterwards, when the gale had abated, a Danish boat, with two of the English sailors, went on board the St. George to bring away the corpses of the admiral and others, but they found the decks had been entirely swept away. Nothing could exceed the hospitality and kindness with which the Danes treated the few who were thrown upon their shore. Nor was the Danish government backward in generosity. The dead were buried with military honours, and the survivors were sent to England without exchange. The following letter from Major General Tellequist, given in his own language, sufficiently shows the deep commiseration felt by the Danish government, as well as by himself, for the lamentable catastrophe which befel the St. George and Defence.

' Randus, the 21st of January, 1812.

' SIR,—Though the grievous misfortune which has happened his great Britannic Majesty's ships of war 'on the Danish coast perhaps already may be known to your Excellency; nevertheless, whereas the opposite case may be possible, I will not omit hereby to make you acquainted with the sorrowful accident, assuring you that I am very compassionating.

'The 24th of last month, in the night, the English ships of the line, St. George and Defence, are splitted upon the western coast of Jutland, and the violent waves made it impossible to bring the wretched crews any assistance. From both ships are saved but thirteen persons, who are cast on shore by the sea with goods of wreck. Some of them are sick, and at present under care. A part of the dead bodies are driven to land, and interred with as much ceremony as the circumstances would admit.

'All possible pains have been taken to find out the bodies of the officers, in order to show them military honours, by the obsequies upon the churchyard.

'Two bodies of officers were found, and buried with military honours. Among these was the body of Captain Atkins, commanding the Defence, which is deposited in a church till I receive the further ordaining from my most gracious sovereign.

'I complain much that the body of Admiral Reynolds has not yet been found, for all the pains which are taken on this purpose.

'Agreeably to the charitable sensibility of the Danish nation, the inhabitants have been very grieved to see the English warriors in such a distress without being able to assist them; and I am very sorry, Sir, that I cannot give your Excellency of this accident an account less sorrowful.

'With great esteem, I remain, Sir,

'&c. &c. &c.,

'TELLEQUIST.

'To Governor Maurice.'

The body of Rear Admiral Reynolds was found a few days after the date of the above letter, and deposited with military honours near that of Captain Atkins, in Rinkum Church.

The surviving officers and men of the St. George were tried by a court-martial at Sheerness, and were acquitted of all blame with reference to the loss of that vessel.

With respect to the loss of the Defence, the court was of opinion that she was lost by getting on shore on the western coast of Jutland, in company with his Majesty's late ship St. George, in consequence of the noble and heroic determination of the captain to stay to the last by his admiral, at a moment of extreme danger and distress, conduct which, in the opinion of the court, will reflect immortal honour on the memory of Captain Atkins.

Rear Admiral Reynolds was an officer of considerable experience, and had distinguished himself on several occasions previous to his melancholy fate on board the St. George.

In the year 1797, he commanded the Amazon, a 36-gun frigate, and was cruizing the 13th of January off Ushant, in company with the Indefatigable, Captain Sir Edward Pellew, when a large ship was descried, steering under easy sail for France. This was a little after twelve o'clock at noon; chase was immediately given, and at four in the afternoon, the stranger was discovered to be a French two-decker, the Droits de l'Homme, of 74 guns.

She had on board, exclusive of her crew of 700 men, about 1050 troops, which, with 50 English prisoners, made 1800 souls.

At a little past five o'clock, the Indefatigable closed with the enemy and began the action; this had lasted about an hour, when the Indefatigable unavoidably shot ahead, on which the Amazon took her place and nobly continued the battle. The Indefatigable, having in the meantime repaired her rigging, again joined in the attack, the British ships placing themselves one on each quarter of their opponent. A continued fire was kept up for upwards of five hours, when they found it absolutely necessary to sheer off, in order to secure their masts. During the action the sea is described as having run so high, that the men on the main decks of the frigates were up to their middles in water. As soon as the masts were secured, the attack was again resumed, and notwithstanding the crews of both ships were almost exhausted with their exertions, it was prolonged for five hours more, when, late in the night, the fire ceased on both sides. The Amazon had now nearly three feet of water in the hold, and was in other respects most severely damaged. The enemy had suffered still more; her foremast was shot away, and the main and mizen-masts left tottering, the decks being strewed with the dead and dying.

At about four o'clock in the morning, an officer on board the Indefatigable reported breakers ahead, and the loss of all three vessels appeared almost inevitable.

The Indefatigable was then close under the starboard quarter of the Droits de l'Homme, and the Amazon as near to her on the larboard bow. The Indefatigable was fortunate enough to avoid the danger by being able to make sail to the southward, and she escaped.

When daylight broke, a terrible spectacle was presented. The Droits de l'Homme had drifted towards the land—broadside on—a tremendous surf beating over her. The position of the Amazon was as precarious, notwithstanding every effort was made by her officers and crew to work her off shore, all proved unavailing, and she struck the ground. The ship's company, with the exception of six men, gained the shore, which proved to be Audierne Bay, where they were all made prisoners.

The melancholy fate of the Droits de l'Homme is described in James's *Naval History*. Already 900 souls had perished, when the fourth night came with renewed horrors,—' weak, distracted, and wanting everything,' says one of the prisoners, a British officer, in his narrative, 'we envied the fate of those whose lifeless corpses no longer needed sustenance. The sense of hunger was already lost, but a parching thirst consumed our vitals.' .... 'Almost lost to a sense of humanity, we no longer looked with pity on those who were the speedy forerunners of our own fate, and a consultation took place, to sacrifice some one to be food to the remainder. The die was going to be cast, when the welcome sight of a man-of-war brig renewed our hopes. A cutter speedily followed, and both anchored at a short distance from the wreck. They then sent their boats to us, and by means of large rafts, about 150, out of nearly 400 who attempted it, were saved by the brig that evening; 380 were left to endure another night's misery,—when, dreadful to relate, about one half were found dead next morning!'

HERO.

WE have next to relate the still more tragical fate of the Hero, of 74 guns. This vessel was lost on the Northern Haaks, under nearly the same circumstances as the Minotaur in the preceding year, but with more fatal results, as every soul on board perished.

The following particulars are derived from the accounts taken from the evidence of Captain Fanshawe, of the Grasshopper, and from the journals of the day.

The Grasshopper sailed from Wingo Sound on the

18th of December, 1811, in company with the Hero, Egeria, and Prince William, and a convoy of about 120 merchantmen. The weather, at the time they commenced their voyage, was stormy and tempestuous. The Egeria and Prince William parted company on the 20th, and on the 23rd the Grasshopper was left in company with the Hero, and about eighteen merchantmen.

At about half-past eleven o'clock, Captain Newman, of the Hero, made signal to the Grasshopper to come within hail; conceiving that they were on the Silver Pitts, he directed the course to be altered to the south-west, which was accordingly done. They continued their course until ten o'clock at night, when the signal was made to alter it two points to port.

The Grasshopper was at this time going at the rate of nine knots an hour; four of the convoy had been kept in view up to this period, but were soon lost sight of in the heavy squall of snow and sleet. At half-past three o'clock all hands were turned up, when the ship being in broken water, she struck with great violence, and suddenly fell into three fathoms water. The best bower was let go, and she was brought to an anchor. In a few minutes the ship struck again, and continued to do so as long as she remained in that position.

The crew of the Grasshopper had now their attention called to the situation of the Hero. It was first supposed that she was at anchor, although she fired several guns, and burnt blue lights, which in about half-an-hour ceased. At daylight it was discovered that both the ships were inside the Northern Haaks, about five or six miles from the Texel Island. About a mile from the Grasshopper was the Hero—a complete wreck—lying on her starboard broadside. The ship's company were all crowded together upon the poop and forecastle; the sea making clean breaches over her. An attempt was made by the crew of the Grasshopper to reach the Hero, but the surf ran so high that it prevented all communication, and they were under the imperious necessity of seeing their comrades perish, without the slightest possibility of being able to render them assistance.

The Hero had hoisted a flag of truce, and fired a gun: in a short time these signals of distress were answered, by several vessels putting out from the Texel to her relief; but owing to the flood-tide, and the strong gale of wind then blowing, the boats were unable to get nearer than three miles.

Notwithstanding that those on board the Grasshopper were themselves in a most precarious position, from the repeated shocks the ship had sustained by striking against the ground, their attention was completely diverted from themselves, in their anxiety for the fate of the Hero. The waves burst with relentless fury over the doomed vessel, every moment snatching a victim from the now almost deserted decks.

As the night was approaching, and the weather still continued boisterous, Captain Fanshawe, having taken the opinion of the officers, judged that there was no other alternative for saving the lives of his crew than by surrendering to the enemy. At four o'clock the cable was cut, and they made sail for the Helder Point, where they surrendered to the Dutch Vice-Admiral, De Wintner.

The Hero went to pieces during the night: in the morning not a vestige of her was to be seen. Every exertion was made by the Dutch squadron to save the crew, but the weather was so stormy, that all their efforts proved abortive, and thus every soul on board perished.

In the year 1798, Captain Newman distinguished himself by a most gallant action which he fought off the coast of Ireland. He was then in command of the

Mermaid, 32-gun frigate, and was cruising in consort
with the Revolutionnaire, of 38 guns, Captain Twysden,
and the Kangaroo, gun-brig, commanded by Captain
Brace. On the 15th October, when near Black Cod
Bay, two very large French frigates were seen and pursued, but they were lost sight of during the night. The
next morning, however, the Mermaid and Kangaroo
made out one of the Frenchmen, and the Kangaroo
came up with her the same afternoon, but was speedily
disabled by the heavy fire of her opponent, and compelled to drop astern. The Mermaid kept on in chase,
and engaged the French vessel, which proved to be the
Loire, 46-gun frigate, on the morning of the 17th
October. Early in the action the French attempted to
board, but were frustrated by the skilful handling of the
Mermaid, which enabled her to close within pistol-shot
of the Loire, when the latter's foretop-mast was soon
shot away, and the fire from her great guns nearly
silenced, though a continuous storm of musketry was
still kept up from her decks. Upon attempting to rake
her opponent, the Mermaid's mizen-mast unfortunately
went by the board, so that she fell off, and the maintop-
mast almost instantly followed. By this time the rigging
of the English frigate was completely cut to pieces, and
her boats destroyed ; she was also making a great deal
of water, having received several shots between wind and
water. In this crippled condition, Captain Newman had
no other alternative but to discontinue the action. This
was done without any attempt on the part of the Loire
to renew the engagement, the French being no doubt
only too glad to get rid of her spirited antagonist, though
she was only half the size of their own vessel.

On the following day the Loire fell in with the Anson
and Kangaroo, and surrendered to the British flag.
Subsequently Captain Newman was appointed to the

Loire, having the proud satisfaction of commanding the vessel in whose capture he had so gallantly assisted.

In 1808, our officer received the command of the unfortunate Hero, which ship, in 1810, formed part of the squadron under Sir James Saumarez, employed for the protection of commerce in the North Sea. Here he continued in the unpleasant duty of convoying merchant vessels backwards and forwards from Dar's Head, the south entrance of the Great Belt, to Sproe Island. On the 25th of September, Captain Newman, in company with the Mars, 74, arrived off Yarmouth, having in charge between five and six hundred merchantmen, the largest convoy that had ever sailed from the Baltic. He again returned to his former station in March, 1811, where he remained until the latter end of the year, when his ship was selected, with others, to convoy the homeward-bound fleet. On this occasion, he appears to have had sad misgivings as to the prudence of sending ships home at so late a period of the year, through the dangerous navigation of the northern seas. On the day previous to the sailing of the squadron from Wingo Sound, he observed, 'I cannot help thinking that we have been detained too long, and it is well if some of us do not share the fate of the Minotaur.'* His words were but too prophetic ; and, ere long, he and two thousand of our brave defenders perished on a foreign strand.

---

* *Naval Chronicle.*

THE DÆDALUS.

HIS Majesty's ship Dædalus, of 38 guns, Captain Murray Maxwell, sailed from Spithead on the 27th of January, 1813, in charge of an East Indian convoy, and made the island of Ceylon, near the Pointe de Galle, on the 1st of July. She passed Dondra Head at sunset, and then steered east by north during the night, in order to pass well outside the Basses. In the morning, the ship's head was pointed to the north, to get near land, a good look-out being kept both from the deck and mast-head for rocks and breakers. The atmosphere was so clear that a ripple might have been seen upon the water for miles around. Nothing appeared to indicate danger; the vessel was supposed to be seven or eight miles off the land, and the master was pointing out to Captain Maxwell her position upon the chart, when they felt her take the ground abaft; but so very easily, that many people on board were not aware that she had touched. Signals were immediately made to warn the convoy of their danger, but before the signals could be answered, the Dædalus swung off into deep water. All sail was set, and strong hopes were entertained that she was not materially injured; but her frame was too slight to sustain any shock whatever without damage, the lower part of the stern-post had given way, occasioning a leak of such magnitude, that although the pumps were instantly manned, and worked with unceasing energy, the water could not be kept under. A signal was made for the convoy to bring to, and to send all their carpenters on board the Dædalus, which was immediately done, but the combined efforts of the whole were unavailing to reduce the leak. The rudder worked

so much that it was found necessary to unship it from
the broken part of the stern-post, and bring it alongside ;
and in order to relieve the ship from the pressure aft,
the guns and other heavy things were carried forward ;
this, however, was of so little avail, that the guns and
anchors were soon thrown overboard. They then prepared a sail with oakum and tar, and got it over the
stern, in order, by passing it under the keel, to stop the
leak.   For a time this seemed to have the desired effect,
and hopes were entertained that they might be able to
carry the ship to Trincomalee ; but these hopes were of
short duration.   In spite of the indefatigable exertions
of every officer and man on board, the water gained upon
them till it rose two feet above the orlop-deck.   The
men had now been working without intermission for
eight hours, and their strength and spirits began to fail,
when, notwithstanding all their efforts, they saw the
water rising to the level of the lower deck.

Captain Maxwell now knew that there was not a
chance of saving his ship, and he felt the painful necessity of leaving her as soon as possible, in order to preserve
the lives of his men, whilst there was yet time.   He
ordered the boys, idlers, and two divisions of seamen and
marines to get into the boats which were alongside,
while the remaining men were employed at the pumps
to keep the ship afloat.   The good order and discipline
which prevailed during this scene are beyond all praise.
'The men behaved,' to use the words of the captain, 'as
if they were moving from one ship to another in any
of the king's ports.'

Such conduct is highly creditable, not only to the
ship's company, but likewise to the captain and officers,
in whom the crew must have reposed most perfect confidence, or such real good order could not have been
maintained at such a time.

The ship was settling fast, when the boats returned to carry away the remainder of the officers and men, they left the pumps and embarked in the boats, taking with them the hammocks and clothes belonging to the ship's company. The last man who stood upon the deck of the sinking ship was her captain. When all others had gone, he too with a heavy heart stepped into the boat which bore him from her side ; sadly and sorrowfully he fixed his gaze upon the wreck of 'his home on the waters.' In a few minutes the ship gave a lurch, and, falling on her beam ends, remained in that position for the space of a minute, then she righted, showing only her quarter-deck ports above water, and then gently and majestically sunk into the bosom of the deep blue sea.

THE PERSIAN.

THE Persian, an 18-gun brig, commanded by Captain Charles Bertram, was lost on the Silver Keys, St. Domingo, in the West Indies, on the 26th of June, 1813. It appears from Captain Bertram's statement, that the Keys were laid down on the chart too far to the southward, or that the ship was carried in that direction by a strong current not mentioned in any of the charts. The Persian struck about five o'clock P.M., by running stem on, upon one of the rocks ; she was at the time going at the rate of three or four knots an hour. Everything was done to back her off; the water was started, most of the guns thrown overboard, the boats were got out, and the anchors cut from the bows. These measures for the moment seemed to have the desired effect; but in paying off, she struck on another rock, and from this it was impossible to move her. Again the same means were resorted to ; the remainder of the guns, spars, &c., were thrown overboard, but to no purpose. The pumps had been kept in active play from the first moment of alarm, but the water gained on them so fast, there was little hope of the vessel keeping afloat till daylight. The Captain, therefore, resolved to prepare for the worst, and he directed a large raft to be made for the safety of some of the ship's company. About seven o'clock, two hours after she first struck, Captain Bertram perceived that she was gradually sinking ; he therefore ordered as many of the ship's company as the boats would hold, to get into the two cutters and the jolly-boat; the cutters were placed under the command of Mr. Norris, the second lieutenant, and Mr. Nicholls, the master ; and the jolly-boat under the superintendence of the gunner. These boats were ordered to remain near the ship, in case anything should occur to render it necessary for the people to return on board.

About half-past nine P.M., Lieutenant Price and the rest of the ship's company, excepting two or three who remained on board with the captain, took their places upon the raft, which was veered by a hawser to leeward of the brig, and directed to remain in that position until the morning. At two o'clock in the morning Captain Bertram, convinced that there was no hope of saving his ship, got into his gig with the men who had stayed with him, and he had scarcely left the side of the Persian ere she slipped off the rock, fell over on the larboard side, and sunk into about seven fathoms water, the tops of the masts only being visible above the waves.

At daylight, Captain Bertram, with the other boats, bore up for the raft, which had broken from the hawser during the night and drifted to some distance. They found her and her crew in a very deplorable state,—the lashings had been cut through by the rocks, and many of the timbers were broken, so that they scarcely held together, and the men had had great difficulty in keeping her from being dashed to pieces against the rocks, and in preserving themselves from being carried away by the surf which washed over them continually.

Here was a great difficulty to be overcome ; the raft was evidently so insecure that it could not be depended upon for an hour, and the only means of saving the men was by distributing them amongst the boats, which were already so overcrowded, that it would be imminently perilous to add to their freight. However, Captain Bertram did not hesitate to brave the danger, but set the example by first taking four men from the raft into his own gig, and directing the other boats to receive the rest amongst them in their relative proportions. His commands were instantly and cheerfully obeyed, but to carry them into effect the boats' crews were obliged to throw overboard the few articles of clothing they had saved, and the greater part of the provisions, in order to enable the boats to bear the additional weight.

It was now between five and six o'clock in the morning; the wind was blowing fresh from the east; the nearest part of St. Domingo was, as far as they could judge, about twenty-five leagues distant, to reach which they supposed they must go through the Mona passage, the most dangerous in the West Indies.

One of the cutters had forty-five men on board, the other forty-two, the jolly-boat twenty-two, and the gig fourteen ; in all, a hundred and twenty-three persons. The wind increased as the day advanced, and became so violent that it seemed almost by a miracle that the boats were enabled to resist the fury of the storm. In the afternoon the danger increased, and the men were obliged to heave overboard the remainder of their bread

and water, and never for an instant could they relax in
their efforts to keep the boats free from water. God in
His mercy preserved those who had shown such trust in
Him; for we can scarcely suppose that such noble acts of
humanity, courage, and self-sacrifice as were evinced by
these men could arise from other than the highest and
holiest principles.

Before the evening closed in, they caught a glimpse of
the land, but too distant for them to make out what
part of the coast it was. The boats were hove to for the
night, and a dreary night it was to these poor men.
They were without food, almost without clothing, weak
from want of nourishment, and exhausted by fatigue;
and in this miserable state they awaited the break of
day, the rain falling in torrents, and the sea breaking
over the boats.

On the morning of the 28th, they again made sail,
and landed the same evening in a small cove of a bay
between Vieux Cap François and Cap Cabron. Here,
to their bitter disappointment, they could get nothing to
eat—not even a spring of fresh water could be found,—
and all the nourishment they had that night was a few
limpets, and the rain water that had remained in the
holes of the rocks,—sorry fare for men who had been
exposed to the inclemency of the weather for two days
and two nights, in open boats, without food.

However, it was a great thing to be on shore; for
many of the people had suffered severely from being so
closely stowed in the bottom of the boats, and their limbs
had been terribly cramped. They now wisely endeavoured to make themselves as comfortable as circumstances allowed, by lighting a fire to keep off the insects,
and to dry their clothes, and then they composed themselves to sleep, which they much needed. The next
morning, being somewhat refreshed, they started across
the bay to a place called Margante, which they reached

about eight o'clock. Here they found the people well disposed towards them, and they were able to purchase some beef and plantains, and plenty of good water, of which they all gladly partook. The inhabitants informed them that it was probable they might find a vessel at Port Plata that could take them to St. Thomas's, that being the nearest port where they were likely to fall in with any of His Majesty's ships. On the 30th of June, they departed from Margante, taking with them a pilot, to guide them to Port Plata. In order to ease the boats, Captain Bertram and part of the ship's company walked along the shore. Towards evening, the people had gone upwards of twenty miles, and were so exhausted, they were obliged to put into a small bay called Scott's Bay (B. Ecossaise), where they came on shore and erected a tent, with the sails of the boats and a few logs of mahogany. With the help of some turtle, the whole of the ship's company were supplied with food; and they remained on shore till the next morning, when the boats were again launched, and all the party embarked in them, as there was no way along the beech. They arrived safely at Port Plata at eleven o'clock that night, and were received with great kindness and humanity. Three houses were provided for the men and one for the officers, and everything was done that could alleviate their sufferings. Unfortunately there was no vessel at Port Plata large enough to convey them to St. Thomas's. With some difficulty, a boat was procured, in which Lieutenant Price was despatched to Turk's Island, with a letter to the naval officer there, describing the situation of the crew of the Persian, and requesting that assistance might be afforded to Lieutenant Price to enable him to hire a vessel to take the crew to St. Thomas's.

Lieutenant Price made a successful voyage, and returned to Port Plata on the 10th of July, with the

K

government schooner Swift, and a hired sloop. Three
days were spent in fitting out these vessels with the
necessary stores, and on the evening of the 13th, the
ship's company, to the number of 112, embarked in
them, and arrived at St. Thomas's on the 22nd. The
crew was by this time in a very sickly state; the crowded
state of the ships had engendered a complaint of which
the surgeon died an hour after they cast anchor; and
there is little doubt that had they been forty-eight hours
longer on their passage, many others would have fallen
victims to the same disease. At St. Thomas's, the sufferers
received the care and attention they required, and were
sent home to England.

We cannot conclude this account without quoting the
following passage from the narrative of Captain Bertram:
—' I most justly attribute the preservation of the ship's
company to very great coolness and persevering exertions
of both officers and men, in keeping the boats free from
the water they shipped, and their great attention in
steering before the sea. I am happy to say that every
man behaved with a regularity that is seldom found on
similar occasions: in fact, when the little clothing the
people had saved, and the remaining bread and water,
were from necessity ordered to be thrown overboard,
there was not a murmur,—they vied with each other
who should obey the order first.'

In the year 1808, Captain Bertram, then a lieutenant,
was appointed to the Emerald, a 36-gun frigate, commanded by Captain the Honourable Frederick Maitland.
On the 13th of March, they were off the harbour of
Vivero, when a large French schooner was discovered at
anchor, under the protection of the batteries. Captain
Maitland determined to attempt to capture or destroy
her, and accordingly he stood in for the harbour at
about five o'clock in the evening. The first fort, which

mounted eight 24-pounders, opened on the ship, as did also another fort about a mile higher up, as soon as the frigate came within range. As it was impossible to place the ship in a position to act upon both batteries, Captain Maitland ordered Lieutenant Bertram, with a party of marines and seamen, to storm the outer fort, whilst he took the ship as near the inner fort as the water would allow. Mr. Bertram succeeded in driving the enemy from the battery, and spiking the guns ; he then made the best of his way by the shore to take possession of the schooner, which had been run upon the rocks. He was joined by Mr. Baird, a midshipman, who had been sent with a party for the same purpose. On the road they were met by a part of the schooner's crew, consisting of about sixty men. These were speedily assailed by the two young officers and their men, and put to flight. Lieutenant Bertram then advanced towards the schooner, which proved to be L'Apropos, of twelve 8-pounder carronades, and he persevered for several hours in his attempts to get her afloat, under a galling fire of musketry from the shore. All his efforts, however, were of no avail, as she had gone on shore at high water ; it therefore became necessary to set her on fire, which was done ; and the lieutenant returned with his party to the Emerald.

In this gallant exploit, nine men belonging to the Emerald were killed, and Lieutenant Bertram and several others wounded.

Captain Bertram has lately accepted the rank of Retired Rear-Admiral.

THE PENELOPE.

WE have now to relate the painful statement of a wreck, which was not only one of the most disastrous, but the most disgraceful in its consequences, of any that we have had to describe.

Unfortunately, the loss of the ship is not the darkest side of the picture; and the insubordination of the crew of the Penelope in the hour of danger was as fatal to themselves as it was rare in its occurrence.

The Penelope, troop-ship, Commander James Galloway, sailed from Spithead for Canada on the 31st of March, 1815, and had a favourable passage to the Banks of Newfoundland. Here she fell in with large masses of ice, fogs, and strong south-east winds, so that the captain considered it unsafe to run in for the land until the weather cleared up. On the 24th of April, they made the Island of Mequilon, and at the same time encountered a very heavy gale from the north-west. On the following day they were surrounded with ice, and were frozen up for nearly twelve hours. When the ice gave way, all sail was set, and the ship entered the Gulf of St. Lawrence, and for the next few days she continued her course in a north-easterly direction, and passed between the Islands of Brion and Magdalen. The frost during this time was so severe, that the furled sails were frozen into a solid body.

On the 29th, they met with large quantities of field ice, which gave the sea the appearance of one entire sheet of ice, but it was not strong enough to stop the ship's way. In the afternoon of that day, the land about Cape Rozier, on the coast of Lower Canada, was visible.

On the 30th, the weather was more moderate, though cloudy; at noon they steered an eastward course, until the ship broke off about three points, when at sunset they tacked, and stood in for the land, which was set by the first lieutenant and the master, at three or four leagues distance.

At eight o'clock, they sounded in seventy-one fathoms; the vessel broke off to the west by north, and the captain ordered the master to go round the ship, and caution the men forward to keep a good look out,—at the same time desiring him on no account to leave the deck. The captain then sent for the first-lieutenant into his cabin, and was in the act of pointing out to him the supposed situation of the vessel on the chart; the line was at the same moment passing forward for another cast of the lead, when the ship took the ground.

'I cannot describe my feelings,' writes Captain Galloway, 'at that moment; for having, for a long time, been almost deprived of my eyesight by night, and also afflicted with rheumatic pains and other complaints, I was unable to judge correctly of the extent of our danger.' The helm was immediately put down, and the sails thrown aback. One boat was then hoisted out to sound, and found two and a half fathoms forward, and about three and a half fathoms aft, having six fathoms a little on the starboard quarter.

All the boats were immediately lowered, and the stream-anchor and cable, with part of the messenger bent on to it, stowed in the pinnace, which, from the strength of the current, was with great difficulty towed to leeward by the other boats, and dropped into five and a-half fathoms water.

On heaving round, the anchor came home, which it continued to do until more than half of the cable was run in, when it held fast, but without altering the position of the vessel. The captain then gave orders to heave overboard the guns, and cut away the anchors from the bows; but all these attempts to lighten the vessel were of no avail. The wind, which had been moderate when she first struck, had increased to a gale, and the ship beat with such violence upon the rocks, that it appeared impossible that she could hold together many hours.

In this condition they were obliged to remain until daylight, exposed to a cold north-east wind, and a pitiless storm of sleet and snow. The officers did all in their power to sustain the courage of the men, but unfortunately in many instances without success. Already symptoms of insubordination had exhibited themselves, several had skulked below to their hammocks, where they remained in defiance of every command and entreaty of their officers.

The topmasts were got over side to shore the ship up, but the motion was so violent that the lashings gave way. At daylight, as the weather did not moderate, and there was no prospect of saving the ship, orders were given to get up the provisions. This, however, had been delayed until it was too late; the water had risen over the orlop deck, and in a short time gained the lower deck. All that was saved was thirty bags of biscuits, and these so damaged by the salt water, that they were totally unfit for use.

The masts were about this time cut away, in order to ease the ship as much as possible; they fell towards the shore about a cable's length from the beach. The master was sent in the cutter to try to fasten a rope to the shore, but the surf ran so high that the boat was stove, and the crew with difficulty gained the beach.

In this condition, with very little prospect of saving the lives of the crew, the captain, anxious for the preservation of the public dispatches, entrusted them to the purser, who, with Captain Moray (aide-de-camp to Lieut. General Sir George Murray), in charge of the military dispatches, embarked in the life-boat, to which a small line was attached. They had, however, no better success than the other boat, for as soon as they reached the surf, the boat capsized, and the two officers swam to the shore with the dispatches tied round their necks.

Another cutter was then sent off in hopes that she would be more successful, but she filled almost immediately; and the rope which was fastened to her was obliged to be abandoned.

. By this time it was impossible to stand upon the deck, the sea made a fair breach over the ship, and the water having rushed into the cabin, the few bags of bread that had been stowed there for protection were destroyed.

The captain being unable from ill health to make any great exertion to save his life, was lowered into the pinnace, into which were already crowded as many men as she could hold, and they took another rope on board, to make a last attempt to form a communication with the shore. The boat had scarcely left the side of the ship before a sea struck and upset her. The captain, supported by two men, made his way through the surf with great difficulty and got on shore, followed by the rest of the boat's crew, who, some by swimming and others by help of oars and spars, saved themselves from destruction. The gig was now the only boat left on board ; she was lowered from the stern, and the first and second lieutenants, with eighteen men, jumped into her. They were all fortunate enough to reach the shore, and some of the men gallantly returned to the vessel, and succeeded in landing about twenty others. Again, the gig repaired to the wreck, and took off some more of the crew, but this time she was unfortunately upset in the surf, though no lives were lost.

When the men left on the wreck saw themselves thus deprived of the last chance of escape, they raised the most piteous cries for assistance, although they knew that their comrades had no means of affording it. It has been said that 'man is a bundle of inconsistencies,' and here was a proof of the assertion. These were in all probability the very men who had betaken themselves to their hammocks a short time before, and had refused to assist in providing for their own safety; they had disobeyed orders, and despised discipline, and now we find them imploring others for that deliverance which they had neglected to provide for themselves. Most of them had been drinking the spirits, and were so stupified that they were incapable of taking advantage of the floating spars and planks to which they might have clung, and so gained the land.

By drunkenness the bed of the ocean has been rendered a foul and gloomy charnel house, where the bones of thousands of our fellow-men await the summons of the Archangel's trumpets, when 'the sea shall give up her dead.' The reckless seamen, though unprepared for another world, hurry themselves into the presence of their Judge, to meet the drunkard's doom.

It has been related that upon one occasion, when the shipwreck of a large packet seemed inevitable, the sailors grew tired of working at the pumps, and shouted 'to the spirit-room!' They saw death staring them in the face, and to drown their terror for the moment, they desired to die drunk. A post-captain in the navy, who was on board the packet, knowing what would be the result if they got at the spirits, took his stand at the door of the spirit-room, with a pistol in each hand, and declared in the most solemn manner, that he would shoot the first man who attempted to enter. The men seeing them-

selves defeated, returned to the pumps, and by the
blessing of God, the vessel was brought in safe with all
her crew.*

Unfortunate as was the situation of the helpless
creatures on the wreck of the Penelope, it was only a few
degrees more wretched than that of the officers and men
on the shore. They had been cast at the base of a steep
mountain, bruised and benumbed by the cold; their
clothes were actually freezing on their backs, and they
were without provisions of any kind. Their first care
was to search for wood and kindle fires, which they at
last succeeded in doing, and then they dried their clothes
—but before they could derive any benefit from the
fire, the intensity of cold had caused many of them
extreme suffering; they were frost-bitten in the hands
and feet, and several lost their toes. Some of the people
were employed in constructing a tent with branches of
trees and blankets, others were searching for provisions
and securing such articles as were washed on shore from
the ship. In the evening, they found about sixty pieces
of pork,—and with this and some melted snow they satisfied the cravings of hunger and thirst. Later in the evening several casks of wine, which had been stowed in the
ward-room, were washed on shore; but this, which
might have proved a blessing to all, was seized by a party
of the men,—who broke open the casks and drank to
such an excess that they fell asleep, and were found
almost frozen to death. During the whole of the day
the unhappy men upon the wreck had never ceased
supplicating their more fortunate comrades to go to
their assistance, but this was impossible; no human
effort could save them. As night drew on, their cries
were redoubled, and were still heard far above the

---

* *Parliamentary Report*, 255.

K 3

howling and roaring of the tempest, when darkness had
hidden the ill-fated vessel from view. About twelve
o'clock three fearful crashes were followed by a still more
fearful sound—the last agonized shriek of many perishing
creatures.

> And then all was hushed,
> Save the wild and remorseless dash
> Of billows.   BYRON.

At daylight, the remains of the Penelope were again
visible, but in three separate pieces ; all that were left
on board had perished, save one man, who was washed
on shore nearly lifeless.

The sufferings of these poor wretches must have been
awful in the extreme, for their agonies of mind appear
to have surpassed those of the body, and to have prolonged their lives by preventing them falling into the
torpor which precedes death from cold. So severe was
the frost, that the wreck had the appearance of huge
masses of ice ; and on shore nothing but the very large
fires that were kept burning could have preserved the
existence of the rest of the crew.

Upon the ship breaking up, the spirits floated on
shore, when there ensued such a scene of tumult and
insubordination as, happily for the honour of the service,
seldom occurs in the British navy. The men broke
open the casks, and before the officers were aware of it,
scarcely a man was to be seen sober. This brought with
it its own punishment; many had drank to such a
degree that they fell lifeless in the snow. The officers
then caused the remainder of the rum to be stove,
excepting a certain quantity placed under their own
care; but when discipline is once broken, it is not easily
restored. The next day, forty-eight men deserted, after
plundering several of their shipmates, and breaking
open every trunk that was washed up. These paid the

penalty of their crimes, for many of them were found
dead in the woods by the Canadians.

We cannot do better than take up the account which
is thus given by one of the surviving officers:—

' With the remaining part of the crew the boats were
hauled up, which we began to repair the best way we
could. Sails were made from a lower and topmast
studding-sail, which were fortunately washed ashore; a
cask of flour was also found, a part of which was made
into dough, and preparations were made to proceed to
Quebec.

' On the third day, a Canadian boat was passing, when
the captain ordered her to be detained to proceed to
that port. With the assistance of the cooking utensils
found in the Canadian boat, all the pork that could be
found was cooked and served out to the different boats,
which was a very short allowance for two days.

' On the sixth day of our misery, the weather moderated,
the boats were launched, and all hands embarked; sixty-
eight persons in all, including two women. The wind
was favourable, but light; with rowing and sailing, we
got to Great Fox River that night, at which place we
were hospitably entertained with potatoes and salt at a
Canadian hut. Next morning we sailed for Gasper
Bay, and reached Douglas Town in the evening.

' The captain and officers were accommodated at
Mr. Johnston's, and the crew lodged at the different
huts around the place. After three days' rest, we walked
nine miles over the ice to where the transports lay;
leaving the sick at Douglas Town. The captain hoisted
his pendant on board the Ann, transport, and put a
lieutenant in each of the others, and an equal number
of men. When the ice broke up, which was seven days
after we got on board, we dropped down to Douglas

Town, and embarked the sick, one of whom died, and two deserted. The next morning we sailed for Quebec, where we arrived on the 28th, many of us not having a change of clothes of any description.'

In concluding the above narrative of the loss of this vessel, we will quote the language of Captain Galloway, who thus deprecates, in strong terms, the disgraceful conduct of the majority of the crew of the Penelope:— 'I feel it my duty,' he says, 'to state to you the infamous conduct of the whole of the crew, with a very few exceptions. From the time that the ship struck, their behaviour was not in the character of British seamen in general; they had neither principle nor humanity; some, in consequence, have suffered severely, and several died from drunkenness.'

Captain Galloway died in 1846.

THE ALCESTE.

AT the close of 1815, the Court of Directors of the East India Company having represented to the British Government the impediments thrown in the way of our trade with China, by the impositions practised by the local authorities at Canton, it was determined to send an embassy to the court of Pekin.

Lord Amherst was selected to undertake the mission, and Mr. Henry Ellis was appointed secretary to the embassy.

The Alceste, a frigate of 46 guns, under the command of Captain, afterwards Sir Murray Maxwell, was fitted up for the reception of the ambassador and his suite.

On the 9th of February, 1816, the expedition sailed

from Spithead, and arrived in the China seas about the middle of July following. It is not in our province to give any account of the proceedings of the embassy, which have already been so ably described, and are well known.

His excellency, having acomplished the object of his mission, took his departure from China on the 9th of January, 1817, arrived at Manilla on the 3rd of February, and finally sailed from thence in the Alceste, on the 9th of the same month.

Captain Maxwell directed the ship's course to be steered towards the Straits of Gaspar, in preference to those of Banca, as affording, at that period of the monsoon, the most convenient and speedy egress from the China seas; and though this passage is not so often taken as that of Banca, the Gaspar Straits appeared by the plans and surveys laid down in the Admiralty charts, as well as in those of the East India Company, to be, not only wider, but to have a much greater depth of water, and to offer fewer difficulties to navigation.

Early on the morning of the 18th of February, they made the Island of Gaspar, and in a short time, Pulo Leat, or Middle Island, was descried from the masthead. The weather was remarkably fine and clear,—a mild breeze blowing from the north-west, and the surface of the water gently agitated by the current, which perpetually sets through the straits, either to the south-east or south-west, according to the monsoon.

The sea, which is usually so clear in these climates, had been greatly discoloured that morning by a quantity of fish spawn, a circumstance of not unfrequent occurrence in those seas; and the navigation being thus rendered more dangerous, unusual precautions were taken for ensuring the safety of the ship. A man was stationed at the foretop-mast head, and others at the fore-yardarms. Captain Maxwell, with the master and other officers, was upon deck, 'steering, under all these guarded circumstances,' (writes an eye-witness,) 'the soundings corresponding so exactly with the charts, and following the express line prescribed by all concurring directions, to clear every danger,—and it was the last danger of this sort between us and England,—when the ship, about half-past seven in the morning, struck with a horrid crash on a reef of sunken rocks, and remained immoveable.' 'What my feelings were,' says Captain Maxwell, 'at this momentary transition from a state of perfect security to all the horrors of a shipwreck, I will not venture to depict; but I must acknowledge, it required whatever mental energy I possessed to control them, and to enable me to give with coolness and firmness the necessary orders preparatory to abandoning the ship,—which a very short period of hard working at all the pumps showed the impracticability of saving.'

The carpenter very soon reported the water above the tanks in the main hold, and in a few minutes more, over the orlop deck.

The quarter boats had been instantly lowered to sound, and reported deep water all round the reef, ten fathoms immediately under the stern, and seventeen about a quarter of a cable further off,—so that it was but too evident that the preservation of the crew depended solely upon the vessel's remaining fast where she was.

The first care of Captain Maxwell was for the safety of Lord Amherst and his suite; the boats were quickly hoisted out, and before half-past eight, he had the melancholy satisfaction of seeing the ambassador and all his attendants safely embarked in them.

For the better protection of the embassy, an officer was sent in the barge, with a guard of marines, to conduct them to Pulo Leat, between three and four miles distant, and from which it was hoped that plenty of water and abundance of tropical fruits might be procured.

Meanwhile the officers and men exerted themselves most indefatigably to save some of the provisions,—a task by no means easy of accomplishment, as the holds and everything in them were submerged in water. Towards the afternoon, the boats returned from the shore, and the men reported that they had had great difficulty in landing his excellency, from the mangrove trees growing out to a considerable distance in the water; and it was not until they had pulled three or four miles from the place where they first attempted to land that they were enabled to reach terra firma. They also stated that neither food nor water could be discovered on the island. Unpromising as appearances were, there was no alternative but to seek shelter on the inhospitable shore. Accordingly, every preparation was made, and by eight o'clock P.M., the people were all landed, excepting one division, who remained on board the wreck, with the captain, first lieutenant, and some other officers.

About midnight, the wind had greatly increased, and the ship became so uneasy from her heeling to windward, that fears were entertained for the safety of those on board. To prevent her falling further over, the topmasts were cut away, and as the wind became more moderate towards daylight, the ship remained stationary, and all apprehensions were removed. The boats did not return to the wreck till between six and seven o'clock in the morning, and they brought no better tidings as to the capabilities of the island to furnish food and other necessaries for the subsistence of so many human beings.

A raft had been constructed during the previous day, upon which the small quantity of provisions they had been able to collect, together with some of the baggage of the embassy, and clothes and bedding of the officers and men, had been transported to the shore.

In the course of the forenoon, Captain Maxwell thought it right to confer with Lord Amherst as to his further movements; he accordingly quitted the wreck, and went on shore. He left the vessel in charge of Mr. Hick, the first lieutenant, with orders that every effort should be made to get at the provisions and the water, and that a boat should remain by the wreck for the safety of the men in case of any emergency. Captain Maxwell reached the shore about half-past eleven A.M., and we may imagine the bitterness of his distress on finding the ambassador, surrounded by his suite, and the officers and men of the Alceste, in the midst of a pestilential salt-water marsh.

The scene is well described by Mr. McLeod. 'The spot in which our party were situated was sufficiently romantic, but seemed, at the same time, the abode of ruin and of havoc. Few of its inhabitants (and among the rest the ambassador) had now more than a shirt or a pair of trousers on. The wreck of books, or, as it was not unaptly termed, 'a literary manure,' was spread about in all directions; whilst parliamentary robes, court dresses, and mandarin habits, intermixed with check shirts and tarry jackets, were hung around in wild confusion on every tree.'

The situation in which Captain Maxwell was placed was, indeed, a most trying one, and such he felt it to be, for, from the lowest seaman to the ambassador himself, every one looked to him for relief and direction in his perilous position. Captain Maxwell was fully competent to meet the emergency; and, said he, 'I had the consolation left me, to feel with confidence that all would follow my advice, and abide by my decision, whatever it might be.'

His first care was for the safety of Lord Amherst; and in a short conference with his excellency and Mr. Ellis, the second commissioner, it was arranged that the embassy should proceed to Batavia in the barge and cutter, with a guard of marines to defend the boats from any attack of the pirates. Mr. Ellis promised that if they arrived safely at Batavia, he would himself return, in the first vessel that should put off, to the assistance of those who remained on the island.

A small quantity of provisions, and nine gallons of water, was all that could be spared from their very scanty store; but at sunset every heart was exhilarated by hope and sympathetic courage, on seeing the ambassador strip, and wade off to the boats, with as much cheerfulness as if he had stepped into them under a salute. At seven o'clock, the barge, under the charge of Lieutenant Hoppner, and the cutter, commanded by Mr. Mayne, the master, containing in all forty-seven persons, took their departure for Batavia, accompanied by the anxious thoughts and good wishes of their fellow-sufferers, who were left to encounter new dangers.

Captain Maxwell's first order was to direct a party to dig in search of water. The men had begun to suffer greatly from thirst, as for the last two days they had had scarcely a pint of water each—one small cask only having been saved from the ship. The next step was to remove their encampment to higher ground, where they could breathe a purer air, and be in greater safety in case of attack.

In a short time the island presented a scene of bustle and activity strangely at variance with the dreary solitude it had exhibited two days before; and the once silent woods resounded with the voices of men, and the strokes of the axe and the hammer. One party was employed in cutting a path to the summit of the hill, another in removing thither their small stock of provisions. A few men were on board the wreck, endeavouring to save every article that might prove of general use.

About midnight, the men who had been employed for so many hours on a most fatiguing and harassing duty, and exposed to the burning rays of a vertical sun, began to suffer most painfully from increased thirst, and it was at that moment when they were almost bereft of hope that they experienced one of the many merciful interpositions of Providence by which the Almighty displays His tender care for His creatures: a plentiful shower of rain fell, which the people caught by spreading out their table cloths and clothes ; and then, by wringing them, a degree of moisture was imparted to their parched lips, and their hearts were revived, and prepared to hear the joyful news, which was communicated by the diggers soon after midnight, that they had found water in the well, and a small bottle of this most dearly prized treasure was handed to the captain.   So great was the excitement of the people on receiving the announcement, that it became necessary to plant sentries, in order to prevent their rushing to the well and impeding the work of the diggers.

On the morning of the 20th, the captain called all hands together, and pointed out to them the critical nature of their position, and the absolute necessity of their uniting as one man to overcome the difficulties by which they were surrounded.   He reminded them that they were still amenable to the regulations of naval discipline, and assured them that discipline would be enforced with even greater rigour, if necessary, than on board ship; and that in serving out the provisions the strictest impartiality should be observed, and all should share alike until the arrival of assistance from Lord Amherst.

During this day, the well afforded a pint of water to each man; the water is said to have tasted like milk and water, and when a little rum was added to it, the men persuaded themselves it resembled milk-punch, and it became a favourite beverage with them.

The people were employed during the 20th much in the same manner as on the previous day, but very few things could be obtained from the ship, every article of value being under water.

On Friday, the 21st, the party stationed on board the wreck observed a number of proahs full of Malays, apparently well armed, coming towards them. Being without a single weapon of defence, they could only jump into their boats without loss of time, and push for the land. The pirates followed closely in pursuit, but retreated when they saw two boats put out from the shore to the assistance of their comrades. The Malays then returned to the ship and took possession of her. In an instant all was activity and excitement in the little camp.

'Under all the depressing circumstances attending shipwreck,' writes Mr. McLeod, 'of hunger, thirst, and fatigue, and menaced by a ruthless foe, it was glorious to see the British spirit stanch and unsubdued. The order was given for every man to arm himself in the best manner he could, and it was obeyed with the utmost promptitude and alacrity. Rude pike staves were formed by cutting down young trees; small swords, dirks, knives, chisels, and even large spike nails sharpened, were firmly fixed to the ends of these poles, and those who could find nothing better hardened the end of the wood in the fire, and bringing it to a sharp point, formed a tolerable weapon. There were, perhaps, a dozen cutlasses; the marines had about thirty muskets and bayonets; but we could muster no more than seventy-five ball cartridges among the whole party.

'We had fortunately preserved some loose powder, drawn from the upper deck guns after the ship had struck (for the magazines were under water in five minutes,) and the marines, by hammering their buttons round, and by rolling up pieces of broken bottles in cartridges, did their best to supply themselves with a sort of shot that would have some effect at close quarters, and strict orders were given not to throw away a single discharge until sure of their aim.

'Mr. Cheffy, the carpenter, and his crew, under the direction of the captain, were busied in forming a sort of abattis by felling trees, and enclosing in a circular shape the ground we occupied; and by interweaving loose branches with the stakes driven in among these, a breastwork was constructed, which afforded us some cover, and must naturally impede the progress of any enemy unsupplied with artillery.'

The Malays had taken possession of some rocks, at no great distance from where the crew of the Alceste were encamped, and here they deposited the plunder they had taken from the wreck. It now became necessary for Captain Maxwell to prepare against an attack. With a very small stock of provisions, which, even if husbanded with the greatest care, could last only a few days, he had to contend, with a handful of men, many of them unarmed, against a host of savages, perhaps the most merciless and inhuman that are to be found in any part of the world.

In the evening a general muster was called, and a rude and motley group presented itself to the eye of the commander. But rough as was the exterior, he well knew that there was that within which would bid defiance to danger and outrage so long as life should last.

So stanch and resolute was the spirit diffused through all the little band, that Mr. McLeod says,—'Even the boys had managed to make fast table-forks on the end of sticks for their defence. One of them, who had been severely bruised by the falling of the masts, and was slung in his hammock between two trees, had been observed carefully fixing, with two sticks and a rope yarn, the blade of an old razor. On being asked what he meant to do with it, he replied, ' You know I cannot stand, but if any of these fellows come within reach of my hammock, I'll mark them.' '

The officers and men were divided into companies, and every precaution adopted to secure the slender garrison from being taken by surprise. The boats were hauled closer up to the landing-place, and put under the charge of an officer and guard.

On Saturday morning, the 22nd, every effort was made to induce the Malays to come to an amicable conference, but without success. Mr. Hay, the second lieutenant, was, therefore, ordered to proceed to the ship, with the barge, cutter, and gig, (armed in the best manner possible under the circumstances,) and to gain possession of her by fair means or by force. No sooner did the pirates see the boats put out towards the wreck, than they left the vessel, though not before they had set fire to her, thus performing an act which was of great service to the crew of the Alceste; for by burning her upperworks and decks, everything buoyant could float up from below and be more easily laid hold of. The ship continued to burn during the night, and the flames, as they darted from her sides, shed a ruddy glare upon the wild scenery around, and breaking through the shade of the thick and lofty trees rested upon a landscape worthy of the pencil of Salvator Rosa.

Upon the summit of a hill, and under the spreading branches of the majestic trees, was a rude encampment, formed by the erection of a few wigwams; whilst here and there, collected together in groups and reclining in different attitudes, were parties of men armed with pikes or cutlasses, in their ragged, unwashed, and unshorn appearance, resembling rather a gang of banditti, than the crew of a British ship of war.

It was with the most painful feelings that both officers and men witnessed the gradual destruction of the gallant ship, which had been their home for so many months.

No one but a sailor can understand the devotion with which a brother sailor regards his ship, and we cannot better describe it than in the words of Captain Basil Hall:—.

' We do truly make the ship our home, and we have no other thoughts of professional duty or of happiness, but what are connected with the vessel in which we swim; we take a pride in her very looks, as we might in those of a daughter; and bring up her crew to honourable deeds, as we should wish to instruct our sons. The rate. of sailing of each ship in a fleet is a subject of never-ending discussion amongst all classes of officers, midshipmen, and crews, every one of whom considers his own individual honour involved in all the ship does or is capable of doing.

' This is true almost universally, but it is most striking, no doubt, in our first ship, which like our first love, is supposed to drink up from our opening feelings the richest drops of sentiment, never to be outdone, or even equalled by future attachments.

' I owe, indeed, much good companionship, and many sincere obligations to other vessels; yet I am sure that if I live to be Lord High Admiral, the old Leander must still be nearest and dearest to my nautical heart. I remember every corner about her, every beam, every cabin, every gun.'

The same feeling, no doubt, existed in the breast of

every man and boy who now stood watching, with painful interest, the fate of the old ship; all had been too actively employed from the time the vessel first struck to think of anything save of providing means for their own preservation; but now, in the dead hour of night, thrown upon a strange shore, and surrounded by enemies, the thought, perhaps, that they might never again see their native land or their beloved kindred, might steal over their hearts, and fill them with sad forebodings. By degrees the fire became less and less vivid; for an instant, at times, a brighter flame illuminated the sky, throwing up a shower of golden sparks—then all was darkness,—a darkness which was felt by all; for it told that nought remained of their old home, save a smouldering hull,—that thus was severed, perhaps, the last link between them and England.

During the night that followed this sad scene, an incident occurred which, though it occasioned considerable alarm at the time, became a source of amusement afterwards.

A sentry, startled by the approach of a very suspicious looking personage, who was making towards him, levelled his musket and fired. In an instant the whole camp was alive with excitement, supposing that they were attacked by the savages, when, behold, the enemy turned out to be a large baboon, one of a race that abounded in the island. These creatures became very troublesome; they were most audacious thieves, and even carried away several ducks which had been saved from the wreck; till at last the poor birds were so frightened that they left their little enclosure and voluntarily sought for safety and protection amongst the people.

From the morning of Sunday, the 23rd, till Wednesday, the 26th, the men were busied in saving whatever they could from the hull of the Alceste, and they were fortunate enough to obtain several casks of flour, a few cases of wine, and a cask of beer, besides between fifty and sixty boarding-pikes, and eighteen muskets, all of which proved most acceptable.

A second well had been sunk, which supplied clearer water, and in great abundance, so that they possessed one of the chief necessaries of life in plenty.

Everything now wore a more favourable aspect. The Malays had retired behind a little island (called Palo Chalacca, or Misfortune's Isle), about two miles distant ; and although they were expected to return speedily with a reinforcement, the crew of the Alceste were better prepared for them. The gunner had been actively employed in forming musket cartridges ; and, by melting down some pewter basons and jugs, with a small quantity of lead obtained from the wreck, balls had been cast, in clay moulds, which not a little increased their confidence and feeling of security.

Under the able command of Captain Maxwell, the greatest regularity and order prevailed amongst the people. Every man appeared happy and contented with his lot ; for each man, from the highest to the lowest, encouraged his neighbour by his own good conduct, whilst he in turn received encouragement from the example of those above him. The provisions were served out with the strictest impartiality. 'The mode adopted by Captain Maxwell,' (writes Mr. M'Leod,) 'to make things go as far as possible, was to chop up the allowance for the day into small pieces, whether fowls, salt beef, pork, or flour, mixing the whole hotch-potch, boiling them together, and serving out a measure to each publicly and openly, and without any distinction. By these means no nourishment was lost : it could be more equally divided than by any other way ; and although necessarily a scanty, it was by no means an unsavoury mess.'

Early on Wednesday morning, Lieutenant Hay, who had charge of the boats, observed two pirate proahs nearing the island, as if to reconnoitre ; he immediately made a dash at them, with the barge, cutter, and gig. The barge closed with the Malays first, and a desperate conflict ensued. There was only one musket in the boat, which Mr. Hay used to some purpose, for he killed two of the savages with his own hand. In the meantime, the other two boats had come up to the assistance of their comrades. One more pirate was shot dead, and another knocked down with the butt-end of a musket ; yet the rest continued to fight with savage ferocity, until, seeing that resistance was fruitless, they jumped into the sea and drowned themselves, choosing to perish rather than yield. During the engagement, an officer who was on the beach, observed a canoe, which had been cut away from one of the proahs, drifting not many yards from the spot where he stood ; and as he thought the prize worth securing, he entered the·water, and swam towards it. He had nearly attained his object, when those who watched him from the shore perceived an enormous shark hovering about. They were almost petrified with horror; anxious to make their friend aware of his danger, yet not daring to call out to warn him, lest a sudden perception of the perils of his situation, and of the proximity of his formidable enemy, should unnerve him, and thus deprive him of the slight chance of escape that remained. Breathless and silent then they stood, and marked the movements of the shark with trembling anxiety. He seemed to be so sure of his prey, that he was in no haste to seize it, but swam leisurely about, crossing and recrossing betwixt the doomed victim and the shore, as if gloating himself, and sharpening his appetite by gazing on the anticipated feast. The officer, too, seemed to be luxuriating in the refreshing coolness

L

of the water, calmly approaching the canoe, happily unconscious of his danger; but the shark followed him closely : his life depended upon a swimmer's stroke, or the whim of a moment. The anxiety of the spectators became agony; but that moment was decisive—the swimmer struck out once more—the canoe was gained, and he was saved.

Then, and then only, did he become aware of the horrible fate that had threatened him, and of the merciful interposition of Providence in his behalf.

In the course of this day fourteen proahs and smaller boats were observed standing towards the island, from the Banca side, and every heart bounded with joy in the full anticipation that it was a party sent by Lord Amherst from Batavia, to their relief. Their joy, however, did not last long, for they soon found that the boats had come only to gather a kind of sea-weed much esteemed by Chinese epicures, who use it, as they do birds' nests, in their soup.

Consultations were held that night as to the policy of negotiating with these people, so as to induce them, by promises of reward, to convey part of the crew of the Alceste to Java—the four remaining boats would then be sufficient for the transport of the rest.

But the morning dawn put all such plans to flight, and revealed the true character of the Malays. No sooner did they perceive the wreck, than they started off to her and plundered the hull of everything they could carry away. No assistance was to be expected from these rapacious thieves; and as the time had elapsed which was required to bring succour from Batavia, measures were taken to repair the launch and to construct a raft to enable the people to leave the island before their provisions should be completely exhausted.

Matters now began to assume a more formidable

aspect, for on Saturday, the 1st of March, the Malay force was increased by the arrival of several proahs, who joined in breaking up the remains of the wreck.

At daybreak on Sunday, the 2nd, the camp was alarmed, and all were called to arms by the yells of the savages, who, firing their partereroes, and beating their gongs, advanced with about twenty of their heaviest vessels towards the landing-place, and anchored within a cable's length of the shore.

After a short deliberation, a boat full of men armed with creeses approached the shore, and was met by a canoe containing an officer and party with a letter from Captain Maxwell, addressed to the chief authority at Minto, stating the situation of the Alceste's crew, and praying that assistance might be sent to them.

The officer placed this letter in the hands of the Malays, repeatedly pronounced the word Minto, and showed them a dollar, to intimate that they would be well rewarded if they returned with an answer. They appeared to understand the mission, and to be willing to execute it; but, as may be supposed, the service was never performed.

Meantime the Malay forces continued to increase; no less than fifty proahs and boats of different sizes were collected, and, on a moderate computation, they had 500 men on board. Their mischievous intentions were too evident; they drew closer and closer to the shore, prevented the escape of any of the ship's boats, and even had recourse to stratagem in order to gain possession of the much-desired booty. One party declared that all the Malays except themselves were hostile, and urged that they might be allowed to go to the camp to guard the crew of the Alceste. This kind offer was of course refused. 'We can trust to ourselves,' was the reply. The plot began to thicken; the odds seemed fearfully against the heroic little band, who, badly armed, and worse provisioned, had to make good their position against a multitude of foes—matchless amongst savages in cunning and cruelty. But in proportion to the imminence of the danger rose the courage of our countrymen.

Mr. M'Leod relates that, in the evening, when Captain Maxwell had assembled, as usual, the men under arms, for the purpose of inspecting them, he addressed them in these words : ' My lads, you must all have observed this day, as well as myself, the great increase of the enemy's force (for enemies we must now consider them), and the threatening position they have assumed. I have, on various grounds, strong reason to believe they will attack us this night. I do not wish to conceal our real state, because I think there is not a man here who is afraid to face any sort of danger. We are now strongly fenced in, and our position in all respects is so good, that armed as we are, we ought to make a formidable defence even against regular troops ; what, then, would be thought of us, if we allowed ourselves to be surprised by a set of naked savages with their spears and their creeses ?

' It is true they have swivels in their boats, but they cannot act here ; I have not observed that they have any matchlocks or muskets ; but if they have, so have we !

' I do not wish to deceive you as to the means of resistance in our power. When we were first thrown together on shore we were almost defenceless. Seventy-five ball-cartridges only could be mustered ; we have now sixteen hundred. They cannot, I believe, send up more than five hundred men, but, with two hundred such as now stand around me, I do not fear a thousand—nay, fifteen hundred of them ! I have the fullest confidence that we shall beat them. The pikemen standing firm,

we can give them such a volley of musketry as they will
be little prepared for, and when we find they are thrown
into confusion, we'll sally out among them, chase them
into the water, and ten to one but we secure their vessels.
Let every man, therefore, be on the alert with his arms
in his hands; and should these barbarians this night
attempt our hill, I trust we shall convince them that
they are dealing with Britons!'

This short but spirited appeal had its full effect upon
the hearts to whom it was addressed. It was answered
by three wild hurras, which were taken up by the piquets
and outposts, and resounded through the woods. The
British cheer struck the savages with terror; they no
doubt thought it preceded an attack, and they were
observed making signals with lights to some of their
tribe behind the islet.

The night passed undisturbed, and daylight discovered
the pirates in the same position, their force increased by
ten proahs, making their number at least six hundred
men. The situation of Captain Maxwell and his party
became hourly more critical; the provisions could not
last long—something must be done—some plan must be
decided on. They had but little choice; they must
either make a dash at the pirates, and seize their boats,
with the certainty of being all butchered should they not
succeed,—and the odds were fearfully against them,—or
they must maintain their present position, in the hope
that aid might be sent from Java, in time to save them
from a scarcely less horrible fate—the lingering death of
famine.

Under these depressing circumstances, the spirits of
the men never for a moment seemed to flag. True
'hearts of oak,' their courage increased with their difficulties, and the prevailing desire amongst them was, to
rush upon the enemy and get possession of their boats,
or perish in the attempt.

But for this day, at least, they were ordered to remain passive; perhaps in coming to this decision, the wise and brave commander of the party may have remembered another captain who was 'in a great strait,' and who said, ' Let us fall now into the hands of the Lord, for His mercies are great, and let me not fall into the hand of man.' The decision, then, was to wait; and the hours rolled on till afternoon, when an officer ascended one of the loftiest trees, and thence he thought he descried a sail at a great distance. The joyful news seemed too good to be true.

A signal-man was sent up with a telescope, to sweep the horizon. The eager and intense anxiety that pervaded the little band, until he could report his observations, may be better imagined than described. At last, he announced that the object was indeed a brig, or a ship, standing towards the island under all sail. The joy was unbounded and overpowering. Men felt as if awaking from some horrible dream; and, doubtless, many an honest heart was uplifted in thankfulness to the Almighty, for the mercy vouchsafed in delivering them from what had appeared, a few minutes before, to be certain destruction.

There remains little more to be told; the vessel proved to be the Ternate, which Lord Amherst had sent to their assistance. The pirates took to flight as soon as they discovered the ship, but not before they had received a volley from the Alceste's people, unfortunately without effect.

It was not till Friday, the 7th of March, that all were embarked on board the Ternate. They arrived safely at Batavia on the 9th, and were most kindly received by Lord Amherst, who converted his table into a general mess for the officers, as well as the embassy; comfortable quarters were also provided for the men; and in their present enjoyment they all soon forgot the hardships they had suffered.

In conclusion, we will quote the following passage from the pen of Mr. M'Leod :—' It is a tribute due to Captain Maxwell to state (and it is a tribute which all will most cheerfully pay) that, by his judicious arrangements, we were preserved from all the horrors of anarchy and confusion. His measures inspired confidence and hope, while his personal example in the hour of danger gave courage and animation to all around him.' Nor ought we to omit the high and well deserved praise which Captain Maxwell bestowed upon the ship's company in his examination before the court martial.

' I should be trespassing far too long upon the time of this court,' said Captain Maxwell, ' were I to bring all before them whose conduct merited applause ; but I can with great veracity assure the court, that from the captain to the smallest boy, all were animated by the spirit of Britons ; and, whatever the cause was, I ought not to regret having been placed in a position to witness all the noble traits of character this extraordinary occasion called forth ; and having seen all my companions in distress fairly embarked, I felt in walking off to the boat that my heart was lifted up with gratitude to a kind Providence that had watched over us.'

Captain Murray Maxwell commenced his naval career under the auspices of Vice-Admiral Sir Samuel Hood, and obtained his first commision as lieutenant in 1796, and was subsequently promoted to the command of the Cyane, in December, 1802.

In the following year he was appointed to the Centaur, and received his post commission on the 4th of August, in the same year. In 1804, Captain Maxwell distinguished himself at the capture of Surinam, and for his conduct on that occasion was highly mentioned in the dispatches.

This officer was constantly employed in the late war, and distinguished himself on so many occasions, that we can only briefly allude to one or two instances where his gallantry was most conspicuous. In 1806, he was appointed to the Alceste, and on the 4th of April, 1808, whilst that vessel, in company with the Mercury, Captain James Alexander Gordon, and the Grasshopper, 18-gun sloop, lay at anchor near Cadiz, a large convoy under the protection of several gun-boats, was seen coming close in shore from the northward.

Captain Maxwell determined to attempt their capture, and accordingly, the Alceste and Mercury attacked the gun-boats, whilst the Grasshopper, stationed close to the batteries of Rota, by a well directed fire, succeeded in driving the Spaniards from their guns. The gun-boats being thrown into confusion, the first-lieutenant of the Alceste, Mr. Allen Stewart, and Lieutenant Watkin Owen Pell of the Mercury, volunteered to board the enemy in the boats. They accordingly dashed in among the convoy, boarded and brought out seven tartans from under the very muzzles of the enemy's guns, though supported by several armed boats sent from Cadiz to their assistance.

Captain Maxwell was actively employed on the coast of Italy until 1811, when we find him cruizing in the Adriatic, in company with the Active, Captain James Alexander Gordon, and a 36-gun frigate, the Unité, Captain Edward Henry Chamberlain. On the morning of the 28th of November, the little squadron was lying in Port St. George, Island of Lissa, when signals were made that there were three suspicious sail south. The three frigates immediately got under weigh, and on the morning of the 29th came within sight of the strange vessels, which proved to be the Pauline, a 40-gun frigate, the Pomone, frigate, and 26-gun ship, Persanne. The French commodore, finding the English force greater than he expected, bore up to the north-west, and the Persanne separated, and stood to the north-east. The Unité was then despatched in chase of the Persanne, and the Alceste and Active continued in pursuit of the French frigates.

In the course of a couple of hours the Alceste commenced action with the Pomone, but an unlucky shot soon afterwards brought down the main-topmast of the Alceste, and she was compelled to drop astern. The Active speedily ranged alongside of the Pomone, and after a spirited conflict, the latter ship was compelled to haul down her colours and surrender.

The Pauline, in the meantime, tacked, and poured her fire into the Alceste, no doubt anticipating an easy victory from her disabled state; but in this she was disappointed, for the fire was returned with such effect, that after a warm conflict of two hours and twenty minutes, the commodore made off to the westward, which, from the crippled state of the Alceste, Captain Maxwell was unable to prevent. In this action the Alceste lost twenty killed and wounded, the Active thirty-five, and Pomone fifty. The gallant captain of the Active had the misfortune to lose his leg, and his first lieutenant, William Bateman Dashwood, had his right arm shot away: the command therefore fell upon the second lieutenant, George Haye, who fought the action, until her opponent surrendered.

In 1813, Captain Maxwell had the misfortune to be wrecked in the Dædalus, and in 1815 was again reappointed to the Alceste. On his passage home, after the loss of that vessel, he touched at St. Helena, and had an interview with Napoleon Buonaparte, who, reminding him of the capture of the Pomone, said, ' Vous étiez très méchant. Eh bien! your government

must not blame you for the loss of the Alceste, for you
have taken one of my frigates.'*

Captain Maxwell was nominated a C.B. in 1815, and
received the honour of knighthood in 1818.

He died in June, 1831.

THE DRAKE.

THE DRAKE, a small schooner, under the command
of Captain Charles Baker, had been despatched by
the commander-in-chief on the Newfoundland station,
upon special duty to Halifax.

Having accomplished the object of her mission there,
she set sail again to return to St. John's, on the morning
of Thursday, the 20th of June, 1822. The weather was
unusually fine, the wind favourable, and everything
promised a short and prosperous voyage.

Nothing occurred to retard the progress of the vessel
until Sunday morning, when the increasing thickness of
the atmosphere betokened the approach of one of those
heavy fogs which so frequently hover over the coast of
Newfoundland.

There are few things more perplexing to the mariner
than to find himself suddenly enveloped in one of these
thick mists: it is impenetrable gloom; night and day
are both alike; the sails, saturated with the watery
vapour, hang heavily, and flap against the masts with
a sad foreboding sound, whilst every heart on board
feels more or less oppressed by the atmospheric influence, and every countenance expresses languor or dis-

---

* Marshall's *Naval Biography*.

content. But these discomforts are minor evils compared with other attendants upon a Newfoundland fog.

It often happens that, in spite of every precaution on the part of the men on the look-out, the bows of the vessel run across some unfortunate fishing boat; and before a single voice can be raised in warning, a sudden shock, a smothered cry, a gurgling of the waves, tell the sad tale! One moment, and all is silent; the ship pursues her course, and no trace is left of the little vessel and her crew, for whom many days and nights will anxious love keep watch ; but those objects of a mother's tenderness and of a wife's affection will never more gladden the eyes of the watchers, till ' the sea shall give up her dead.'

Would that such calamities were of less frequent occurrence. There is one curious characteristic of these fogs, which in some degree mitigates the evil of them: they sometimes do not extend beyond a few miles, having the appearance of a huge wall of dense cloud or mist. A vessel, after beating about for hours, will suddenly emerge from almost total darkness, the clouds break away, and all hearts are gladdened by finding themselves once more beneath the rays of the glorious sun.

Captain Basil Hall gives an amusing instance of such an occurrence. The Cambrian ' had run in from sea towards the coast, enveloped in one of these dense fogs. Of course they took it for granted that the light-house and the adjacent land—Halifax included—were likewise covered with an impenetrable cloud of mist; but it so chanced, by what freak of Dame Nature I know not, that the fog on that day was confined to the deep water, so that we who were in the port could see it at the distance of several miles from the coast, lying on the ocean like a huge stratum of snow, with an abrupt face fronting the shore.

'The Cambrian, lost in the midst of this fog-bank, supposing herself to be near land, fired a gun. To this the light-house replied; and so the ship and the light-house went on pelting away gun for gun during half the day, without seeing one another.

'The people at the light-house had no means of communicating to the frigate, that if she would only stand on a little further, she would disentangle herself from the cloud, in which, like Jupiter Olympus of old, she was wasting her thunder. At last, the captain, hopeless of its clearing up, gave orders to pipe to dinner; but as the weather, in all respects except this abominable haze, was quite fine, and the ship was still in deep water, he directed her to be steered towards the shore, and the lead kept constantly going. As one o'clock approached, he began to feel uneasy, from the water shoaling, and the light-house guns sounding closer and closer; but being unwilling to disturb the men at their dinner, he resolved to stand on for the remaining ten minutes of the hour. Lo and behold! however, they had not sailed half a mile further before the flying gib-boom end emerged from the wall of mist, then the bowsprit shot into daylight, and lastly, the ship herself glided out of the cloud into the full blaze of a bright and 'sunshine holiday.' All hands were instantly turned up to make sail; and the men, as they flew on deck, could scarcely believe their senses when they saw behind them the fog-bank—right ahead the harbour's mouth, with the bold cliffs of Cape Sambro on the left—and further still, the ships at their moorings, with their ensigns and pendants blowing out light and dry in the breeze.'

But to return to our sad tale. Towards noon, the weather cleared up for about a quarter of an hour, allowing just sufficient time to get a good observation of the latitude, which, according to Captain Baker's reckoning, made their position to be about ninety-one miles from Cape Race, and fifty-one from Cape St. Mary's.

They continued to steer east till about six o'clock in the evening, when the breeze rather freshening, and the ship having run sixty miles since noon, she was hauled off to south-east.

The fog was then so dense that the men could not see more than twenty yards beyond the ship, but as Captain Baker's orders were to use the utmost dispatch, he determined to make the best of his way. Every precaution was taken, by using the lead, and by keeping a vigilant look-out from every part of the ship. In this manner they proceeded, carefully feeling the way, until about half-past seven o'clock, when the look-out man shouted, ' Breakers ahead! Hard a-starboard!' The ship was instantly hauled to the wind, but not being able to clear the danger on that tack, every effort was made to stay the vessel, but from the heavy sea, and whilst in stays, her stern took the breakers, and she immediately fell broadside on, the sea breaking completely over her.

At the moment the ship struck, every man was on deck, and there was such a universal feeling of confidence in the commander, that notwithstanding their extreme peril, not the slightest confusion ensued. Captain Baker's first order was to cut away the masts, so as to lighten the vessel, and perhaps afford means of saving some of the crew. The order was promptly executed, but unhappily without producing the desired result, for in a few moments the ship bilged, and the destruction of the whole crew appeared to be inevitable.

Captain Baker then ordered the cutter to be launched, but they had scarcely got her over the gangway before she sank. It was a time of terrible anxiety for both officers and men; for, from the denseness of the fog, they could not form a conjecture as to their actual position, whilst the crashing of the masts, the strain of the vessel upon the rocks, and the roar of the waters, as they swept over the decks, added to the horrors of the scene.

Captain Baker was as calm and self-possessed as if nothing unusual had occurred, whilst the eyes of the men were fixed upon him, and they were ready to obey every command with the same promptitude as when performing the usual routine of ship's duty.

Fortunately a small rock was discerned through the mist, and as it seemed to be at no great distance, it presented a means of escape from the most pressing danger. Without a moment's hesitation, a man of the name of Lennard sprang forward, and seizing a lead-line, jumped into the sea; but the current setting directly against him to the northward, his efforts were unavailing, and with difficulty he was dragged on board again.

It might be supposed that Lennard's failure would have damped the spirits of the men, and deterred them from a second attempt. But it seems to have had a contrary effect, and to have stirred them up to renewed exertion. A consultation was held as to the next steps to be taken. The only hope that remained was in the gig, (the jolly-boat having been washed away,) when Turner, the boatswain, as brave a fellow as ever breathed, volunteered to make the attempt. He secured a rope round his body, and was then lowered into the boat. The tackling was let go, the men gave a cheer, and the boat, with its occupant, was borne away by the current.

With intense anxiety the men on the wreck watched the progress of Turner, who had been carried in the boat to within a few feet of the rock; then the watchers saw it balanced upon the crest of a huge wave, and the next moment it was dashed to pieces upon the rock; the boatswain, however, retained his presence of mind; he kept hold of the rope when dashed out of the boat, and succeeded in scrambling up the cliff.

In the meantime, the waves were making heavy breaches over the ship; the crew clung by the ropes on the forecastle; each succeeding wave threatened them all with destruction, when a tremendous sea lifted her quarter over the rock on which she had at first struck, and carried her close to that on which the boatswain stood. The forecastle, which up to this time had been the only sheltered part of the ship, was now abandoned for the poop; and as Captain Baker saw no chance of saving the vessel, he determined to remove the people from her if possible.

Calling around him his officers and men, he communicated to them his intentions, and pointed out the best means of securing their safety. He then ordered every man to make the best of his way from the wreck to the rock. Now, for the first time, his orders were not promptly obeyed; all the crew to a man refused to leave the wreck unless Captain Baker would precede them. There was a simultaneous burst of feeling that did honour alike to the commander and the men. To the former, in that he had so gained the affection and respect of his people; and to the latter, inasmuch as they knew how to appreciate such an officer.

Never was good discipline displayed in a more conspicuous manner. No argument or entreaty could prevail on Captain Baker to change his resolution. He again directed the men to quit the vessel, calmly observing that his life was the least and last consideration. The men, upon hearing this reiterated command, stepped severally from the poop to the rock with as much order as if they had been leaving a ship under ordinary circumstances. Unhappily, a few of them perished in the attempt; amongst these was Lieutenant Stanley, who, being benumbed with cold, was unable to get a firm

footing, and was swept away by the current, his companions, with every inclination, had not the power to
save him; he struggled for a few moments—was dashed
with irresistible force against the rocks, and the receding
wave engulfed its victim.

When he had seen every man clear of the wreck, and
not till then, did Captain Baker join his crew.

As soon as they had time to look about them, the
ship's company perceived that they were on an isolated
rock, separated from the mainland by a few fathoms.
The rock rose some feet above the sea, but to their
horror they perceived that it would be covered at high-
water. It seemed as if they were rescued from one fearful catastrophe, only to perish by a more cruel and pro-
tracted fate. They watched the waters rise inch by inch
around them, appalled by the feeling that those waters
must sooner or later close over them for ever, and that
nothing could save them except the outstretched arm of
Him who could bid the waves be stayed, and say to the
stormy winds, be still. Every man is more or less
courageous under circumstances of danger, when it is
attended by excitement,—such as that of the battle-
field. There is a courage which springs from companionship in danger, and a courage derived from the fear of
shame; but the test of true valour is a scene like that we
have described. *There* was no room for a display of the
adventitious bravery which often becomes in reality the
thing it strives to appear. No man *there* could reproach
his neighbour if his cheek should blanch and his lip quiver;
all are alike appalled, but the well-regulated mind rises
superior to the rest. Such was the case with Captain
Baker. Although he could not conceal from himself
that their condition was almost hopeless, he continued
with his voice to encourage the timid, and by his arm to
support the weak.

By degrees the fog had partially dispersed, and as the

dawn began to break, a dreary prospect was displayed. The haggard countenances and lacerated limbs of the men told the sufferings they had endured, whilst the breakers, which they had only heard before, became distinctly visible. Still the devoted crew, following the example of their commander, uttered no complaint. They were ready to meet death, yet they felt it hard to die without a struggle. The tide was rising rapidly, and if anything was to be done, it must be done instantly. The boatswain, who had never lost hold of the rope, determined at all hazards to make another effort to save his comrades, or to perish in the attempt.

Having caused one end of the rope to be made fast round his body, and committing himself to the protection of the Almighty, he plunged into the sea, and struck out in the direction of the opposite shore.

It was an awful moment to those who were left behind ; and in breathless suspense they waited the result of the daring attempt. All depended upon the strength of his arm. At one moment he was seen rising on the crest of the wave, at the next he disappeared in the trough of the sea ; but in spite of the raging surf, and of every other obstacle, he reached the shore, and an inspiring cheer announced his safety to his comrades.

As soon as he had recovered his breath and strength, he went to the nearest point opposite the rock, and, watching his opportunity, he cast one end of the line across to his companions. Fortunately it reached the rock, and was gladly seized, but it proved to be only long enough to allow of one man holding it on the shore, and another on the rock, at arm's length. It may be imagined with what joy this slender means of deliverance was welcomed by all. The tide had made rapid advances ; the waves, as if impatient for their prey, threw the white surf aloft, and dashed over the rock.

Would that we could do justice to the noble courage

and conduct displayed by the crew of the Drake.
Instead of rushing to the rope, as many would have
done under similar circumstances, not a man moved
until he was commanded to do so by Captain Baker.
Had the slightest hesitation appeared on the part of the
commander, or any want of presence of mind in the
men, a tumultuous rush would have ensued, the rope,
held as it was with difficulty by the outstretched hand,
would inevitably have been lost in the struggle, and
then all would have perished.

But good order, good discipline, and good feeling
triumphed over every selfish fear and natural instinct of
self-preservation, and to the honour of British sailors be
it recorded, that each individual man of the crew, before
he availed himself of the means of rescue, urged his
captain to provide for his own safety first, by leading the
way. But Captain Baker turned a deaf ear to every
persuasion, and gave but one answer to all—' I will
never leave the rock until every soul is safe.'

In vain the men redoubled their entreaties that he
would go; they were of no avail; the intrepid officer was
steadfast in his purpose. There was no time for further
discussion or delay. One by one the men slipped from
the rock upon the rope, and by this assistance forty-four
out of fifty succeeded in gaining the opposite shore.
Unfortunately, amongst the six who remained, one was
a woman. This poor creature, completely prostrate from
the sufferings she had endured, lay stretched upon the
cold rock almost lifeless. To desert her was impossible ;
to convey her to the shore seemed equally impossible.
Each moment of delay was fraught with destruction.
A brave fellow, in the generosity of despair, when his
turn came to quit the rock, took the woman in his arms,
grasped the rope, and began the perilous transit. Alas !
he was not permitted to gain the desired shore. When
he had made about half the distance, the rope parted—

not being strong enough to sustain the additional weight and strain, it broke ; the seaman and his burden were seen but for an instant, and then swallowed up in the foaming eddies. With them perished the last means of preservation that remained for Captain Baker and those who were with. him on the rock. Their communication with the mainland was cut off; the water rose, and the surf increased every moment; all hope was gone, and for them a few minutes more must end ' life's long voyage.'

The men on shore tried every means in their power to save them. They tied every handkerchief and available material together to replace the lost rope, but their efforts were fruitless ; they could not get length enough to reach the rock. A party was despatched in search of help. They found a farm-house ; and while they were in search of a rope, those who stayed to watch the fate of their loved and respected commander and his three companions, saw wave after wave rise higher and higher. At one moment the sufferers disappeared in the foam and spray ; the bravest shuddered, and closed his eyes on the scene. Again, as spell-bound, he looked ; the wave had receded—they still lived, and rose above the waters. Again and again it was thus; but hope grew fainter and fainter. We can scarcely bring our narrative to an end; tears moisten our page; but the painful sequel must be told. The fatal billow came at last which bore them from time into eternity—all was over. When the party returned from their inland search, not a vestige of the rock, or of those devoted men, was to be seen.

> And is he dead, whose glorious mind
> Lifts thine on high?
> To live in hearts we leave behind,
> Is not to die.   CAMPBELL.

We feel how inadequate have been our efforts to depict the self-devotion of Captain Baker, and the courage and constancy of his crew. The following letter, addressed to Lieutenant Booth, formerly an officer of the Drake, will go farther than any panegyric we can offer, to display the right feeling of the ship's company, and their just appreciation of their brave and faithful commander.

'SIR,—Your being an old officer of ours in a former ship, and being our first lieutenant in H.M. ship Drake, leads us to beg that you will have the goodness to represent to our Lords Commissioners of the Admiralty the very high sense of gratitude we, the surviving petty officers and crew of his Majesty's late ship Drake, feel due to the memory of our late much lamented, and most worthy commander, who, at the moment he saw death staring him in the face on one side, and the certainty of escape was pointed out to him on the other, most stanchly and frequently refused to attempt procuring his own safety, until every man and boy had been rescued from the impending danger. Indeed, the manliness and fortitude displayed by the late Captain Baker on the melancholy occasion of our wreck was such as never before was heard of. It was not as that of a moment, but his courage was tried for many hours, and his last determination of not crossing from the rock, on which he was every moment in danger of being washed away, was made with more firmness, if possible, than the first. In fact, during the whole business he proved himself to be a man whose name and last conduct ought ever to be held in the highest estimation by a crew who feel it their duty to ask from the Lords Commissioners of the Admiralty that, which they otherwise have not the means of obtaining, that is, a public and lasting record of the lion-hearted, generous, and very unexampled way in which our late noble commander sacrificed his life in the evening of the 23rd of June.'

The above letter was signed by the surviving crew of the Drake.

We need not add that their request was complied with, and a monument erected to the memory of Captain Baker, in the chapel of the Royal Dockyard at Portsmouth.

At the request of the author, a friend, to whom he related the pathetic story of the captain of the Drake, composed the following verses on his untimely and romantic fate:—

THE LOSS OF THE DRAKE.

1.

THERE'S a garden full of roses, there's a cottage by the Dove;
And the trout stream flows and frets beneath the hanging crags
    above;
There's a seat beneath the tulip-tree, the sunbeams never scorch;
There's jasmine on those cottage walls, there's woodbine round
    the porch.
A gallant seaman planted them—he perished long ago;
He perished on the ocean-wave, but not against the foe.

2.

He parted with his little ones beneath that tulip-tree;
His boy was by his father's side, his darling on his knee.
' Heaven bless thee, little Emma; night and morning you must
    pray
To Him on high, who'll shield thee, love, when I am far away.
Nay, weep not!—if He wills it, I shall soon be back from sea;
Then how we'll laugh, and romp, and dance around the tulip-
    tree!

3.

' Heaven bless thee, too, my gallant boy! The God who rules
    the main
Can only tell if you and I shall ever meet again.
If I perish on the ocean-wave, when I am dead and gone
You'll be left with little Emma in a heartless world alone:
Your home must be her home, my boy, whenever you're a man;
You must love her, you must guard her, as a brother only can.

4.

' There's no such thing as fear, my boy, to those who trust on
     high ;
But to part with all we prize on earth brings moisture to the eye.
There's a grave in Ilam Church-yard, there's a rose-tree marks
     that grave ;
'Tis thy mother's : go and pray there when I'm sailing o'er the
     wave.
Think, too, sometimes of thy father, when thou kneel'st upon
     that sod,
How he lived but for his children, for his country, and his God.'

5.

Farewell, farewell, thou gallant ship ! thy course will soon be
     o'er ;
There are mournful hearts on board thee, there are breaking
     hearts on shore.
The mother mourned her sailor boy, the maiden mourned her
     love ;
And one, on deck, was musing on a cottage near the Dove :
But his features were unmoved, as if all feeling lay congealed ;
They little knew how soft a heart that manly form concealed.

6.

Beware, beware, thou gallant ship ! there's many a rock ahead,
And the mist is mantling round thee, like a shroud around the
     dead.
The listless crew lay idly grouped, and idly flapped the sail,
And the sea-bird pierced the vapour with a melancholy wail.
So hushed the scene, they little deemed that danger was at hand,
Till they heard the distant breakers as they rolled upon the strand.

7.

The winds were roused, the mist cleared off, the mighty tempest
     rose,
And cheeks were blanched that never yet had paled before their
     foes :
For the waves that heaved beneath them bore them headlong
     to the rock,
And face to face with death they stood, in terror of the shock.
A crash was heard—the ocean yawned—then foamed upon the
     deck,
And the gallant Drake, dismasted, on the waters lay a wreck !

8.

On that rock they've found a refuge; but the waves that dash
  its side
They know, must sweep them from it at the flowing of the tide.
With the giant crags before them, and the boiling surge between,
There was one alone stood dauntless midst the horrors of the scene.
They watched the waters rising, each with aspect of dismay;
They looked upon their fearless chief, and terror passed away.

9.

There's a gallant seaman battling with the perils of the main;
They saw the waves o'erwhelm him thrice, but thrice he rose again.
He bears a rope around him that may link them with the beach:
One struggle more, thou valiant man! the shore's within thy
  reach.
Now blest be He who rules on high; though some may die to-
  night,
There are more will live to brave again the tempest and the fight.

10.

They gathered round their gallant chief, they urged him to
  descend,
For they loved him as their father, and he loved them as a friend.
' Nay, go ye first, my faithful crew; to love is to obey,—
'Gainst the cutlass or the cannon would I gladly lead the way;
But I stir not hence till all are safe, since danger's in the rear;
While I live, I claim obedience; if I die, I ask a tear.'

11.

With a smile to cheer the timid, and a hand to help the weak,
There was firmness in his accents, there was hope upon his cheek.
A hundred men are safe on shore, but one is left behind;
There's a shriek is mingling wildly with the wailing of the wind.
The rope has snapped! Almighty God! the noble and the brave
Is left alone to perish at the flowing of the wave.

12.

'Midst the foaming of the breakers and the howling of the storm,
'Midst the crashing of the timbers, stood a solitary form;
He thought upon his distant home, then raised his look on high,
And thought upon another home—a home beyond the sky.
Sublimer than the elements, his spirit was at rest,
And calm as if his little-one was nestling on his breast.

13.

In agony they watched him, as each feature grew elate,
As with folded arms and fearless mien he waited for his fate;
Now seen above the breakers, and now hidden by the spray,
As stealthily, yet surely, heaved the ocean to its prey.
A fiercer wave rolled onward with the wild gust in its wake,
And lifeless on the billows lay the Captain of the Drake.

J. HENEAGE JESSE.

FURY.

IN the year 1824, notwithstanding the repeated failures which had attended the expeditions to the Polar Seas, the British government determined to make another attempt to discover a passage between the Atlantic and Pacific Oceans; for this purpose Captain, now Sir Edward Parry was appointed to the command of the Hecla, and a second vessel was commissioned by Captain Hoppner, who was directed to put himself under the orders of the beforenamed officer.

The vessels being fully equipped and furnished with provisions and stores for two years, sailed from England on the 16th of May. Their progress had been unexpectedly slow, from the quantity and magnitude of the ice, which had kept the people constantly employed in heaving, warping, or sawing through it, so that they did not arrive at the entrance of Lancaster Sound until nearly the middle of September.

There was no doubt that the more than ordinary difficulties which they encountered in crossing the barrier of ice in Baffin's Bay was owing to a season of very unusual severity; indeed, Captain Parry was of opinion, that but for Phillips's capstan, the Hecla and Fury would have been obliged to winter in the middle of Baffin's Bay.

The season was now too far advanced to give any hopes of the ships being able to penetrate to the westward, according to their instructions, during the present year; Captain Parry determined, therefore, to push on as far as the present season would permit, and devote the whole of the next summer to the fulfilment of the object of the expedition.

It is not our intention to enter into a detailed description of the many difficulties which they met in their passage; it is enough to say that their toils were incessant, and nothing but the most unwearied vigilance and perseverance could have prevented the ships being materially damaged by the enormous pressure of the ice.

Both officers and men were constantly employed, one time in getting out the boats to tow or cut through the ice, at another, at what is termed ' sallying,' or causing the ship to roll, by the men running in a body from side to side, so as to relieve her from the adhesion and friction of the young ice. It sometimes happened, also, that their labour was in vain; for during the night a westerly wind would spring up, and that, combined with a strong current, would drive the vessels several leagues to eastward, thus compelling them to recommence their work over again.

On the 27th of September they found themselves in a tolerably open sea, and assisted by a fine working breeze they reached Port Bowen, in Regent's Inlet. Here Captain Parry determined to make his winter harbour, being convinced that it would be safer to remain there, than run the risk of any further attempt at navigation during the present year.

'To those who read,' writes Sir Edward Parry, ' as well as those who describe, the account of a winter passed in these regions can no longer be expected to afford the interest of novelty it once possessed; more especially in

M

a station already delineated with tolerable geographical precision on our maps, and thus, as it were, brought near to our firesides at home.'

Here it may be perhaps asked, why tell a thrice-told tale ?—why go over ground that has been so often trod before ? The answer is, we are not only writing for the information of the general reader, but also for the seaman, in the hope that these examples may afford encouragement to him, if ever thrown under similar circumstances to those which befel the crews of the Hecla and Fury.

In a short time, the ships became embedded in ice, and in this remote part of the globe were they destined to remain, in all probability, for nine months, during the greater part of which they would not see the light of the sun.

To the seaman, whose happiness is dependent upon a life of excitement and adventure, such a change must be almost insupportable. As far as the eye could reach, nothing was to be seen but trackless wilds of snow ; an awful stillness reigned around ; even the indigenous animals had for a time fled ; and out of his ship, which is the world to him, not a living creature breathed in this dreary desert. In order to procure occupation and amusement for the men, it was necessary to hit upon some expedient to keep their spirits from flagging. This was found, by a proposal from Captain Hoppner, that they should attempt a masquerade, in which both officers and men should join. The happy thought was at once seized upon, the ship's tailor was placed in requisition, admirably dressed characters were enacted, and mirth and merriment rang through the decks of the Hecla. These réunions took place once a month, alternately on board each ship, and not one instance is related of anything occurring which could interfere with the regular discipline of the ship, or at all weaken the respect of the men towards their superiors. But an occupation which was of benefit as much to the mind as to the body, was found in the establishment of a school on board each of the ships. These were superintended by Mr. Hooper, in the Hecla, and Mr. Mogg, in the Fury. The men gladly seized this opportunity of instruction which was afforded them, and in many a long winter evening the lower deck was made a scene of rational employment, which was not only a lasting benefit to themselves, but assisted materially in passing away the time, which otherwise would have hung heavily on their hands.

We cannot refrain here from offering a few observations upon the good results of education to the seaman.

In the beginning of the present century, and even in a much later date, the majority of our seamen could neither read nor write ; in the present day it is quite the reverse. We may affirm, without exaggeration, that two-thirds of them are more or less educated. Experience has taught those placed at the head of naval affairs the advantages arising from the improvement of the minds of the seamen of our navy ; every ship has now a seaman schoolmaster, and a well selected library ; and there is no doubt that the moral effect thus produced, adds in no small degree to the preservation of that discipline which is so necessary for the comfort and welfare of a ship's company.

In corroboration of the above, we cannot do better than quote the words of Sir Edward Parry :—'And I do not speak lightly when I express my thorough persuasion that to the moral effect thus produced upon the minds of the men were owing to a very high degree the constant yet sober cheerfulness, the uninterrupted good order, and even in some measure the extraordinary state of health which prevailed among us during winter.'

With the amusement before mentioned, varied now and then, as the days grew longer, by the excitement of

killing a bear, entrapping foxes, or shooting grouse, the
men continued to pass the winter months. To the officers,
higher and more intellectual enjoyments were afforded by
making observations, studying astronomy, and witnessing
the brilliant appearance of the Aurora Borealis.

About the end of March, or beginning of April, 1825,
thin flakes of snow, lying upon painted wood or metal,
exposed to the sun's direct rays, began to melt. These
signs of returning spring were hailed as indications of
their approaching deliverance from their winter quarters.
Towards the middle of June, information was brought
that the sea was clear of ice about twenty miles from
Port Bowen. On the 12th of July, the ice began to
break away, leaving the ship about one mile and a
quarter from the open sea. All hands were set to work
to saw through this barrier, the men being employed
from seven in the morning, till seven in the evening. On
the 19th, after the most incessant labour, which was
performed with the greatest cheerfulness and alacrity,
Captain Parry had the satisfaction of seeing the two
vessels once more floating in their proper element.

After a winter of unusual severity, but of unprece-
dented good health, they sailed out of Port Bowen on
the 20th of July, the expedition being in every respect
in the most perfect condition, and the season remarkably
forward and fine. Pushing over to the west coast of
Prince Regent's Inlet, which it was Captain Parry's
intention to coast northward and then westward, till they
could strike off to the continental shore, the prospect
seemed as favourable as could possibly be expected. The
season continued unusually warm, and channels of open
water always occurred along the shore with particular
winds. The ice was entirely detached from the shores,
very much broken up, and lighter than they had yet
navigated.

Proceeding as usual, taking advantage of every opening, and sheltering the ships on shore when the ice
closed, the Fury, on the 1st of August, was unfortunately pressed by the ice in such a manner, while she
also took the ground, that her main keel, stern-post,
and cutwater were immediately broken, and four pumps
were necessary to keep her free.

It was now evidently impossible to proceed without
heaving the Fury down to repair, her officers and men
being in a few days almost exhausted with excessive
fatigue ; the men's hands having become so sore from
the constant friction of the ropes, that they could hardly
handle them any longer without the use of mittens.

The shore being a straight and exposed one, the principal difficulty consisted in securing the ship from the
inroads of the ice during the operation. There was little
hopes of discovering a harbour for this purpose, and the
only alternative was to endeavour to make one. This
was done by passing lower cables round grounded masses
of ice, and setting them up to anchors buried on the
beach, so as to form a basin for the reception of the
ships.

We have now arrived at the period when the labour
of heaving down the Fury commenced ; and, for the
better information of the reader, we will at once lay
before him the account of the future proceedings, as
related by Sir Edward Parry.*

'The ice remaining quite close, on the 6th every individual in both ships, with the exception of those at the
pumps, was employed in landing provisions from the
Fury, together with the spars, boats, and everything from

---

* The loss of the Fury is taken from Sir Edward Parry's
Voyage to the North Pole, published by Mr. Murray, who has
kindly allowed it to be inserted in this work.

off her upper deck. The ice coming in in the afternoon
with a degree of pressure which usually attended a
northerly wind on this coast, twisted the Fury's rudder
so forcibly against a mass of ice lying under her stern,
that it was for some hours in great danger of being
damaged, and was, indeed,. only saved by the efforts of
Captain Hoppner and his officers, who, without breaking
off the men from their other occupations, themselves
worked at the ice-saw.

' On the following day, the ice remaining as before, the
work was continued without intermission, and a great
quantity of things landed. The two carpenters, Messrs.
Pulfer and Fiddis, took the Fury's boats in hand themselves, their men being required as part of our physical
strength in clearing the ship. The armourer was also
set to work on the beach in forging bolts for the mar-
tingales of the outriggers. In short, every living creature
among us was somehow or other employed, not even
excepting our dogs, which were set to drag up the stores
on the beach, so that our little dockyard soon exhibited
the most animated scene imaginable. The quickest
method of landing casks, and other things not too
weighty, was that adopted by Captain Hoppner, and
consisted of a hawser secured to the ship's mainmast
head, and set up as tight as possible to the anchor on
the beach,—the casks being hooked to a block traversing
on this as a jack stay, were made to run down with
great velocity. By this means, more than two were got
on shore for every one handed by the boats; the latter,
however, being constantly employed in addition. The
Fury was thus so much lightened in the course of the
day, that two pumps were now nearly sufficient to keep
her free, and this number continued requisite until she
was hove down. Her spirit room was now entirely clear,
and on examination the water was found to be rushing

in through two or three holes that happened to be in the ceiling, and which were immediately plugged up. Indeed it was now very evident that nothing but the lightness of the Fury's diagonal ceiling had so long kept her afloat, and that any ship not thus fortified within could not possibly have been kept free by the pumps.

'At night, just as the people were going to rest, the ice began to move to the southward, and soon after came in towards the shore, again endangering the Fury's rudder, and pressing her over on her side to so alarming a degree, as to warn us that it would not be safe to lighten her much more in her present insecure situation.

'One of our bergs also shifted its position by this pressure, so as to weaken our confidence in the pier heads of our intended basin; and a long 'tongue' of one of them, forcing itself under the Hecla's fore-foot, while the drift-ice was also pressing her forcibly from astern, she once more sewed three or four feet forward at low water, and continued to do so, notwithstanding repeated endeavours to haul her off, for four successive tides, the ice remaining so close, and so much doubled under the ship, as to render it impossible to move her a single inch.

'Notwithstanding the state of the ice, however, we did not remain idle on the 8th, all hands being employed in unrigging the Fury, and landing all her spars, sails, booms, boats, and other top weight.

'The ice still continuing very close on the 9th, all hands were employed in attempting, by saws and axes, to clear the Hecla, which still grounded on the tongue of ice every tide. After four hours' labour, they succeeded in making four or five feet of room astern, when the ship suddenly slided down off the tongue with considerable force, and became once more afloat. We then got on shore the Hecla's cables and hawsers for the accommodation of the Fury's men in our tiers during the heaving

down; struck our topmasts, which would be required as
shores and outriggers; and, in short, continued to occupy
every individual in some preparation or other.

'These being entirely completed at an early hour in the
afternoon, we ventured to go on with the landing of
the coals and provisions from the Fury, preferring to run
the risk which would thus be incurred, to the loss of
even a few hours in the accomplishment of our present
object. As it very opportunely happened, however, the
external ice slackened to the distance of about a hundred
yards outside of us, on the morning of the 10th, enabling
us by a most tedious and laborious operation, to clear
the ice out of our basin piece by piece. The difficulty
of this apparently simple process consisted in the heavy
pressure having repeatedly doubled one mass under
another, a position in which it requires great power to
move them, and also by the corners locking in with the
sides of the bergs.

'Our next business was to tighten the cables sufficiently
by means of purchases, and to finish the floating of them
in the manner and for the purpose before described.
After this had been completed, the ships had only a few
feet in length, and nothing in breadth to spare, but we
had now great hopes of going on with our work with
increased confidence and security. The Fury, which was
placed inside, had something less than eighteen feet at
low water; the Hecla lay in four fathoms, the bottom
being strewed with large and small fragments of lime-
stone.

'While thus employed in securing the ships, the
smoothness of the water enabled us to see, in some
degree, the nature of the Fury's damage; and it may be
conceived how much pain it occasioned us, plainly to
discover that both the stern-post and fore-foot were
broken and turned up on one side with the pressure.

We could also perceive, as far as we were able to see along the main-keel, that it was much torn, and we had therefore reason to conclude that the damage would altogether prove very serious. We also discovered that several feet of the Hecla's false keel were torn away abreast of the fore chains, in consequence of her grounding forward so frequently.

'The ships being now as well secured as our means permitted from the immediate danger of ice, the clearing of the Fury went on with increased confidence, though greater alacrity was impossible, for nothing could exceed the spirit and zealous activity of every individual, and as things had turned out, the ice had not obliged us to wait a moment except at the actual times of its pressure. Being favoured with fine weather, we continued our work very quickly, so that on the 12th every cask was landed, and also the powder; and the spare sails and clothing put on board the Hecla.

' On the 13th, we found that a mass of heavy ice which had been aground with the Fury, had now floated alongside of her at high water, still further contracting her already narrow basin, and leaving the ship no room for turning round. At the next high water, therefore, we got a purchase on it, and hove it out of the way, so that at night it drifted off altogether.

'The coals and preserved meats were the principal things now remaining on board the Fury, and these we continued landing by every method we could devise as the most expeditious. The tide rose so considerably at night, new moon occurring within an hour of high water, that we were much afraid of our bergs floating ; they remained firm, however, even though the ice came in with so much force as to break one of our hand-masts, a fir spar of twelve inches in diameter. As the high tides, and the lightening of the Fury, now gave us suf-

M 3

ficient depth of water for unshipping the rudders, we
did so, and laid them upon the small berg astern of us,
for fear of their being damaged by any pressure of the
ice.

'Early on the morning of the 14th, the ice slackening
a little in our neighbourhood, we took advantage of it,
though the people were much fagged, to tighten the
cables, which had stretched and yielded considerably by
the late pressure. It was well that we did so, for in the
course of this day we were several times interrupted in
our work by the ice coming with a tremendous strain
on the north cables, the wind blowing strong from the
N.N.W., and the whole 'pack' outside of us setting
rapidly to the southward. Indeed, notwithstanding the
recent tightening and re-adjustment of the cables, the
bight was pressed in so much, as to force the Fury
against the berg astern of her, twice in the course of the
day. Mr. Waller, who was in the hold the second time
that this occurred, reported that the coals about the
keelson were moved by it, imparting the sensation of part
of the ship's bottom falling down ; and one of the men
at work there was so strongly impressed with that belief,
that he thought it high time to make a spring for the
hatchway. From this circumstance, it seemed more
probable that the main keel had received some serious
damage near the middle of the ship.

'From this trial of the efficacy of our means of security,
it was plain that the Fury could not possibly be hove down
under circumstances of such frequent and imminent risk.
I therefore directed a fourth anchor, with two additional
cables, to be disposed, with the hope of breaking some of
the force of the ice, by its offering a more oblique resistance
than the other, and thus by degrees turning the direction
of the pressure from the ships. We had scarcely completed this new defence, when the largest floe we had

seen since leaving Port Bowen came sweeping along
the shore, having a motion to the southward of not less
than a mile and a half an hour, threatened to overturn
it, and would certainly have dislodged it from its situation but from the cable recently attached to it.

'A second similar occurrence took place with a smaller
mass of ice about midnight, and near the top of an
unusually high spring tide, which seemed ready to float
away every security from us. For three hours about the
time of this high water, our situation was a most critical
one, for had the bergs, or, indeed, any one of them, been
carried away or broken, both ships must inevitably have
been driven on shore by the very next mass of ice that
should come in. Happily, however, they did not suffer
any further material disturbance, and the main body
keeping at a short distance from the land until the tide
had fallen, the bergs seemed to be once more firmly
resting on the ground. The only mischief, therefore,
occasioned by this disturbance was the slackening of our
cables by the alteration in the position of the several
grounded masses, and the consequent necessity of employing more time, which nothing but absolute necessity
could induce us to bestow, in adjusting and tightening
the whole of them afresh.

'The wind veering to the W.N.W. on the morning of
the 15th, and still continuing to blow strong, the ice was
forced three or four miles off the land in the course of a
few hours, leaving us a quiet day for continuing our
work, but exciting no very pleasant sensations, when we
considered what progress we might have been making
had we been at liberty to pursue our object.

'The land was indeed so clear of ice to the southward,
that Dr. Neill, who walked a considerable distance in
that direction, could see nothing but an open channel in
shore to the utmost extent of his view. We took

advantage of this open water to send the launch for the
Fury's ironwork, left at the former station ; for though
the few men thus employed could very ill be spared, we
were obliged to arrange everything with reference to the
ultimate saving of time ; and it would have occupied
both ships' companies more than a whole day to carry
the things round by land.

' The Fury being completely cleared at an early hour,
on the 16th, we were all busily employed in ' winding'
the ship, and in preparing the outriggers, shores, purchases, and additional rigging.   Though we purposely
selected the time of high water for turning the ship
round, we had scarcely a foot of space for doing it, and
indeed, as it was, her forefoot touched the ground, and
loosened the broken part of the wood so much as to
enable us to pull it up with ropes, when we found the
fragments to consist of the whole of the gripe, and most
of the ' cutwater.'   The strong breeze continuing, and
the sea rising as the open water increased in extent, our
bergs were sadly washed and wasted ; every hour producing a sensible and serious diminution in their bulk.
As, however, the main body of ice still kept off, we were
in hopes, now that our preparations were so near completed, we should have been enabled in a few hours to
see the extent of the damage, and repair it sufficiently to
allow us to proceed.

' In the evening we received the Fury's crew on board
the Hecla, every arrangement and regulation having
been previously made for their personal comfort, and for
the preservation of cleanliness, ventilation, and dry
warmth throughout the ship.   The officers of the Fury,
by their own choice, pitched a tent on shore for messing
and sleeping in, as our accommodation for two sets of
officers was necessarily confined.   On the 17th, when
every preparation was completed, the cables were found

again so slack, by the wasting of the bergs, in consequence
of the continued sea, and possibly also in part by the
masses being moved somewhat in shore, that we were
obliged to occupy several hours in putting them to rights,
as we should soon require all our strength at the purchases. One berg also had, at the last low water, fallen
over on its side, in consequence of its substance being
undermined by the sea, and the cable surrounding it
was thus forced so low under water as no longer to afford
protection from the ice should it again come in. In
tightening the cables, we found it to have the effect of
bringing the bergs in towards the shore, still further
contracting our narrow basin ; but anything was better
than suffering them to go adrift.

'This work being finished at ten P.M., the people were
allowed three hours' rest only, it being necessary to
heave the ship down at, or near, high water, as there
was not sufficient depth to allow her to take her distance
at any other time of tide. Every preparation being
made, at three A.M., on the 18th, we began to heave her
down on the larboard side ; but when the purchases
were nearly a-block, we found that the strops under the
Hecla's bottom, as well as some of the Fury's shore-fasts,
had stretched or yielded so much, that they could bring
the keel out of water within three or four feet. We
immediately eased her up again, and re-adjusted everything as requisite, hauling her further in shore than
before by keeping a considerable keel upon her, so as to
make less depth of water necessary ; and we were then
in the act of once more heaving her down, when a snow
storm came on, and blew with such violence off the land,
as to raise a considerable sea. The ships had now so
much motion as to strain the gear very much, and even
to make the lower mast of the Fury bend in spite of the
shores. We were, therefore, most unwillingly compelled

to desist until the sea should go down, keeping everything
ready to recommence the instant we could possibly do so
with safety. The officers and men were now literally so
harassed and fatigued as to be scarcely capable of further
exertion without some rest; and on this and one or two
other occasions, I noticed more than a single instance of
stupor amounting to a certain degree of failure in intellect, rendering the individual so affected quite unable at
first to comprehend the meaning of an order, though
still as willing as ever to obey it. It was, therefore,
perhaps, a fortunate necessity which produced the intermission of labour which the strength of every individual
seemed to require.

'The gale rather increasing than otherwise, during the
whole day and night of the 18th, had, on the following
morning, when the wind and sea still continued un-
abated, so destroyed the bergs on which our sole dependence was placed, that they no longer remained aground
at low water; the cables had again become slack about
them, and the basin we had taken so much pains in
forming had now lost all its defences, at least during a
portion of every tide. It will be plain, too, if I have
succeeded in giving a distinct description of our situation,
that independently of the security of the ships, there was
now nothing left to seaward by which the Hecla could
be held out in that direction while heaving the Fury
down, so that our preparations in this way were no longer
available.

'After a night of most anxious consideration and consultation with Captain Hoppner, who was now my mess-
mate in the Hecla, it appeared but too plain that, should
the ice again come in, neither ship could any longer be
secured from driving on shore. It was therefore determined instantly to prepare the Hecla for sea, making
her thoroughly effective in every respect; so that we

might at least push her out into comparative safety among the ice, when it closed again, taking every person on board her; securing the Fury in the best manner we could, and returning to her the instant we were able to do so, to endeavour to get her out, and to carry her to some place of security for heaving down. If, after the Hecla was ready, time should still be allowed us, it was proposed immediately to put into the Fury all that was requisite, or at least as much as she could safely carry, and towing her out into the ice, to try the effect of 'foldering' the leaks, by sails under those parts of her keel which we knew to be damaged, until some more effectual means could be resorted to.

'Having communicated to the assembled officers and ships' companies my views and intentions, and moreover given them to understand that I hoped to see the Hecla's top-gallant yards across before we slept, we commenced our work, and such was the hearty good-will and indefatigable energy with which it was carried on, that by midnight the whole was accomplished, and a bower-anchor and cable carried out in the offing, for the double purpose of hauling out the Hecla when requisite, and as some security to the Fury if we were obliged to leave her. The people were once more quite exhausted by these exertions, especially those belonging to the Fury, who had never thoroughly recovered their first fatigues. The ice being barely in sight, we were enabled to enjoy seven hours of undisturbed rest; but the wind becoming light, and afterwards shifting to the N.N.E., we had reason to expect the ice would soon close the shore, and were, therefore, most anxious to continue our work.

'On the 20th, therefore, the re-loading of the Fury commenced with recruited strength and spirits, such articles being in the first place selected for putting on board as were essentially requisite for her re-equipment;

for it was my full determination, could we succeed in
completing this, not to wait even for rigging a topmast,
or getting a lower yard up, in the event of the ice coming
in, but to tow her out among the ice, and there put
everything sufficiently to rights for carrying her to some
place of security. At the same time, the end of the sea-
cable was taken on board the Fury, by way of offering
some resistance to the ice, which was now more plainly
seen, though still about five miles distant. A few hands
were also spared, consisting chiefly of two or three con-
valescents and some of the officers, to thrum a sail for
putting under the Fury's keel; for we were very anxious
to relieve the men at the pumps, which constantly
required the labour of eight to twelve hands to keep
her free. In the course of the day several heavy masses
of ice came drifting by with a breeze from the north-
east, which is here about two points upon the land, and
made a considerable swell. One mass came in contact
with our bergs, which, though only held by the cables,
brought it up in time to prevent mischief. By a long
and hard day's labour, the people not going to rest till
two o'clock on the morning of the 21st, we got about
fifty tons weight of coals and provisions on board the
Fury, which, in case of necessity, we considered sufficient
to give her stability.

'While we were thus employed, the ice, though
evidently inclined to come in, did not approach us
much; and it may be conceived with what anxiety we
longed to be allowed one more day's labour, on which
the ultimate saving of the ship might almost be considered as depending. Having hauled the ships out a
little from the shore, and prepared the Hecla for casting
by a spring at a moment's notice, all the people except
those at the pumps were sent to rest, which, however,
they had not enjoyed for two hours, when, at four A.M.

on the 21st, another heavy mass coming violently in contact with the bergs and cables, threatened to sweep away every remaining security. Our situation, with this additional strain,—the mass which had disturbed us fixing itself upon the weather-cable, and an increasing wind and swell setting considerably on the shore,— became more and more precarious; and indeed, under circumstances as critical as can well be imagined, nothing but the urgency and importance of the object we had in view—that of saving the Fury, if she was to be saved— could have prevented my making sail, and keeping the Hecla under way till matters mended. More hawsers were run out, however, and enabled us still to hold out: and after six hours of disturbed rest, all hands were again set to work to get the Fury's anchors, cables, rudder, and spars on board, these things being absolutely necessary for her equipment, should we be able to get her out. At two P.M. the crews were called on board to dinner, which they had not finished, when several not very large masses of ice drove along the shore near us at a quick rate, and two or three successively coming in violent contact either with the Hecla or the bergs to which she was attached, convinced me that very little additional pressure would tear everything away, and drive both ships on shore. I saw that the moment had arrived when the Hecla could no longer be kept in her present situation with the smallest chance of safety, and there- fore immediately got under sail, despatching Captain Hoppner, with every individual, except a few for working the ship, to continue getting the things on board the Fury, while the Hecla stood off and on. It was a quarter-past three P.M. when we cast off, the wind then blowing fresh from the north-east, or about two points on the land, which caused some surf on the beach. Captain Hoppner had scarcely been an hour on board

the Fury, and was busily engaged in getting the anchors
and cables on board, when we observed some large pieces
of not very heavy ice closing in with the land near her ;
and at twenty minutes after the Hecla had cast off, I
was informed, by signal, that the Fury was on shore.
Making a tack in shore, but not being able, even under
a press of canvass, to get very near her, owing to a strong
southerly current which prevailed within a mile or two
of the land, I perceived that she had been apparently
driven up the beach by two or three of the grounded
masses forcing her onwards before them, and these, as
well as the ship, seemed now so firmly a-ground, as
entirely to block her in on the seaward side. We also
observed that the bergs outside of her had been torn
away, and set adrift by the ice. As the navigating of
the Hecla with only ten men on board required constant
attention and care, I could not at this time with pro-
priety leave the ship to go on board the Fury. This,
however, I the less regretted, as Captain Hoppner was
thoroughly acquainted with all my views and intentions,
and I felt confident that, under his direction, nothing
would be left undone to endeavour to save the ship.   I,
therefore, directed him by telegraph, ' if he thought
nothing could be done at present, to return on board
with all hands until the wind changed ;' for this alone,
as far as I could see the state of the Fury, seemed to
offer the smallest chance of clearing the shore, so as to
enable us to proceed with our work, or to attempt
hauling the ship off the ground.

'About seven P.M., Captain Hoppner returned to the
Hecla, accompanied by all hands, except an officer with
a party at the pumps, reporting to me that the Fury
had been forced aground by the ice pressing on the
masses lying near her, and bringing home, if not breaking, the seaward anchor, so that the ship was soon found

to have swerved from two to three feet fore and aft. The
several masses of ice had, moreover, so disposed themselves, as almost to surround her on every side where
there was sufficient depth of water for hauling her off.
With the ship thus situated, and masses of heavy ice
constantly coming in, it was Captain Hoppner's decided
opinion, as well as that of Lieutenants Austin and Ross,
that to have laid out another anchor to seaward would
have only been to expose it to the same danger as there
was reason to suppose had been incurred with the other,
without the most distant hope of doing any service,
especially as the ship had been driven on shore by a
most unfortunate coincidence, just as the tide was beginning to fall. Indeed, in the present state of the Fury,
nothing short of chopping and sawing up a part of the
ice under her stern could by any possibility have effected
her release, even if she had been already afloat. Under
such circumstances, hopeless as, for the time, every seaman will allow them to have been, Captain Hoppner
judiciously determined to return for the present, as
directed by my telegraphic communication; but being
anxious to keep the ship free from water as long as
possible, he left an officer and a small party of men to
continue working at the pumps, so long as a communication could be kept up between the Hecla and the shore.
Every moment, however, decreased the practicability of
doing this; and finding, soon after Captain Hoppner's
return, that the current swept the Hecla a long way to
the southward while hoisting up the boats, and that more
ice was drifting in towards the shore, I was under the
painful necessity of recalling the party at the pumps,
rather than incur the risk, now an inevitable one, of
parting company with them altogether. Accordingly
Mr. Bird, with the last of the people, came on board at
eight o'clock in the evening, having left eighteen inches

water in the well, and four pumps being requisite to keep her free. In three hours after Mr. Bird's return, more than half a mile of closely packed ice intervened between the Fury and the open water in which we were beating, and before the morning this barrier had increased to four or five miles in breadth.

'We carried a press of canvas all night, with a fresh breeze from the north, to enable us to keep abreast of the Fury, which, on account of the strong southerly current, we could only do by beating at some distance from the land. The breadth of the ice inshore continued increasing during the day, but we could see no end to the water in which we were beating, either to the southward or eastward. Advantage was taken of the little leisure now allowed us to let the people mend and wash their clothes, which they had scarcely had a moment to do for the last three weeks. We also completed the thrumming of a second sail for putting under the Fury's keel, whenever we should be enabled to haul her off the shore. It fell quite calm in the evening, when the breadth of the ice inshore had increased to six or seven miles. We did not, during the day, perceive any current setting to the southward, but in the course of the night we were drifted four or five leagues to the south-westward, in which situation we had a distinct view of a large extent of land, which had before been seen for the first time by some of our gentlemen, who walked from where the Fury lay. This land trends very much to the westward, a little beyond the Fury Point, the name by which I have distinguished that headland, near which we had attempted to heave the Fury down, and which is very near the southern part of the coast seen in the year 1819. It then sweeps round into a large bay, formed by a long, low beach, several miles in extent, afterwards joining higher land, and running in a south-easterly direction to

a point which terminated our view of it in that quarter,
and which bore from us S. 58° W., distant six or seven
leagues. This headland I named Cape Garry, after my
worthy friend, Nicholas Garry, Esq., one of the most
active members of the Hudson's Bay Company, and a
gentleman most warmly interested in everything connected with northern discovery. The whole of the bays
which I named after my much esteemed friend, Francis
Cresswell, Esq., as well as the land to the southward,
was free from ice for several miles ; and to the southward
and eastward scarcely any was to be seen, while a dark
water-sky indicated a perfectly navigable sea in that
direction ; but between us and the Fury there was a
compact body of ice eight or nine miles in breadth. Had
we now been at liberty to take advantage of the favourable prospect before us, I have little doubt we could,
without much difficulty, have made considerable progress.

' A southerly breeze enabling us to regain our northing,
we ran along the margin of the ice, but were led so
much to the eastward by it, that we could approach the
ship no nearer than before during the whole day. She
appeared to us, at this distance, to have a much greater
heel than when the people left her, which made us still
more anxious to get near her. A south-west wind gave
us hopes of the ice setting off from the land, but it produced no good effect during the whole of the 24th. We
therefore beat again to the southward, to see if we could
manage to get in with the land anywhere about the
shores of the bay; but this was now impracticable, the ice
being once more closely packed there. We could only
wait, therefore, in patience for some alteration in our
favour. The latitude at noon was 72° 34' 57", making
our distance from the Fury twelve miles, which by the
following morning had increased to at least five leagues,
the ice continuing to pack between us and the shore.

The wind, however, now gradually drew round to the westward, giving us hopes of a change, and we continued to ply about the margin of the ice in constant readiness for taking advantage of any opening that might occur. It favoured us so much by streaming off in the course of the day, that by seven P.M. we had nearly reached a channel of clear water which kept open for seven or eight miles from the land. Being impatient to obtain a sight of the Fury, and the wind becoming light, Captain Hoppner and myself left the Hecla in two boats, and reached the ship at half-past nine, or about three-quarters of an hour before high water, being the most favourable time of tide for arriving to examine her condition.

' We found her heeling so much outward, that her main-channels were within a foot of the water ; and the large floe-piece which was still alongside of her, seemed alone to support her below water, and to prevent her falling over still more considerably. The ship had been forced much farther up the beach than before, and she had now in her bilge above nine feet of water, which reached higher than the lower-deck beams. On looking down the stern-post, which, seen against the light-coloured ground, and in shoal water, was now very distinctly visible, we found that she had pushed the stones at the bottom up before her, and that the broken keel, stern-post, and dead wood had, by the recent pressure, been more damaged and turned up than before. She appeared principally to hang upon the ground abreast the gangway, where, at high water, the depth was eleven feet alongside her keel ; forward and aft, from thirteen to sixteen feet ; so that at low tide, allowing the usual fall of five or six feet, she would be lying in a depth of from five to ten feet only. The first hour's inspection of the Fury's condition too plainly assured me, that, exposed as she was, and forcibly pressed up upon an open and stony beach, her holds full of water, and the damage of her hull, to all appearance and in all probability, more considerable than before, without any adequate means of hauling her off to the seaward, or securing her from the incursions of the ice, every endeavour of ours to get her off, or *if* got off, to float her to any known place of safety, would at once be utterly hopeless in itself, and productive of extreme risk of our remaining ship.

' Being anxious, however, in a case of so much importance, to avail myself of the judgment and experience of others, I directed Captain Hoppner, in conjunction with Lieutenants Austin and Sherer, and Mr. Pulfer, carpenter, being the officers who accompanied me to the Fury, to hold a survey upon her, and to report their opinions to me. And to prevent the possibility of the officers receiving any bias from my own opinion, the order was given to them the moment we arrived on board the Fury.

' Captain Hoppner and the other officers, after spending several hours in attentively examining every part of the ship, both within and without, and maturely weighing all the circumstances of her situation, gave it as their opinion that it would be quite impracticable to make her sea-worthy, even if she could be hauled off, which would first require the water to be got out of the ship, and the holds to be once more entirely cleared. Mr. Pulfer, the carpenter of the Fury, considered that it would occupy five days to clear the ship of water; that if she were got off, all the pumps would not be sufficient to keep her free, in consequence of the additional damage she seemed to have sustained : and that, if even hove down, twenty days' work, with the means we possessed, would be required for making her sea-worthy. Captain Hoppner and the other officers were therefore of opinion, that an absolute necessity existed for abandoning the Fury. My own opinion being thus confirmed as to the utter hopelessness of saving her, and feeling more strongly than ever the responsibility which attached to me of preserving the Hecla unhurt, it was with extreme pain and regret that I made the signal for the Fury's officers and men to be sent for their clothes, most of which had been put on shore with the stores.

'The Hecla's bower-anchor, which had been placed on the beach, was sent on board as soon as the people came on shore; but her remaining cable was too much entangled with the grounded ice to be disengaged without great loss of time. Having allowed the officers and men an hour for packing up their clothes, and what else belonging to them the water in the ship had not covered, the Fury's boats were hauled up on the beach, and at two A.M. I left her, and was followed by Captain Hoppner, Lieutenant Austin, and the last of the people in half an hour after.

'The whole of the Fury's stores were, of necessity, left either on board her or on shore; every spare corner that we could find in the Hecla being now absolutely required for the accommodation of our double complement of officers and men, whose cleanliness and health could only be maintained by keeping the decks as clear and well ventilated as our limited space would permit. The spot where the Fury was left is in latitude 72° 42′ 30″; the longitude by chronometers is 91° 50′ 05″; the dip of the magnetic needle, 88° 19′ 22″; and the variation 129° 25′ westerly.'

There now remains little more to be told—the accident that befel the Fury, the lateness of the season, and the crowded state of the Hecla, deprived Sir Edward Parry of all hopes of being able that season of accomplishing the object for which the expedition had been despatched.

Under all these untoward circumstances, he determined

to return to England, and on the 2nd of September the crew of the Fury were taken on board the Hecla, the boats hoisted up, the anchor stowed, and the ship's head put to the north-eastward.

After a prosperous voyage, the whole of the Hecla and Fury's crews, with but two exceptions, returned in safety to their native country, arriving at Sheerness on the 20th of October, in as good health as when they quitted England eighteen months before.

Lieutenant, now Captain Austin has, since these pages were written, been appointed to the command of an expedition in search of Sir John Franklin and his brave companions.

Captain Sir Edward Parry at present holds the appointment of Superintendent of the Royal Clarence Victualling Yard, and Haslar Hospital, Portsmouth.

THE MAGPIE.

IT is a common and no less apposite remark that truth is stranger than fiction, and the longer we live, the more are we convinced of the force of the above axiom.

The story which we are about to relate is one of the most remarkable incidents in a sailor's life, and, as a tale of horror, cannot be exceeded even in the pages of romance.

In the year 1826, the Magpie, a small schooner under the command of Lieutenant Edward Smith, had been despatched in search of a piratical vessel, which had committed serious depredations on the western shores of the Island of Cuba.

In the prosecution of this object, she was cruizing

N

on the 27th of August, off the Colorados Roads, at
the western extremity of the Island. The day had
been extremely sultry, and towards the evening the
schooner lay becalmed, awaiting the springing up of
the land breeze, a blessing which only those can appreciate who have enjoyed its refreshing coolness after passing many hours beneath the burning rays of a tropical
sun.

About eight o'clock a slight breeze sprung up from
the westward, and the vessel was standing under reefed
mainsail, whole foresail, and topsail, and jib. Towards
nine, the wind shifted to the southward, and a small dark
cloud was observed hovering over the land. This ominous
appearance, as is well known, is often the precursor of a
coming squall, and seems as if sent as a warning by
Providence.

The lurid vapour did not escape the practised eye of
the mate of the watch, who immediately reported the
circumstance to Mr. Smith. All hands were turned up,
and in a few minutes the schooner was placed in readiness to encounter the threatened danger.

In the meantime, the cloud had gradually increased
in size and density. The slight breeze had died away, and
a boding stillness reigned around. Suddenly a rushing,
roaring sound was heard, the surface of the water, which
a moment before was almost without a ripple, was now
covered with one white sheet of foam, the schooner
was taken aback; in vain her commander gave the
order to cut away the masts—it was too late, and in less
than three minutes from the first burst of the squall, the
devoted vessel sunk to rise no more.

At this fearful juncture, a vivid flash of lightning darted
from the heavens, displaying for a moment, the pale
faces of the crew struggling in the water; the wind
ceased as suddenly as it had begun, and the ocean, as if

unconscious of the fearful tragedy that had so lately
been enacted upon its surface, subsided into its former
repose.

At the moment of the vessel going down, a gunner's
mate, of the name of Meldrum, struck out and succeeded
in reaching a pair of oars that were floating in the water,
—to these he clung, and having divested himself of a part
of his clothing, he awaited in dreadful anxiety the fate
of his companions.

Not a sound met his ear, in vain his anxious gaze
endeavoured to pierce the gloom, but the darkness was
too intense. Minutes appeared like hours, and still the
awful silence remained unbroken; he felt, and the
thought was agony, that out of the twenty-four human
beings who had so lately trod the deck of the schooner,
he alone was left. This terrible suspense became almost
beyond the power of endurance, and he already began
to envy the fate of his companions, when he heard a
voice at no great distance inquiring if there was any one
near. He answered in the affirmative, and pushing out
in the direction from whence the sound proceeded, he
reached a boat, to which seven persons were clinging;
amongst whom was Lieutenant Smith, the commander
of the sloop.

So far this was a subject of congratulation; he was no
longer alone; but yet the chances of his ultimate preservation were as distant as ever.

The boat, which had been placed on the booms of the
schooner, had fortunately escaped clear of the sinking
vessel, and if the men had waited patiently, was large
enough to have saved them all; but the suddenness of
the calamity had deprived them of both thought and
prudence. Several men had attempted to climb in on
one side,—the consequence was, the boat heeled over, became half filled with water, and then turned keel upper-

most; and when Meldrum reached her, he found some
stretched across the keel and others hanging on by the
sides.

Matters could not last long in this way, and Mr.
Smith, seeing the impossibility of any of the party
being saved, if they continued in their present position,
endeavoured to bring them to reason, by pointing out
the absurdity of their conduct. To the honour of the
men, they listened with the same respect to their commander, as if they had been on board the schooner;
those on the keel immediately relinquished their hold,
and succeeded, with the assistance of their comrades, in
righting the boat. Two of their number got into her
and commenced baling with their hats, whilst the others
remained in the water, supporting themselves by the
gunwales.

Order being restored, their spirits began to revive, and
they entertained hopes of escaping from their present
peril; but this was of short duration, and the sufferings
which they had as yet endured, were nothing in comparison with what they had now to undergo.

The two men had scarcely commenced baling, when
the cry was heard of—'A shark! a shark!' No words can
describe the consternation which ensued: it is well
known the horror sailors have of these voracious animals, who seem apprised by instinct when their prey is
at hand. All order was at an end, the boat again capsized,
and the men were left struggling in the waters. The
general safety was neglected, and it was every man for
himself; no sooner had one got hold of the boat, than
he was pushed away by another, and in this fruitless
contest more than one life was nearly sacrificed.

Even in this terrible hour, their commander remained
cool and collected; his voice was still raised in words of
encouragement, and as the dreaded enemy did not make

its appearance, he again succeeded in persuading them to renew their efforts to clear the boat. The night had passed away—it was about ten o'clock on the morning of the 28th; the baling had progressed without interruption; a little more exertion, and the boat would have been cleared, when again was heard the cry of—'The sharks! the sharks!' But this was no false alarm; the boat a second time capsized, and the unhappy men were literally cast amongst a shoal of these terrible monsters.

The men, for a few minutes, remained uninjured, but not untouched; for the sharks actually rubbed against their victims, and, to use the exact words of one of the survivors, 'frequently passed over the boat and between us, whilst resting on the gunwale.' This, however, did not last long; a shriek soon told the fate of one of the men; a shark had seized him by the leg, dying the water with his blood; another shriek followed, and another man disappeared.

But these facts are almost too horrible to dwell upon; human nature revolts from so terrible a picture; we will therefore hurry over this part of our tale.

Smith had witnessed the sufferings of his followers with the deepest distress; and although aware that in all probability he must soon share the same fate, he never for a moment appeared to think of himself. There were but six men left, and these he endeavoured to sustain by his example, cheering them on to further exertions. They had once more recommenced their labours to clear out the boat, when one of his legs was seized by a shark. Even whilst suffering the most horrible torture, he restrained the expression of his feelings, for fear of increasing the alarm of the men. But the powers of his endurance were doomed to be tried to the utmost; another limb was scrunched from his body, and uttering a deep groan, he was about to let go his hold, when he

was seized by two of his men, and placed in the stern
sheets.

Yet when his whole frame was convulsed with agony,
the energies of his mind remained as strong as ever, his
own pain was disregarded, he thought only of the preservation of his crew. Calling to his side a lad of the
name of Wilson, who appeared to be the strongest of the
remaining few, he exhorted him, in the event of his
surviving, to inform the admiral that he was going to
Cape Ontario in search of the pirate when the unfortunate accident occurred; 'Tell him,' he continued, 'that
my men have done their duty, and that no blame is
attached to them. I have but one favour to ask, and
that is, that he will promote Meldrum to be a gunner.'

He then shook each man by the hand, and bade
them farewell. By degrees his strength began to fail,
and at last became so exhausted, that he was unable
to speak. He remained in this state until the sunset,
when another panic seized the men, from a reappearance
of the sharks. The boat gave a lurch, and the gallant
commander found an end to his sufferings in a watery
grave.

Thus perished an officer, who, if it had pleased Providence to preserve, would, in all probability, have been
one of the brightest ornaments of the service. His
character combined the three great qualities which are
essential for an officer and a seaman—courage, coolness,
and decision: opportunity only was wanting to display
these parts. If he had succeeded in capturing the pirate,
promotion would without doubt have followed, and a
bright and honourable career have been open to him.
But the ways of Providence are inscrutable; it was
ordained that he should undergo sufferings from which
the bravest would have shrunk with horror. Had he
fallen in battle, his name would have been recorded in

history. We hope that our feeble efforts to rescue the memory of this brave seaman from sinking into oblivion will not have been in vain, and that his name may find an honourable place with others who have died in the performance of their duty.

The death of their commander was sensibly felt by all, for they had long known his kindness and courage, and when his body sank below the waves, their hopes sank also. Mr. Maclean, a mate, and now the commanding officer, took upon himself to direct the efforts of his comrades, and did all that lay in his power to revive their spirits; he assured them that if they once succeeded in righting the boat, that there was every chance of falling in with some vessel. But twenty hours of constant fatigue, hunger, and thirst had made fearful ravages upon the strength of the men. Night was again approaching, and Maclean could not conceal from himself, that when darkness came on, the chances of their being seen by any vessel passing near were further removed than ever. The sharks had for a time taken their departure, but they might return at any moment; for having once tasted blood, they were not likely to be debarred from making another attack. Two more of the men, either worn out from fatigue, or anxious to escape from further suffering, threw themselves from their support, and were drowned.

The burning sun again set beneath the horizon, but as yet no sail had been seen upon the waters. Again the land-breeze passed over the ocean, but it brought no refreshing coolness; it only reminded them of the weary hours that had elapsed since it was so anxiously expected, though its results were then far different from what they had hoped.

There were but four men left—Maclean, Meldrum, (the gunner's mate,) Wilson, and another man. These had, by their united efforts, almost managed to clear the boat of water, when, about three o'clock in the morning, the two latter became delirious, sprung overboard, and were either seized by the sharks or drowned. It will be remembered, that it was Wilson who was selected by poor Smith to convey his last message to the admiral.

The two survivors for a time forgot their own sufferings in the horrible scene which they had just witnessed; but this did not last long; their thoughts soon returned to the necessity of preserving their own lives. They once more resumed their labours, and, though nearly exhausted, did not desist until the boat was almost dry. They then lay down to rest, in comparative security, and, let us hope, with their hearts filled with gratitude for the mercies which had already been vouchsafed to them, and remembering those words of our beautiful Liturgy: ' That it may please Thee to succour, help, and comfort all that are in danger, necessity, or tribulation.'

It is said that sometimes the criminal, the night before his execution, forgets the fate that awaits him in a deep and refreshing slumber. These two men, in spite of the horrors they had undergone, fell into a sound sleep, from which they did not awake until the sun was high in the heavens; when the horrors of their situation broke upon them, rendered doubly painful by the temporary oblivion of the last few hours.

The sun darted its scorching rays upon the two solitary beings, who had planted themselves, one in the bows, and the other in the stern of the boat, with neither oars, mast, sail, nor provisions of any kind. In vain they strained their gaze in every direction; nothing was to be seen but a boundless expanse of waters. Their eyes met, but it needed no words to tell the hopeless despair which was gnawing at their hearts. No longer was the loss of their companions regarded with horror;

they envied the fate which had spared them the torture which they themselves were doomed to suffer:—

> Famine, despair, cold, thirst, and heat had done
> Their work on them by turns.   BYRON.

Death at that moment would have been welcome.

Hour after hour passed away, but still the boat remained motionless on the waters. Neither spoke; their hearts were too full for utterance: in rapid succession, every thought and action of their lives passed across their minds; home, kindred, friends, all would be remembered, only again to be banished by the pangs of hunger and thirst.

Towards eight o'clock in the morning, the energies of Maclean and his companion had almost sunk under the accumulated load of suffering; it was more in despair than with any expectation of success, that they once again cast their eyes around. But this time it was not in vain; a white speck was seen in the distance: both exclaimed, 'A sail! a sail!' and the extravagance of joy was now equal to their former despair. Still the vessel was several miles distant, and unless those on board kept a vigilant look-out, it was more than probable that they would escape observation.

Of all the ills to which the human frame is liable, the agony of suspense is the most intolerable. Hope and fear rose alternately in their breasts; at one moment, the ship appeared to be nearing, at another, she seemed further off than ever. The vessel sped slowly on its course, but to their excited minds the time seemed interminable. First the white canvas was seen, then the dark hull became visible; but as yet no signs gave token that those on board were aware of their proximity.

The brig, for such she now appeared, could not have been above half a mile distant, when she suddenly altered

her course. In vain they both hailed at once, and waved
their jackets as a signal, but no notice was taken ; then,
indeed, every hope was dispelled, and the bitterness of
despair returned with redoubled force.

At this juncture, Meldrum resolved, at all hazards, to
attempt to swim to the vessel. If he remained in the
boat, certain death would be the fate of himself and his
companion : on the other hand, he might perish in the
sea, but if he reached the brig, both would be saved.
Without a moment's hesitation, he communicated his
design to Maclean, and then, committing himself to the
pretection of the Almighty, sprang overboard.

The idea of solitude is so repugnant to human nature,
that even death would be preferable. It can be therefore easily imagined that it was with feelings almost
amounting to agony that Maclean saw himself separated
from his last friend. His first impulse was to follow his
companion, but better judgment prevailed, and he determined to await the result. Never for a single instant
did his eyes turn from the bold swimmer : they followed
his every stroke. At one time, he thought he had sunk ;
at another, the ripple of a wave appeared to his distorted
imagination like the fin of a shark. Anxiety for the
fate of his companion kept his mind on the stretch until
distance rendered the object no longer visible. ' Then,
indeed, did he feel that he was alone.'

Meldrum was naturally a good swimmer, and every
nerve was strained in this last struggle for life ; buoyed
up by hope, he had accomplished about two-thirds of his
weary task when his strength began to fail, his dying
eyes turned towards the brig, and with one last effort he
raised his voice. He was heard : a boat was lowered
from the brig, and he was taken on board. The perilous
situation of his comrade was made known ; and thus by his

gallant exertions were preserved the lives of the two survivors of the ill-fated Magpie.

This tale might almost be discredited, but the facts
from which it was taken bear the signature of the
officers composing the court-martial who sat upon the
two remaining men. Mr. Maclean is at the present
moment alive, and is now serving as a lieutenant in the
coast-guard. Meldrum was promoted for his gallantry to
the rank of gunner, and died two years ago.

THE THETIS.

HIS Majesty's ship, Thetis, Captain Samuel Burgess,
sailed from Rio Janeiro on the evening of the 4th
of December, 1830, having a large amount of treasure on
board. The weather was so thick, that as they worked
out of the harbour, the islands at its entrance were not
visible ; but as the evening was tolerably fine, with the
exception of the fog, Captain Burgess determined to
persevere in his course. The following morning the fog
dispersed, but it was soon succeeded by such heavy rain,
that the obscurity was nearly as great as before. The ship
continued her course with the wind upon the starboard
tack, until half-past one in the afternoon, when, from the
reckoning, they supposed Cape Frio to be about thirty-eight
miles distant, lying north 36° east. From the hour of their
departure from Rio Janeiro, till the time of which we speak,
neither sun, moon, nor stars had been visible. On account
of the cross sea, which appeared to impede the progress of
the vessel, and the lightness of the wind, her course was
kept east by north until two o'clock, when it was changed

to E.N.E. At four o'clock P.M. it was calculated that they had run about nineteen miles, and that they must be nearly abreast of Cape Frio, and about twenty-four miles distant from it. The weather clearing up at that time, they discovered a large ship, with all sail set, standing in shore, and no land being visible, they concluded that they were still further from land than they had reckoned, and therefore they changed their course again to N.E. by E. At five o'clock the people were mustered at quarters, and then a looming of land was seen to the N.N.W., which, according to their calculation, was the direction Cape Frio would bear; and there being no land near it that could have the same appearance, the reckoning was considered correct, and a prudent proportion of sail was made, regard being had to the state of the weather, and the course they were steering. Between six and seven o'clock P.M. the rain again began to fall; the fog returned, and became gradually so thick, that it was impossible to see the length of the ship.

At eight P.M. the watch was mustered, and the men placed at their stations to keep a vigilant look-out, while the officer of the watch went forward himself to see that the sails were well trimmed, and that every one was on the alert. At half-past eight, when the captain had retired to his cabin, and was waiting for the usual evening report from the master, a midshipman entered with the startling intelligence that land had been seen close a-head, the ship at the time going at the rate of eight or nine miles an hour.

Captain Burgess was on deck in a moment; he ordered the helm to be put 'hard a-port,' and was told it had been done. The next instant the jib-booms and bowsprit were heard to crash; the captain hastened to the gangway, and was just in time to see the foremast go. Scarcely had he called to the men to stand clear, when

all the three masts fell aft, one after the other, covering
the deck with masts, yards, sails, and rigging, and in
their fall killing some and dreadfully mangling others.
Within a few feet of the ship rose a stupendous black
rock, against which the surf was raging violently. The
rock was so perpendicular, that both the fore and main
yardarms were (before they fell) scraping against the
granite cliff. The hull, however, did not appear to come
in contact with the rock; but, as if answering the helm,
her head turned off shore, and as she swung round, the
larboard quarter boat was completely smashed between
the ship's side and the rock. Nothing could exceed the
alarm that prevailed on board for a few minutes after the
sudden crash. The decks were covered with spars and
rigging, lying pell-mell upon the bodies of those who had
been injured by their fall. The man at the helm had
been killed at his post, and the wheel itself was shivered
to atoms; whilst the darkness of the night, and the roar
of the breakers against the cliff, added to the horrors of
a catastrophe of which the suddenness alone was sufficient
to paralyse the energies of the men.

Captain Burgess saw that everything depended upon
promptitude and decision: he quickly rallied his people,
and order was soon restored: he then gave directions
that the well should be sounded, and that the men
should stand by the small bower anchor.

A sentinel was placed to guard the spirit-room, and
two small sails were run up the fore and main-masts, the
stumps of which were from twelve to fifteen feet above
the deck, and the helm was put to starboard. The
winches were next manned, and guns, rockets, and blue
lights let off in rapid succession.

The well was reported dry; orders were given for the
small bower anchor to be let go, but it was found covered
with the wreck of the bowsprit, and it was necessary to

cut away the best bower in order to keep the ship off
shore; and for the same purpose every spar that could
be obtained was made use of to bear her off the rocky
cliffs, but in vain, for from the depth of the water, the
anchor did not reach the bottom, and the stern tailed
upon a shelving rock in spite of all their efforts. The
men were next ordered to clear away the boats and get
them ready—but they were found totally destroyed.
Those on the quarters had been smashed by the rocks,
and those on the booms and stern by the falling of the
masts. During the whole of this anxious period, the
conduct of the men was most exemplary. Aware that all
depended upon individual exertion, each one appeared
to emulate the example set by his officers, and worked
with hearty good will; not a single instance of anything
like bad conduct occurred.

Their condition was most disheartening; the boats
were no longer available; the water was gaining on the
vessel; and the rockets and blue lights, as they darted
into the air, served but to show them the rugged face of
the high rocks, which appeared to afford no footing by
which the summit could be gained, even if they should
be so fortunate as to reach them at all.

Whilst all on board were weighing these chances of
destruction or of safety, the vessel's head had gone
round off, and a few succeeding heavy surfs threw her
again with her starboard quarter upon the rock, and
whilst she was in this position, there appeared a possibility of getting some of the people on shore. Captain
Burgess, therefore, ordered Lieutenant Hamilton to do
everything in his power to facilitate such a proceeding,
and shortly afterwards that officer, Mr. Mends, midshipman, and about seventy others, effected a landing by
jumping either from the broken end of the main-yard,
which was lying across the ship, or from the hammock

netting abaft the mizenmast; several others who attempted to land in the same way were less fortunate some were crushed to death, and some drawn back by the recoil of the surf and drowned.

From the time the ship first struck, the current had been carrying her along the cliffs at the rate of at least a quarter of a mile an hour; it now carried her off the rock, and she drifted along shore, a helpless wreck, at the mercy of the winds and waves. The captain saw that nothing more could be done for the vessel, and therefore he directed all his energies to the preservation of the crew. The marine who had been appointed to guard the spirit-room still remained at his post, and never left it till commanded to do so by his superior officer, even after the water had burst open the hatch. We mention this as an instance of the effect of good discipline in times of the greatest peril.

The vessel, or rather the wreck, was now carried towards a small cove, into which she happily drifted; she struck heavily against the rocks, then gave some tremendous yauls, and gradually sunk until nothing was left above water but the bows, the broken bowsprit, and the wreck of the masts as they laid on the booms.

All on board deemed that the crisis of their fate had arrived,—and they prepared for the final struggle between life and death. There were some moments of awful suspense, for every lurch the ill-fated vessel gave, was expected to be the last; but when she seemed to sink no deeper, there came the hope that her keel had touched the bottom, and that they should not all be engulfed in a watery grave.

Before she sunk, the frigate's bows had gone so close into the rocks as to enable some sixty or seventy people to jump on shore; and a hawser was got out and fixed to a rock, by which several others were saved; but by a tremendous surge, the piece of rock to which the hawser was fastened was broken away, and for a time all communication with the land was suspended. They tried every means that could be devised to convey a rope from the ship to the land, but for a long time without success, until Mr. Geach, the boatswain, swung himself on the stump of the bowsprit, and by making fast two belaying pins to the end of a line, he succeeded in throwing it on shore. To this a stronger cable was bent, and it was dragged through the surf by the people on the rocks, who then kept it taut.

Although a few words only are required to describe the mode by which a communication was established between the ship and the shore, yet it had been a work of toil, time, and danger. The boatswain had more than once nearly lost his life by being washed away by the waves as they swept over the wreck ; the captain, who directed his proceedings, was standing up to his middle in water, upon one foot only, frequently losing his hold, and with great difficulty regaining his position.

The boatswain, when the preparations were completed, suggested that, in order to test the strength of the cable, a boy should be the first to make a trial of it ; accordingly, a young lad was firmly secured to a sort of cradle or bowling knot, and drawn on shore in safety. The success of the attempt was announced by a loud cheer from the strand, and the captain then took upon himself to direct the landing of the rest of the crew by the same means. He stationed himself on the knight head, so as to prevent a general rush being made ; he then called each man separately, and one by one they slung themselves upon the rope and were swung on shore. Nothing could exceed the good conduct displayed by the whole of the ship's company, every order was promptly obeyed, and the utmost patience and firmness exhibited by every individual.

When the greater part of the people had quitted the wreck, there still remained several who could not be induced even by the earnest and repeated entreaties of their commander to leave their *dry* position on the yards. The strength of the captain and boatswain was almost exhausted, and as they could not persuade any more of the men to avail themselves of the proffered means of safety, they were obliged, though very reluctantly, to leave them on the wreck, and they themselves joined the crew on the rocks.

In the course of an hour or two, however, the party who had stayed by the wreck, took courage and ventured upon the rope ; but as the stump of the bowsprit, which was over the larboard. cathead, rendered it extremely hazardous to come forward, they did not all get on shore till daylight. In the morning, Captain Burgess's first care was to muster his men, and a melancholy spectacle presented itself. Sixteen were missing, and of those who were gathered around him, many had been dreadfully bruised and lacerated in their efforts to reach the shore. Amongst those who perished was a fine spirited lad, the son of Captain Bingham, late commander of the Thetis. But a few months before, Captain Bingham himself had been drowned in the Guayaquil : thus father and son lay far from their native land, beneath the western flood.

> The warlike of the isles,
> The men of field and wave,
> Are not the rocks their funeral piles,
> The seas and shores their grave ?
> Go, stranger ! track the deep—
> Free, free, the white sail spread ;
> Wind may not rove, nor billows sweep,
> Where rest not England's dead.

The crew of the Thetis had now time to look around them, and to consider what was next to be done. The prospect was a sad one. Before them, and almost hidden by the white foam, lay the once noble frigate, now a complete wreck; the cove into which she had drifted was bound by lofty and precipitous crags, arising abruptly from the sea, and varying in height from 80 to 194 feet. The men and officers were perched in groups on points of the rocks; few of them had clothing enough to cover them, and scarcely any had shoes. There seemed to be no means of ascending the precipice; but to do so must be their first object; and anxiously they sought for some part which might offer a surer footing, and a less perilous and perpendicular ascent. At last they succeeded in casting a rope round one of the projecting crags, and by help of this some of the strongest of the party climbed the giddy height, and then assisted in hauling up their weaker comrades.

To give some idea of the difficulties which they had to surmount, and their almost miraculous escape, we subjoin the following description of the place from the pen of Captain Dickenson:—

'The coast is formed of rugged and almost perpendicular rocks, varying from 80 to 194 feet in height, a peak rising at each point, and another in nearly the centre of the north-eastern side.

'On viewing this terrific place, with the knowledge that at the time of the shipwreck the wind was from the southward, I was struck with astonishment, and it appeared quite a mystery that so great a number of lives could have been saved; and indeed it will never cease to be so, for that part on which the crew landed is so difficult of access, that (even in fine weather) after being placed by a boat on a rock at the base, it required considerable strength and agility, with the assistance of a man-rope, to climb the precipitous face of the cliff, and I am certain that in the hour of extreme peril, when

excess of exertion was called forth, there must have been
a most extraordinary display of it by a few for the benefit
of the whole.'

When the party were all safely landed on the top of
the rocks, they perceived that they were on an island
without inhabitants, and affording no shelter, except a
few huts, that had been erected for the convenience of
the natives curing fish. Fortunately these huts contained a considerable quantity of salt fish and farina.
This was placed in charge of the purser, and immediately distributed amongst the ship's company, who
stood in great need of refreshment. As soon as the
men were sufficiently recovered from their fatigues,
they were despatched in parties in all directions, to
discover means of communicating with the mainland,
from which the island was a few miles distant. Most
of them soon returned with the tidings that no means of
transport could be procured. This was a very disheartening announcement ; but its effects were quickly
dispelled by the appearance of a canoe coming into the
little cove where the huts were situated.

The seamen made signals to the men in the canoe,
inviting them to approach, which they did ; and when
they came up, they communicated the welcome intelligence, that round a point to the left, on the mainland,
there was a village which afforded all kinds of accommodation.

Captain Burgess then ordered Lieutenant Hamilton
to go in a canoe, with two or three of his men, to this
village, and there to make arrangements for proceeding
to the commander-in-chief at Rio Janeiro, and to send
off as many canoes as he could procure to convey the
ship's company to the mainland.

In a short time several canoes arrived at the island,
and Mr. Drake, the purser of the Thetis, was amongst

the first sent off to the village, with directions to despatch a sufficient quantity of provisions for the people on
the rock; but after making two or three trips between
the parties, Mr. Wilson, the master's assistant, returned
in one of the canoes to say, that the natives refused to
come again without being paid. In this dilemma, Captain Burgess went across himself, and by dint of persuasion and promises of payment, he at last induced some
of the natives to go to the assistance of his people; and
in the course of a few hours as many were conveyed to
the village as was deemed prudent. It was necessary to
leave some men to look after the wreck; and to this
duty Lieutenant Otway, Mr. Mends, midshipman, the
gunner, carpenter, four marines, and thirty-three seamen,
were appointed: they therefore remained on the island;
and before night Captain Burgess had the satisfaction of
seeing all the rest of his crew, if not very comfortably
lodged, at least safe and under shelter. In the evening,
Lieutenant Hamilton set out overland to Rio Janeiro to
apprise the commander-in-chief of the loss of the Thetis,
and the distressing situation of her men.

The following morning the people had great difficulty
in hiring canoes, and only one could be obtained, in
which Lieutenant West and the boatswain went off to
the wreck, where they were for several days actively employed. None of the men were allowed to be idle, for
they had full occupation in carrying wood and water,
which were only to be found at a great distance.

The behaviour of the local authorities was disgraceful
in the extreme; although fully aware of the destitute
condition of the Englishmen who had been cast upon
their shores, they denied them the most trifling assistance, and turned a deaf ear to every entreaty and remon-
strance.

Money! money! was the constant cry. In vain

Captain Burgess assured them that the little he had saved was almost expended; but that as soon as assistance should arrive from his countrymen, every article should be paid for. All his arguments and promises were thrown away upon the natives, whose rapacity knew no bounds; they would give nothing without payment, and their charges were exorbitant.

Captain Burgess was so exasperated at one of these natives, who had agreed to let the crew have a small bullock, but, upon finding there was no money to pay for it, had driven it away, that he thought it almost justifiable to desire his men to help themselves. There was, however, one bright exception to this universal hard-heartedness. A sergeant, named Antonio das Santos, who commanded a small fort of three guns, seeing the unwillingness of the natives to render any aid to the strangers, came forward and asked if anything was wanted that he could supply. Captain Burgess replied, that both his officers and men stood in great need of food, and that a loan of money for present use would be very acceptable. The sergeant immediately placed in the captain's hands forty milreas in copper, and most generously put at his disposal everything he possessed. The example of this noble-hearted fellow had no effect on the conduct of the rest; their great object seemed to be to make as much gain as possible by the misfortunes of their fellow-creatures, and they went so far as to plunder the wreck, breaking open the chests, and taking possession of their contents whenever an opportunity occurred.

In order to attract the notice of vessels passing near, two flag-staffs had been erected upon the heights, with the ensign downwards; but day after day passed on, and no friendly sail appeared. The cupidity of the natives was insatiable, and provisions became more and more scarce. It was not until the 15th of December, ten days after the loss of the Thetis, that a vessel was seen in the offing. She proved to be the Algerine, which arrived most opportunely, when they were almost reduced to extremity, and brought them the articles of which they were in greatest need.

The next day, just after the Algerine had entered the harbour of Cape Frio, Admiral Baker arrived with a necessary supply of money. He had attempted the sea-passage from Rio Janeiro, for three days, in his barge, but had been obliged to put back on account of the current, and had then performed the journey of seventy miles overland in forty-eight hours. From the admiral, Captain Burgess had the satisfaction of hearing that the Druid, Clio, Adelaide, and a French brig of war might be hourly expected.

These all arrived in due course, and took on board the officers and men of the late Thetis, who were safely landed at Rio Janeiro on the 24th of December.

In conclusion, we cannot refrain from noticing the firmness and presence of mind evinced by Captain Burgess under the most appalling circumstances. After having adopted every available means for saving the ship without effect, he superintended for many hours the disembarkation of the crew, and during all that tedious process he was standing in a heavy surf up to the middle in water; nor could he be persuaded to quit the wreck until not one more of his officers or men would consent to go before him. Respecting the conduct of the officers and men, we cannot do better than lay before our readers Captain Burgess's own estimate of its merits.

'I owe,' he says, 'to the whole of my officers and men (and which most sincerely and unreservedly I render,) the meed of praise due to the conduct of every one, without exception. It was their prompt obedience to all my orders, and the firmness, fortitude, and alacrity which they perseveringly as well as patiently displayed amidst their great perils, sufferings, and privations, through the whole of this trying scene, that contributed, under Providence, to the saving of so many of their lives.

'Their subsequent orderly and excellent conduct on shore as much bespeaks my approbation ; and, in truth, the general character of their conduct throughout has induced an esteem in me which it is impossible can ever cease but with my life.'*

Captain Samuel Burgess entered the navy in 1790, and served on board the Impregnable at the victory of the 1st of June, 1794. He was almost constantly employed from that time until the year 1804, when he was appointed a lieutenant on board the Prince, of 98 guns, in which ship he was present at the battle of Trafalgar.

He next served on board the Dreadnought, 98, and subsequently was appointed to the command of the Pincher, a 12-gun brig, employed in the North Sea and Baltic. Whilst in command of this vessel, Lieutenant Burgess distinguished himself on many occasions, particularly in assisting Lord George Stuart in reducing the batteries of Cuxhaven and Bremerleke. His next appointment was to the Vixen gun-brig; and although he might well have expected promotion for his services, he remained lieutenant until the year 1816, when he was appointed to the Queen Charlotte, in which ship he served as flag-lieutenant to Lord Exmouth at the bom-

---

* The greater part of the treasure lost with the Thetis (806,000 dollars) has subsequently been recovered. An interesting description of the means used for raising it will be found in a volume published by Captain Dickenson.

bardment of Algiers. Upon the arrival of the dispatches in England, Lieutenant Burgess was promoted to the rank of commander. He received his post rank on the 27th November, 1830, when he took the command of the Thetis.

A more lengthened statement of the services of this officer will be found in O'Byrne's *Naval Biography*, to which work we are indebted for the above sketch.

THE FIREFLY.

THE Firefly, a small schooner, with a crew of about fifty men, was proceeding on her voyage from Belize to Jamaica, on the 27th of February, 1835. The wind had been moderate during the day, and as they were steering a course laid down in the chart, no danger was anticipated.

Between nine and ten o'clock at night, the greater part of the crew, with the exception of those whose duty it was to be upon deck, had retired below, when the seaman in charge of the watch reported to the commander, Lieutenant Julius McDonnell, that it was very dark ahead. He instantly went upon deck, when the sound of surf breaking upon rocks was distinctly heard. The helm was put down, under the hopes of staying the vessel, but as the wind was light, and a heavy swell setting in at the time, she did not come round, but getting stern-way, struck with a shock which made every timber vibrate, and appeared to threaten instant destruction to the vessel. All were in a moment upon deck; the sweeps were got out on the larboard side, the best

bower anchor let go, and the boats hoisted out, and
ordered to sound, whilst the cutter was sent to carry out
the stream anchor. The cable was then held taut, but
snapped almost immediately: the best bower came home,
and the small bower was let go. In the meantime, the
wind had shifted to the northward, and was blowing in
heavy squalls, and their small bower anchor, which was
their sole dependence, came home.

Everything that could be done was put into practice
to save the vessel, but all in vain; and when daylight
broke, her commander saw that there was nothing now
left him but to take measures for preserving the lives of
the crew.

For this purpose, all the officers and men were set to
work to construct rafts, as the boats were not sufficient
to contain the whole of the crew. Between six and
seven o'clock in the morning, one raft was completed,
and the cutter and gig prepared to receive the men.
The vessel was all this time rapidly breaking up; the
bolts of her keelson and the sternpost had started; the
deck was broken in, and there was but little hope of
her holding together many hours.

One officer, Mr. Nopps, the master's assistant, had
been placed in the cutter, to prevent the men from
taking away anything save the clothes they had on.
Eighteen were already in the boat, including Captain
West (an engineer officer) and his son, and fifteen were
mustered in the raft, which was lashed to the larboard
of the wreck, when from some accident the raft got
adrift, and was carried away by the current. This proved
most unfortunate, as the raft was their great resource;
and all on board of her would inevitably have perished,
had not the cutter pushed out to their assistance. A
rope was fastened to the raft, and they attempted to tow
her back to the schooner; but as the cutter had only

o

four oars, and the wind set so strong to the southward, they were unable to reach the schooner.

Those who remained upon the wreck had only the gig left; and as this could contain but a few, Lieutenant McDonnell thought it advisable to direct an officer to take on board the sick, and proceed for assistance to Belize, and if he fell in with the cutter to send her back to the schooner. The gig accordingly shoved off, but again returned, in consequence of an accident having happened to the mast; this being remedied, she again pulled away from the wreck and having fallen in with the cutter, communicated the orders of Mr. McDonnell for her return. This, as has before been shown, was impossible, and the gig having taken on board Captain West and his son, parted from the cutter, with the intention of proceeding to Belize.

When Lieutenant McDonnell saw that the cutter did not return, he directed and assisted the men who remained upon the wreck to construct a second raft. This, after considerable labour, was completed by the following morning: it was then launched overboard, and made fast to the rocks within the reef. As the wreck still held together, Mr. McDonnell considered it prudent to remain by her as long as possible, in the hope that some assistance might arrive from Belize: but in this he was disappointed. In the meantime, another and stronger raft had been formed from the after part of the quarter-deck, which had been broken up by the sea; this also was launched, and brought forward under the bows. The men almost hoped against hope, but yet no assistance arrived. Fortunately, the weather was partially moderate, but still the sufferings, from exposure to the weather, and the deprivation of proper food, were severely felt; and Lieutenant McDonnell determined, under all these circumstances, to wait no longer, and on the 4th of March everything was in readiness to quit the wreck. A small barrel of bread was placed on the raft, but this was immediately washed off into the sea. A beaker one-third full of rum was then fastened more securely, and this was the only thing that they could take with them.

All having embarked, they started with the intention of steering towards a cay which was in sight, but the current proved too strong, and the raft was swept into deep water. The sail was then set, and they steered in the direction of what was supposed to be a wreck, or vessel, in the same situation as themselves; but on nearing, it proved to be a sand-bore, on which people were distinctly seen walking to and fro. They immediately conjectured that these must be the crew of one of the boats, a supposition which afterwards proved to be correct. Every effort was made to gain the bank, but the current was too strong, and they found it impossible to reach any part of the reef.

Lieutenant McDonnell, who had been suffering some days from ill health, was now so exhausted that he was obliged to be supported upon the raft. He was, therefore, unable to give any commands; and, after a short consultation, it was considered best to stand out to sea, in the hopes of falling in with some vessel. The night had set in, and they steered a course westward. On the following morning a white bottom was seen, but immediately afterwards the raft was again in deep water. All this time they had nothing to eat; their sole subsistence being a small quantity of rum, which was served out at stated intervals.

The following morning, about eight o'clock, land was observed right a-head, and they endeavoured to steer in that direction; but their progress, from the heavy construction of the raft, was necessarily very slow, and it was not until sunset that they found themselves about nine or ten miles from the shore. All the next night they stood in the same direction ; and about four or five o'clock in the morning, as near as they could guess, they were cast by the surf upon the beach. Utterly prostrate with the fatigues they had undergone, they threw themselves upon the sand, and soon found in sleep a brief forgetfulness of their past cares and troubles. They did not awake for many hours, when, upon looking around, they discovered that the commander was absent. This, however, gave them no uneasiness, as it was supposed that he had gone in search of assistance. The first object was to proceed in quest of water, of which they stood in most need. They had gone for more than a mile without finding anything to moisten their lips, or any signs of habitation, when one of the men discovered a cocoa-nut tree : here was both food and drink, and with avidity they seized upon the fruit, and found relief from their most urgent wants.

Amongst the party who were cast on shore were Mr. Malcolm, a master's assistant, and Mr. Price, a merchant ; these, with the rest of the men, proceeding a little further into the woods, became so fatigued that they were obliged to return to the place where they were first cast, whilst their companions prosecuted the search for Lieutenant McDonnell, whose continued absence had given the greatest alarm.

About one o'clock, some of the men returned, but brought no tidings of the commander ; they said that the rest of the men had determined to walk round the cay, as they conjectured the place on which they were cast was Ambegris Cay, and more especially as Mr. Price, who had been long a resident at Honduras, had assured them that to the south-east there was a plantation belonging to one of his friends.

About two hours afterwards the men returned, but neither their endeavours to find . a habitation nor any traces of Lieutenant McDonnell had been successful. They said that it had been their intention to walk round the cay, but from the appearance of the coast, they did not think it was possible to do so that day. It was then proposed that they should rest where they were during night, and renew their search at an early hour next morning.

Whilst they were sitting on the beach, one of the men thought he saw Mr. McDonnell running in the surf, about half a mile distant. Ritchie, the gunner's mate, immediately proceeded in the direction where he was supposed to be, and found that unfortunate officer in a state of delirium. He endeavoured to persuade him to come down to where the rest of the men were assembled, but a few incoherent words were his only reply. Ritchie was, therefore, obliged to return to his comrades for assistance; and having communicated the sad condition of their officer, they all proceeded together to the spot where he was last seen, but found no traces of the commander. Search was made in every direction, but in vain; and as night was approaching, they were reluctantly obliged to return to the place which they had fixed upon as their rendezvous. In their way thither they gathered some more cocoa-nuts, and having satisfied their hunger and thirst, lay down to rest, under the canopy of heaven, and with no softer bed than what the sandy beach afforded.

The next morning the men again declared their intention of walking in search of the plantation mentioned by Mr. Price. Mr. Malcolm, who had become the senior officer in the absence of Mr. McDonnell, advised them to remain where they were, and to build a hut, and dig a well for water; he assured them that, as long as there was a plentiful supply of cocoa-nuts, they could not starve, and that the chances were, assistance would arrive. All was, however, to no purpose; they would not listen to any argument, and even disregarded his authority. It was as much as he could do to insist upon their first going in search of their commander.

After a long time employed for this purpose, they discovered Mr. McDonnell asleep beneath a parmetta tree. Upon hearing footsteps approaching, he awoke, but in such a feeble state that he was unable to rise without assistance, and from the wildness of his manner, there was too much reason to fear that his reason had fled. They gave him some cocoa-nut milk, which he eagerly drank, and this appeared to give him some relief. With difficulty they made him comprehend that they intended to proceed to the plantation for assistance, but he refused to join them, alleging that a boat was coming for him. In a short time he appeared a little more collected, and agreed to join the expedition. There still remained a small supply of rum, and a portion of this being poured into some empty cocoa-nuts, it was distributed equally amongst the men, and they all commenced their journey, the men about 200 yards ahead, and Mr. McDonnell, supported by Malcolm and Mr. Price, brought up the rear.

After proceeding in this way about two miles, Mr. McDonnell's strength utterly failed, and he sank down upon the ground, declaring that he could go no further; every entreaty was urged to persuade him to make another effort, but both the powers of the mind and body had deserted the unfortunate officer, and Malcolm and his companion were at a loss to know what course to pursue. After a brief consultation they determined to leave Mr. McDonnell, and as soon as they reached the plantation, which Mr. Price declared could not be far distant, return with assistance.

They then once more resumed their journey, the men proceeding a-head as before; in the middle of the day they stopped to rest, and again resumed their march until about an hour before sunset, when they arrived at two cocoa-nut trees; and as these formed not only a place of shelter, but also a means of procuring food, they determined to remain there for the night. The men who had climbed up the trees, and were gathering fruit, descried a pond, or creek, in the wood, about half a mile distant. Mr. Price then observed, if that was the case, they were on the mainland, and not on Ambegris Cay.

They were now in a great dilemma, for they were uncertain which way to proceed, and Mr. Malcolm endeavoured to persuade the men to return to the beach, assuring them that it was quite useless their proceeding any further, for they did not know where they were going; but they turned a deaf ear to every argument, declaring that they would walk as long as they were able. Mr. Price, the merchant, agreed with the rest of the men, and urged them to continue their journey, in the hopes that they might be seen by some coasting boats going to Belize. This was Saturday night; and after toiling all day, they had only walked ten miles from where they had left Mr. McDonnell. The next morning Mr. Malcolm again entreated the men to remain, but it was of no avail, and they recommenced their march.

The men continued to walk together until Tuesday evening, subsisting upon cocoa-nuts, which they gathered on their way, when Malcolm was obliged to be left behind, as he was unable to walk any further. The next morning he was found by some natives, and taken to Ambegris Cay, where the men had arrived the previous evening.

We must now return to the fate of the cutter, which

it will be remembered left the wreck on the morning of
the 28th of February, taking the raft in tow. They
endeavoured to return to the schooner, but the current
proving too strong, they were obliged to abandon the
attempt, and ran before the wind until they made a
sand-bore, on the south end of the reef, about an hour
afterwards.

They then cut the raft adrift, and landed the men that
were in the cutter, sending the boat back with two men
to carry the rest off the raft, as it was impossible to bring
the raft to the sand-bore. It was about seven o'clock in
the evening when they were all safely landed, the cutter
being at this time in such a condition, that she could not
have floated, even in smooth water, without baling.

They then dragged the boat up the beach, where they
remained until daylight next morning, the 1st of March.
Mr. Nopps, master's-assistant, who was the commanding
officer of the party, determined to leave the majority of
the men on the sand-bore, and proceed to the wreck; he
accordingly started with five men in the cutter, in hopes
of reaching the schooner, but as it blew strongly from
the northward, and the boat had no jib or mizen, and
the mainmast and sprit sprung, they found it impossible to beat to windward. In this condition, as there
was no appearance of the wind abating, and nothing to
eat except some salt pork, and only two beakers of water,
one of which had been drunk during the night, Mr.
Nopps considered it his duty to take the boat with these
five men, and run for the first place they could fetch,
hoping to reach Belize, which was nearly before the
wind.

For two days they scudded before the wind, without
being able to set any sail, and had passed at least forty
miles to the southward of Belize, before the wind abated;
during this time they suffered severely from want of

water, the last beaker having been finished, and the salt pork increasing their thirst. It was not until twelve o'clock on Tuesday, the 3rd of March, that they arrived in Belize roads, and were taken on board the Fly.

Here they received every attention that was necessary, and Mr. Rogers, the master of the Fly, accompanied by Mr. Nopps, was despatched in the Governor's schooner to the assistance of the men who were left on the sand-bore, and of the others who were still supposed to be upon the wreck.

On the following Friday, the 6th of March, they reached the sand-bore, and having taken off the men, proceeded to the wreck, where they found only two men, from whom they learnt that Lieutenant McDonnell, and the rest of the people, had quitted the wreck two days previously. Pilot boats were then sent in search, and another party explored the coast; and after visiting Long Bay, without hearing any tidings, returned to Belize.

In the course of two days, a boat arrived with the eight men who had been with McDonnell, who reported that they had left that officer, almost dead, in the wood.

Mr. Nopps again departed in a pilot-boat in search of his commander, but when he reached Ambegris Cay, the boat was unable to beat up outside the breakers, and it came on to blow so violently during the night, that they were prevented from landing; the following day they were more successful, and Mr. Nopps walked up the coast. For two days his search proved useless, but on the third he had the pleasure of finding Mr. McDonnell still alive, in a hut, under the care of some Indians. After the lapse of two days, he was so far recovered as to be taken on board the pilot-boat, and arrived next morning at Belize Bay.

It would have been happy if all connected with the

Firefly had been equally fortunate. The gig, which had been sent from the wreck to Belize for assistance, was found several days afterwards cast upon the beach, broken in two, and all in her must have perished.

Lieutenant McDonnell was promoted to the rank of commander in 1846, and at present is unemployed.

THE AVENGER.

THE Avenger, a steam frigate, with an armament of 6 heavy guns and 280 men, sailed from Gibraltar on the afternoon of the 17th of December, 1847. As her commander, Captain Charles G. E. Napier, was anxious to spare the coal, the steam was reduced to the least possible degree, leaving sufficient to work the wheels up to the rate of sailing. On Monday, the 20th, the steamer was running with square yards, at the rate of eight or nine knots an hour, steering about east by south, under double-reefed topsails and reefed foresail. At eight o'clock in the evening the usual watch was placed, with directions to keep a careful look-out. The night was dark and squally, with a high sea running, and occasionally loud peals of thunder were heard, accompanied with vivid flashes of lightning.

Most of the officers were collected in the gun-room, with the exception of the captain, who had retired to his sleeping cabin. He had directed his steward to request the attendance of the master, and of Mr. Betts, the second master, who soon joined him in the cabin, where they remained for a few minutes examining the charts. The captain's steward relates, that the above officers went upon deck, when Captain Napier desired him to take away the light, and to leave a small lamp burning in the fore-cabin, which was always kept alight at sea during the night. He accordingly did so, and returned to his berth. In about half-an-hour afterwards he heard some one come down from the quarter-deck, and go into the captain's cabin. In about five minutes the captain went upon deck, where he remained for a short time, and again returned to his cabin, but had scarcely closed the door, before he was summoned upon deck by the officer of the watch.

The officers in the gun-room were upon the point of retiring to their berths, when they were startled by a sudden jerk, which they at first supposed to be a gun broken adrift, but the next moment the ship gave a heavy lurch, as if filling, and her whole frame appeared shaken, and every beam loosened. It would be in vain to attempt to describe the dismay of the crew of the ill-fated Avenger, when thus roused from a sense of comparative security, to find themselves in an instant upon the verge of destruction. Already the deck was crowded with people, most of them only partially clothed, and the rest almost naked. On the bridge between the paddle-boxes stood the captain and master; Mr. Ayling, the master's assistant, the quarter-master, and two seamen were at the wheel. In another minute the ship gave a heavy lurch to starboard, and the sea poured over the forecastle. The captain then gave the order, 'Out boats —lower away the boats.' These were his last words, for he was immediately afterwards washed overboard and drowned.

Lieutenant Rooke, who never appears to have lost his presence of mind, immediately went forward to assist in lowering the boats, but under the firm impression that the ship was fast sinking, and with little hope that there was time enough to get out the boats, or even if lowered, that they could live in such a heavy sea. He saw, however, if anything was to be done, it must be done immediately; he therefore went amongst the men endeavouring to persuade them to lower the starboard cutter; Mr. Betts, the second master, at the same time attempted to lower the port one. Every entreaty and persuasion that Lieutenant Rooke could use was, however, of no avail; the men seemed paralysed with the sudden panic and the apparent helplessness of their situation. Instead of affording assistance, they clustered together, exclaiming, 'Oh, my God, Sir, we are lost—we are lost!' Mr. Rooke, finding that all his arguments were of no avail, crossed the deck to the port side for the purpose of helping Mr. Betts in lowering the port cutter. In his way he met Larcom, the gunner, who had just come from below, with his clothes under his arm, having been in bed when the ship struck. Hastily acquainting him with his intention, they made the best of their way to the cutter, where they were joined by Dr. Steel, the surgeon, Mr. Ayling, master's-assistant, John Owen, a stoker, James Morley, a boy, and W. Hills, captain's steward. At this moment, Lieutenant Marryat made his appearance, his manner calm and self-possessed; he was in the act of addressing himself to one of the party, when the ship gave a heavy lurch to starboard, and the gallant young officer lost his footing, and was washed overboard.

Whilst they were in the act of lowering the cutter, an accident occurred, which was nearly proving fatal to all their hopes of preservation.

In lowering the boat, the foremost fall got jammed, and the after one going freely, the boat had her stern in the water, and her bows in the air; at this moment, Dr.

Steel threw in his cloak, which fortunately got into the sleave-hole of the after fall, and stopped it.

Just as the boat touched the water, and before the tackles were unhooked, the ship struck again heavily, and began swinging broadside to the sea, falling over to starboard at the same time, which, from the cutter being the port one, made her crash with great violence against the ship's side; however, by dint of great exertion, the boat was got free from the tackles, and pulled clear of the ship.

The Avenger now lay broadside to the sea, with her head towards Africa, falling at the same time to windward, with her deck exposed; the foremast, mainmast, and mizen topmast falling over the starboard side, and the funnel on the gangway, no doubt killing many of the crew as it fell. As the boat left the ship's side, some one attempted to burn a blue-light, but it went out immediately. The sea was now occasionally seen to break over the forecastle and quarter, and Mr. Rooke, in the hope of saving some of the crew, gave orders to lie on their oars, and keep the boat's bow to the ship, to be ready to pick up any of the survivors in the event of the ship's falling to pieces. Lieutenant Rooke and his little party* remained by the ship for about an hour and a half, the moon at intervals shining out brightly from behind the heavy clouds, and discovering the Island of Galita, apparently at about ten or twelve miles distant. The weather now became more tempestuous; the rain poured in torrents; and all being almost exhausted with pulling against a strong current, and being gradually drawn

---

* The party in the boat consisted of Lieutenant Rooke; Mr. Betts, second master; Mr. Ayling, master's assistant; Mr. Larcom, gunner; Dr. Steel, the surgeon; Wm. Hills, captain's steward; John Owen, stoker; and the boy Morley.

away from the ship, Lieutenant Rooke considered it most
advisable to run under the lee of Galita, and there, if
possible, remain on their oars until there was daylight
sufficient to land, and seek assistance for the ship, in the
event of the island being inhabited.

All being of the same opinion, the boat's head was
turned towards Galita, and they took a last look of the
Avenger, which appeared to be firmly fixed, and likely
to hold together for some time.

The weather grew worse and worse; the boat, under a
close-reefed mizen on the bumpkin stepped as a foremast, was steered with an oar by the second master.
When they had arrived within about two miles of the
island, the wind shifted to a very severe squall, accompanied with lightning, thunder, and a heavy hail-storm.
Mr. Larcom, the gunner, now took the place of the
second master in steering the boat, which was scarcely
got round, before the wind caught her with such violence,
that it seemed impossible the boat could live.

The squall continued without intermission for two
hours and a half, when the moon again emerged from
the clouds, and the Island of Galita was discovered on
the port quarter. Some in the boat exclaimed, 'That
is the island!' which, at the time, they supposed to be
long out of sight, as the boat appeared to be going
rapidly through the water; this naturally led to a conjecture that a strong current set to the northward and
eastward. The wind still continued to veer about, and
at one time they thought that they must have passed the
ship, but the night was too dark to enable them to
discern anything clearly many yards beyond the boat.

In this manner they passed the long hours of night,
exposed to cold, hunger, and exhaustion ; and, as Lieutenant Rooke afterwards observed, with the full expecta-

tion that they would be unable to survive until morning. The second master appeared to have lost all reason. Upon being questioned as to whereabouts they were, or in what direction it was necessary to steer, he seemed to be scarcely aware that he was addressed. The doctor, the master's assistant, and the boy Morley, were lying at the bottom of the boat during the whole night, and the stoker, John Owen, was wrapped in his jacket, and appeared, if possible, in a worse condition than the second master. When asked to do anything, he only replied by vacant answers, and before morning became an idiot. At last the wished-for day broke, and the coast of Africa was discerned about eight or nine miles distant. As Lieutenant Rooke considered that the boat could not be kept above water much longer, he determined upon attempting a landing, and accordingly he himself steered her towards a small spot of sand, apparently clear of the rocks, and slightly sheltered by a reef running out into the sea.

This officer, from the time the boat quitted the Avenger, had, notwithstanding his own personal sufferings, set a noble example to his comrades, by exerting every effort to sustain their drooping spirits. As he approached the shore, he exclaimed in a cheerful voice, 'This is something like Don Juan's shipwreck; I only hope we shall find a Haidee.' It must not be supposed that this was said out of bravado, or because he was not perfectly aware of the danger, but from the necessity of his duty, as their commanding officer, to infuse a new spirit into his exhausted crew, and to encourage them in the approaching struggle, which he well knew would be 'life or death.' On hearing the above words, poor Steel, the doctor, exclaimed, 'Rooke! Rooke! there are other things to think of now.' The words were prophetic, for

before many minutes had elapsed, he had ceased to exist.
As they approached the shore, the sail was shifted from the
port side to the starboard, and the sheet which had been
held by Hills, the captain's steward, for ten hours, was
fastened to the thwarts.

Mr. Rooke now again resigned his place as steerer to
Larcom, the gunner, and assisted the others in baling out
the boat, which had shipped a heavy sea on the quarter.
The boat was steered within about one hundred and fifty
yards of the beach, when the rollers caught her, first
lifting her upright, and, as there was not water enough
to float her whole length, she filled and capsized. Larcom,
Lieutenant Rooke, Hills, the captain's steward, and the
boy Morley, succeeded in gaining the beach, but the
rest of their unfortunate comrades perished.

We should here mention that this was the second
occasion on which the boy Morley narrowly escaped a
watery grave.

When the Avenger was at Lisbon, the boy fell overboard, and would have perished, had it not been for
Lieutenant Marryat, who, at the risk of his own life,
sprung into the sea, and rescued the boy.

In a few minutes a Bedouin Arab, who had been
watching the boat from some high ground, came toward
them and conducted them to his hut, where he supplied
them with some milk; and having lighted a fire, they
were enabled to dry their clothes.

They remained with their hospitable entertainer
during that day, and in the evening made a supper of
maize-cake and sour milk. In the meantime, Mr. Rooke
had made the Arab understand their situation, and
their wish to get to Tunis; and after some trouble and
promise of reward, he agreed to conduct them next
morning to Biserta. The wearied men then threw

themselves on the ground, where they passed the night
in company with dogs, cows, and goats, exposed to a
violent wind and pouring rain.

Their subsequent proceedings are thus related by
Lieutenant Rooke :—

'Wednesday, December 22nd.—At about 9 A.M. we
started. Our road lay at first over a ridge of high hills,
from which we saw nothing of the ship. We then
crossed a sandy plain covered with the cactus, which
severely wounded my feet. Afterwards passed through
some wooded ravines, and over an extensive marsh inter-
sected with brooks. Towards the evening a horseman
overtook us, who seeing the tired condition of the
steward, his feet bleeding, and also suffering from a gash
on his head, received whilst landing, carried him for
about four miles, and when his road lay in a different
direction, gave our guide his gun, and a piece of silver
for us.

'The night being now dark, and all of us exhausted,
we stopped at a Bedouin encampment, and asked for
shelter, which after some time was granted. We had
been walking about ten hours, and got over more than
thirty miles of broken ground, having stopped once for a
few minutes to pick the berries off some arbutus trees,
being our only food since breakfast till late that night.
We were wet, coverless, and all except myself shoeless.

'They gave us some maize-cake and milk. Seeing
horses, I made them understand that they would be
well paid if they let us have them to take us on to
Biserta that night, when they made signs that the gates
were locked, but that we should have them in the
morning.

'Thursday, December 23rd.—At daylight we set out,
but none of us could walk from swollen feet. After a

ride of about fifteen miles, sometimes fording streams,
and at others nearly up to our horses' knees in mud, we
arrived about ten A.M., at Biserta, and went to the house
of our consular agent, an Italian, whom I immediately
asked to prepare a boat for Tunis.

'The boats here were all too small to send to the wreck,
and for which the wind was foul, with a fresh breeze.
About 1 P.M. I started for Tunis, and arrived about 11
P.M. at the Goletta, where I landed, and sent to our Vice-
Consul, who after some difficulty, owing to the port
regulations, came to see me, and tried to pass me through
the gates, but did not succeed. He promised to get two
vessels ready, as unfortunately there were no steamers
here at the time of our arrival. In one I meant to have
sent Mr. Larcom to Galita, and the other I intended to
take to the wreck.

'Friday, December 24th.—At daylight, when the
gates opened, I entered a carriage, and drove up to our
consul-general, who ordered his agent to forward my
views in every way, sending his son to hurry matters,
whilst he communicated with the Bey, who ordered his
squadron to sea.

'Whilst my boat was preparing (a Maltese speronara,
with a crew of twelve men, selected for their knowledge
of the coast,) I wrote two letters, one to Malta, and the
other to Lisbon, stating the loss of the ship. Not having
slept for four nights, and being thoroughly tired, would
account for the vague statement I sent. I then break-
fasted, and started about two P.M., having put on board
such provisions as my hurried departure admitted of—
tea, coffee, biscuits, and spirits, in case I should be fortunate enough to save anybody.

'Saturday, December 25th, on my passage, and at
daylight on Sunday I was close to the spot where the

Avenger was wrecked, although there was no broken or discoloured water to mark it. I cruised about till satisfied she had either broken up or sunk. Whilst here I saw two steamers (Lavoisier and Pasha) come up and cruise about Galita together: a merchant ship, and a gun-boat of the Bey's, with which I communicated, asking them to take me to Galita, which I wished to examine personally, as also to speak the steamers, my own crew, with whom I had great trouble, refusing to do so. They declined, when I asked them to take half my crew out, and lend me two men, to which request I also received a negative; so I returned to Tunis, arriving at about 1 A.M. on the morning of Tuesday, December 28th. Sir Thomas Reade took all to his house, and made it a home for us. I went on board the French steamer Lavoisier, to thank the captain for his assistance, and also waited on the governor for the same purpose.'

During the summer of the present year, the French government directed Captain Bouchet Riviere to make a survey of the Sorelle. In conclusion, therefore, we will give the following extract from that officer's letter, as it throws some light upon the circumstances which led to the loss of the Avenger:—

'The English frigate, Avenger, was lost on the two Sorelle; I saw between the two heads of rocks, which are aptly named 'Sisters,' her entire engine, two anchors, a shell gun, and some loose parts of the wreck. I recovered and took on board some pieces of iron from the bed of the engine, and a boarding cutlass. The engine lies in a medium depth of ten metres (thirty-three feet).

'From information which has been given me by boats which saw the Avenger at sea the day of her loss, and adding the observations which I was enabled to make

on the spot itself, I have every reason to believe that
the event happened in the following manner:—

'The Avenger had, during the day, run along the coast
of Algeria, but on the approach of night, being then north
of Calle, and the weather having suddenly become very
bad, with a great deal of wind from the north-west, the
captain of the Avenger altered her course immediately to
the northward, in order not to be caught in the middle
of a dangerous channel. As soon as he thought that the
ship had passed the parallel of the Sorelle, he resumed
his course to the eastward, satisfied that he would pass
several miles to the northward of them. He had not calculated on the currents which I have found at this dangerous spot, and which, with a north-west wind, set to
the south-eastward with a rapidity of about 3 miles an
hour. The track of the Avenger must have been materially altered by this cause. When she steered east, she
was only in the latitude of the Sorelle, and was shortly
afterwards, on a very dark night, shattered against these
rocks. The first shock must have been dreadful. It
took place on the point south-east of the north-west rock;
when she cleared this rock, which is at this spot thirteen
feet below the surface, leaving a large white furrow,
she ran a hundred and sixty feet further, and struck on
the south-east rock, which is only about four feet (one
metre twenty centimetres) below the surface. She again
marked the rock very distinctly. The sea, which is
often very rough on this spot, has left nothing remaining
but the massive part of the engine, where it can be perceived between the two rocks, covered with thick weed.

'The dangerous Sorelle are formed by two tables of
rocks, distant about a hundred and sixty feet from each
other, and separated by a channel of a medium depth
of thirty-nine to forty-nine feet (twelve to fifteen metres).

These two tables of rocks extend from the north-west to the south-east. The north-west one has a diameter of 66 English feet (twenty metres), its highest point is to the eastward, 16 feet under water (five metres). The south-eastern has a diameter of 197 feet (sixty metres), and its highest point is only at a depth of 4 feet. This last point is situated, according to my observations, which agree with the position laid down in the chart of Admiral Berard, in 37° 24′ of north latitude, and 6° 16′ 25″ of east longitude from Paris, (or 8° 36′ 45″ east of Greenwich); 17′·4 miles S. 65° 15′ W. of the east point of the Island of Galita, and 27′·3 miles N. 0° 30′ E. of Cape Roux.'

The fate of the Avenger leads to many sad reflections. The last of the wrecks described in this volume, one of yesterday, as it were, was more disastrous than many others. It is painful to contemplate the scene of dismay, when the ship struck, so unlike the presence of mind and calm deportment which we have recorded on similar occasions. But every allowance is to be made for the panic which followed a catastrophe so sudden and so overwhelming. The night was dark and tempestuous, the sea was running high, and all the elements were in a state of uproar. The paralyzing effect of this accumulation of horrors appears in the fact, that even after the small party of eight had so far secured their preservation as to be in possession of the cutter, and were within sight of the Island of Galita, two of them were found to be bereft of their reason.

The first crash, and the rapid plunge of the ship into the gulf that opened for her, and the loss of their captain among the first that perished, left the crew without that guidance and control to which seamen are in the habit of looking for support.

But though we have to regret the consternation that prevailed, there was no gross neglect or misconduct to throw a darker shade over the last hours of the Avenger. Captain Napier had been in consultation in his cabin with the master and second-master, examining the charts, and had also been on deck, giving directions to the officer of the watch, but a short time before the first alarm. When the panic was at its height, there was no act of dastardly selfishness for personal preservation, to the disregard of the safety of others. The officers are not accused of losing their composure. Lieut. Marryat is stated to have been ' calm and self-possessed ;' and Mr. Rooke's strenuous efforts to lower the cutter, and his manly resolution to remain by the ship, as long as there was any chance of saving the lives of some of the survivors, attest his devotion to his duty to the very last.

The French officer, Captain Bouchier Rivière, who made a survey of the Sorelle after the wreck, and who deliberately considered all the circumstances, imputes no blame to the officers of the Avenger, but generously accounts for the misfortune by referring to the dangers of the spot, the force of the currents, the wildness of the weather, and the darkness of the night. ' The first shock,' says he, ' must have been dreadful.'

It would have been humiliating and afflicting, had this record of the Shipwrecks of the Royal Navy, in which there is so much to admire, been closed with the details of a calamity in any way disgraceful to the service. Truth has required that the words ' *dismay*' and '*panic*' should be used in the foregoing relation; but the terrible suddenness of the event, the instantaneous shock which broke up the Avenger in a moment, without the preparatory warning of ' breakers a-head,' or the previous notice of rocks or shoals in sight, will more than account

for the helplessness to which the crew were reduced.
They had not time to brace up their shattered nerves.
The noble bearing of the two lieutenants, Rooke and
Marryat, cool as they were, and in full command of their
energies in the midst of crashing timbers and perishing
men, places the character of the British seaman in its
true light, and winds up our narrative with two more
examples of naval heroism.

LIST OF THE SHIPWRECKS OF THE ROYAL NAVY,

BETWEEN 1793 AND 1850.

Name of Ship.	Guns.	Date.	Commanding Officer's Name.	No. of men.	Number of lost.	Where lost.
Advice, Cutter	4	June 1, 1793	Edward Tyrell	30	None	Bokell Key, Honduras.
Amphitrite	24	Jan. 20, 1794	Anthony Hunt	160	None	On a sunken rock in the Mediterranean.
Ardent	64	April, 1794	Robert M. Sutton	500	All	Blown up or burnt off Corsica.
Amethyst	44	Dec. 29, 1795	Thomas Affleck	300	None	Striking on rocks off Guernsey.
Arab, Sloop	14	June 10, 1796	Stephen Seymour	96	Captain	Rocks off the Glenan Isles, near Brest.
Active	32	Sept. 15, 1796	Ed. Leveson Gower	215	None	Running on shore at Anticosti River St. Lawrence.
Amphion	32	Sept. 22, 1796	Isaac Pellew	215	Greater part of crew	Burnt by accident, and blown up in Hamoaze Harbour.
Albion	64	April 27, 1797	Henry Savage	491	None	Striking on Middle Sand in the Swin.
Artois	32	July 31, 1797	Sir Edmund Nagle	284	None	Running on Ballien Rocks.
Amazon	32	Jan. 14, 1797	Robert C. Reynolds	264	None	Engaged with the Droits des Hommes, and ran on shore in Audernie Bay, coast of France.
Aigle	36	July 18, 1797	Charles Tyler	274	None	Off Farina, coast of Spain.
Apollo	38	Jan. 7, 1797	Peter Halkett	284	None	Running on Haak Sand, coast of Holland.
Amaranthe, Sloop	14	Oct. 25, 1799	George Hans Blake	86	22	Coast of Florida.
Augustus, G. Boat	50	July 7, 1801	James Scott	86	None	In the Sound, on the Hoe.
Assistance	50	Mar. 29, 1802	Richard Lee	345	None	Between Dunkerque and Gravelines.
Avenger, Sloop	14	Dec. 5, 1803	F. Jackson Snell	80	None	Running on sand bank at the mouth of the River Jade, Heligoland.
Apollo	36	April 2, 1804	J. W. Taylor Dixon	264	62	Running on shore in Mondego Bay, Portugal.

Ship	Guns	Commander	Date			Remarks
Athenienne . .	64	Robert Raynsford ·	Oct. 20, 1806	491	350	On the Esquerques, off Sicily.
Adder, Gun Brig	12	Molyneux Shuldham	Dec. 9, 1806	600	None	Driven on shore on coast of France.
Ajax . . .	74	Hon. Hy. Blackwood	Feb. 14, 1807		250	Burnt by accident in the Dardanelles.
Atalanta, Sloop.	14	John Bowker . .	Feb. 12, 1807	110	None	On La Grande Blanche, Island of Rhe, France.
Anson . .	44	Charles Lydiard .	Dec. 29, 1807	330	60	On sand-bank off Helstone, Falmouth.
Astrea . . .	32	Edmund Heywood	Mar. 23, 1808	215	4	On a reef, Island of Anegada, West Indies.
Alcmene . . .	32	W. Henry Tremlett	April 20, 1809	254	None	On a shoal at the mouth of the Loire.
Agamemnon . .	64	Jonas Rose . .	June 16, 1809	491	None	Ran on shore in Maldonado Roads, Rio de la Plata.
Achates, Sloop .	14	Thomas Pinto .	Feb. 7, 1810	76	None	On Englishman's Head, Guadaloupe.
Amethyst . .	38	Jacob Walton . .	Feb. 15, 1811	284	8	On Cony Cliffs, Plymouth Sound.
Avenger, Sloop.	18	Urry Johnson . .	Oct. 8, 1812	80	None	In the narrows of St. John's Harbour, Newfoundland.
Algerine, Schooner.	10	Daniel Carpenter .	May 20, 1812	70	None	On the Galapagos Roads, West Indies.
Atalante . . .	18	Frederick Hickey .	Nov. 10, 1813	121	None	In a fog on the Sisters' Rocks, Halifax.
Anacreon, Sloop	18	John Davis . .	Feb. 28, 1814	121	None	Foundered in the Channel.
Alceste . . .	38	Murray Maxwell (Sir)	Feb. 18, 1817	315	None	Off Island of Pulo Leat, China Seas.
Arab, Sloop . .	18	William Holmes .	Dec. 12, 1823	100	All	Near Belmullett, Westport.
Algerine . . .	10	Charles Wemyss .	Jan. 9, 1826	75	All	In a squall in the Mediterranean.
Acorn, Sloop .	18	Edward Gordon .	April 14, 1828	115	All	On Halifax Station.
Avenger, Steam-ship	6	Edw. G. E. Napier	Dec. 20, 1847	250	246	On the Sorelle Rocks, Mediterranean.
Boyne . . .	98	George Grey . .	May 1, 1795	750	11	Accidentally burnt at Spithead.
Bombay Castle .	74	Thomas Sotheby .	Dec. 21, 1796	590	None	In the Tagus.
Berbice, Schooner .	20	John Tresahar .	Nov. 1796	42	None	Off the coast of Dominique, West Indies.
Break, Sloop . .	14	James Drew . .	May 23, 1798	86	35	Foundered in the Delaware.
Blanche . . .	16	John Ayscough .	Sept. 28, 1799	121	None	In Scalp Gat, in the Texel.

Name of Ship.	Date.	Guns.	Commanding Officer's Name.	No. of men.	Number of lost.	Where lost.
Brazen, Sloop . . .	Jan. 26, 1800	14	James Hanson . .	116	1	Near Brighton.
Bonetta . . .	Oct. 13, 1801	16	Thomas New . .	121	None	On a shoal east of the Jardines, Cuba.
Babet . . .	Unknown, 1801	24	Jemmett Mainwaring	155	All	Foundered in the West Indies.
Barracouta, Schooner	Oct. 2, 1805	10	Joel Orchard . .	48	None	On the south side of the Island of Cuba, (running on shore.)
Biter, Gun-brig .	Nov. 10, 1805		Geo. Thos. Wingate	50	None	Near Calais.
Bouncer, Gun-brig .	Feb. 1805		Samuel Bassan .	50	None	Off Dieppe.
Brave . . .	April 2, 1806		Edmund Boger .		None	Foundered in passage from Jamaica to England.
Boreas . . .	Dec. 5, 1807	28	George Scott .	195	127	On the Hannois Rocks, Guernsey.
Blenheim . .	1807	74	Sir Thomas Trowbridge, V.-Admiral, Austin Bissell, Capt.	590	All	Foundered, date unknown, off the Island of Rodrigue, Indian Ocean.
Blanche . . .	Mar. 4, 1807	38	Sir T. Lavie .	284	45	Off Ushant.
Busy, Sloop . .	1807	18	Richard Keilley .	121	All	Foundered on the Halifax Station, date unknown.
Bolina . . .	Nov. 3, 1807	12	Edward Claributt .	121	1	Driven on shore, Peran Porth.
Bermuda, Sloop .	April 22, 1808	12	Wm. Henry Byam .	121	None	On Little Bahama Bank.
Bustler, Gun-brig .	Dec. 26, 1808	10	Richard Welsh .	50	None	On shore, Cape Grisnez, France.
Bauterer . .	Dec. 29, 1808	22	Alexander Sheppard	155	None	In the river St. Lawrence.
Bassora, Brig . .	Feb. 13, 1808	12	James Violett .	50	None	Near Carthagena.
Barbadoes . .	Sept. 29, 1812	28	Thomas Huskisson .	195	1	Sable Island, Bermuda.
Belette, Sloop . .	Nov. 24, 1812	18	David Sloane .	121	116	On rocks off Island of Lessoe, in the Kattegat.
Bold, Sloop . .	Sept. 27, 1813	10	John Shekel .	55		On Prince Edward's Island.
Bermuda, Sloop .	Nov. 24, 1816	10	John Pakenham .	76	1	On Passage from Gulf of Mexico.

Ship	Date	Guns	Captain	Crew	Saved/Lost	Remarks
Briseis, Sloop	Nov. 5, 1816		Geo. Domett	76	None	On reef off Point Pedras, Cuba.
Bermuda, Schooner	March, 1821			33	All	Passage from Halifax to Bermuda.
Briseis, Packet	1838	6	John Downey		All	Falmouth to Halifax.
Buffalo, Store-ship	July 28, 1841		James Wood		2	In Mercury Bay, Bay of Islands, New Zealand.
Convert	Feb. 8, 1794	32	John Lawford		None	On the Grand Caymanes, West Indies.
Ca Ira	April 11, 1796	80	Chas. Dudley Pater		4	Burnt by accident, and blown up in St. Fiorenzo Bay.
Courageux	Dec. 10, 1796	74	Capt. B. Hallowell	640	440	Struck on rocks under Apes' Hill, coast of Barbary.
Cormorant, Sloop	Dec. 24, 1796	16	Thomas Gott	121	95	Burnt and blown up by accident, at Port-au-Prince, St. Domingo.
Curlew, Sloop	Dec. 31, 1796	16	Jas. Ventris Field	90	All	Foundered in North Sea.
Charlotte, Brig	Dec. 11, 1797		John Thukness		None	Off the Island of Cuba.
Crash, Gun-boat	Aug. 26, 1798	50	Berkeley Mackworth	50	None	Blown on shore on the Island of Vlieland, Holland.
Colossus	Dec. 9, 1798	74	George Murray	640	None	Off the Island of Scilly.
Contest, Gun-boat	Aug. 28, 1799		John Ides Short	50	None	Driven on shore in the Helder.
Cormorant, Sloop	May 20, 1800	24	C. Boyle, (Hon.)	155	None	On a shoal near Rosetta, coast of Egypt.
Chance, Sloop	Oct. 9, 1800	14	George S. Stovin	121	116	Foundered.
Charlotte, Schooner	Mar. 28, 1801		John Williams	60	None	Running on reef of rocks near Ash, (Island of.)
Calypso	Aug. 1803	16	William Venour	121	All	Foundered in a gale, coming from Jamaica.
Circe	Nov. 16, 1803	28	Chas. Fielding	195	None	On the Leman and Ower, North Sea.
Creole	Jan. 2, 1804	38	Austin Russell		None	Foundered in passage from Jamaica.
Cerbére, Gun-boat	Feb. 20, 1804		John Patey	50	None	Rocks near Berry Head.
Condict, Gun-boat	Oct. 24, 1804		Chas. Cutts Ormsby	50	None	Near Newport, Isle of Wight.
Clinker, Sloop	Dec. 1806	14	John Salmon	50	All	Foundered in a cruize off Havre.

Name of Ship.	Date.	Guns.	Commanding Officer's Name.	No. of men.	Number of lost.	Where lost.
Cassandra, Cutter .	May 13, 1807	10	Geo. Le Blanc . .	35	11	By upsetting in a sudden squall off Bourdeaux.
Capelin, Schooner .	June 28, 1808	6	Josias Bray . . .	20	1	Sunken rock off entrance of Brest Harbour.
Crane, Brig . . .	Oct. 26, 1808	4	Joseph Tindale . .	20	None	Running on a rock to the W. of the Hoe, Plymouth.
Crescent . . .	Dec. 5, 1808	36	John Temple . .	280	220	On the coast of Jutland, in a heavy gale.
Carrier, Cutter .	Jan. 24, 1808	4	W. Milner . . .	20	None	On a sand-bank near Boulogne.
Carieux, Sloop . .	Sept. 25, 1809	18	Henry Geo. Moysey	110	None	Off Petit Terre, Island of Marigalante, West Indies.
Contest . . .	1809		John Gregory . .		All	Foundered, as is supposed, in passage from America.
Claudia, Brig . .	Jan. 20, 1809	10	Anth. Bliss, W. Lord	42	None	Off Norway.
Cuckoo, Brig . .	April 4, 1810	4	Silas Hiscutt Paddon	20	2	Haaks, off Texel.
Conflict, Brig . .	Nov. 9, 1810	10	Joseph B. Batt . .	50	All	Foundered in the Bay of Biscay.
Chichester . .	May, 2, 1811		William Kirby . .	88	2	In Madras Roads.
Centinel, Gun-boat .	Oct. 10, 1812		W. Elletson King .	45	None	North-east end of the Island of Rugen, Baltic.
Chubb, Gun-boat .	Aug. 14, 1812		Samuel Nisbett .	20	All	Foundered near Halifax.
Calibre, Sloop . .	Aug. 23, 1813	16	John Thomson . .	100	None	In crossing the bar of Port Royal, Jamaica.
Captain . . .	Mar. 22, 1813	74	In Ordinary . . .	590	None	Burnt in Hamoaze, Plymouth.
Crane, Sloop . .	Sept. 30, 1814	14	Robert Stanley . .	121	All	Foundered in the West Indies.
Cuttle, Gun-boat .	1814	4		20	All	Exact date unknown, on the Halifax Station.
Cygnet, Sloop . .	1815	16	Robert Russel . .	121	All	Date unknown, off the Courantine River.
Comus . . .	Nov. 4, 1816	22	J. John G. Bremer	175	None	Off Cape Pine, Newfoundland.

Ship	Date	Commander				Remarks
Carron	July, 6, 1820	John Furneaux		135	19	Four miles to the north of the Black Pagoda, Poorie.
Confiance, Sloop	April 21, 1822	W. T. Morgan	18	100		Between Moyin Head and Three Castle Head, Crookhaven.
Columbine, Sloop	Jan. 25, 1824	Chas. Abbott	18	100	None	In harbour of Port Longue, Island of Sapienza.
Cynthian, Pack.-brig	June 6, 1827	John White	6	28	None	Off the Island of Barbados.
Cambrian	Jan. 31, 1828	G. W. Hamilton	48	275	None	Off Carabusa, Mediterranean, in attacking Pirates.
Contest, Gun-boat	April 14, 1828	Edw. Plaggenborg	12	50	All	On Halifax Station.
Calypso, Packet	1833	H. Peyton	6	30	All	In passage from Halifax to England.
Challenger	May, 19, 1835	Michael Seymour	28	160	2	Coast of Moquilla, Conception, Chili.
Diomede	Aug. 2, 1795	Matthew Smith	44	294		Striking on a sunken rock off Trincomalee.
Deux Amis, Schoon.	May 23, 1799.	Mr. Samuel Wilson	20		None	In Great Chine, Isle of Wight.
Dromedary, Store-sh.	Aug. 10, 1800	Bridges W. Taylor	16	120	None	Parasol Rock, Island of Trinidad.
Diligence	Oct. 8, 1800	Charles H. B. Ross		121	None	On a shoal on the coast of Havannah.
Determinée	Mar. 25, 1803	Alexander Becher	26	145	19	Striking on a sunken rock off the Island of Jersey.
Drake, Sloop	July 12, 1804	William King	14	86	None	On a shoal off the Island of Nevis.
De Ruyter	Sept. 4, 1804	Joseph Beckett	32	250	None	In a hurricane in Deep Bay, Antigua.
Doria	Jan. 12, 1805	Patrick Campbell	36	264	None	On a sunken rock in Quiberon Bay.
Dover, Mar. Barr.	Aug. 20, 1806					Burnt at Woolwich.
Delphinen	Aug. 4, 1808	Richard Harward	16	100	None	On the South-west part of Vieland, Holland.
Delight, Sloop	Jan. 31, 1808	Philip C. Handfield	16	95	All	On the coast of Calabria.
Defender, Brig	Dec. 14, 1809	John George Nops	10	50	None	Near Folkestone.
Dominica, Brig	Aug. 1809	Charles Welsh	10	65	62	Foundered near Tortola.

Name of Ship.	Date.	Guns.	Commanding Officer's Name.	No. of men.	Number of lost.	Where lost.
Diana, Cutter	May, 1810	10	Wm. Kempthorne	50	None	At the Island of Rodrigue, East Indies.
Dover	May 2, 1811	38	Edward Tucker	300	2	In Madras Roads.
Defence	Dec. 24, 1811	74	David Atkins	593	587	Off the coast of Jutland.
Dædalus	July 2, 1813	38	Murray Maxwell	315	None	Off Island of Ceylon.
Dart, Cutter	1814	10	Thomas Allen	40		Foundered, exact date unknown.
Dominica, Schooner	Aug. 15, 1815	14	Richard Crauford		Commander & others	Near Bermuda.
Drake, Sloop	June 20, 1822		Charles Baker	76		Off the coast of Newfoundland.
Delight	Feb. 23, 1824	10	Robert Hay	75	All	In a hurricane at the Mauritius.
Dwarf	Mar. 3, 1824	10	Nicholas Gould	60	1	Ran against the Pier in Kingstown Harbour.
Etrusco, Store-ship	Aug. 23, 1798	26	George Reynolds	125	None	Foundered in the West Indies.
Espion	Nov. 17, 1799	18	Jonas Rose		None	In Goodwin Sands.
Ethalion	Dec. 25, 1799	38	John Clark Searle	284	None	On the Saints.
Explosion, Bomb.	Sept. 10, 1807	10	Edward Elliot	57	None	On reef near Sandy Island, Heligoland.
Elizabeth, Schooner	1807	12	John Sedley	55	All	Foundered, date unknown, in West Indies.
Electra, Sloop	Mar. 23, 1808	16	George Trolloppe	95	None	On a reef at the entrance of Port Augusta, Sicily.
Ephira, Sloop	Dec. 26, 1811	14	Thomas Everard	76	None	On Cochinos Rocks, in passage between Cadiz and Tarifa.
Encounter, Brig	July 11, 1812	10	S. H. Talbot	60		Attempting to cut out some vessels, on coast of Spain.
Emulous, Sloop	Aug. 2, 1812	18	W. Howe Mulcaster	121	None	Ragged Island, Nova Scotia.
Exertion, Gun-boat	July 8, 1812		James Murray	60	None	In the Elbe.
Elizabeth, Schooner	Oct. 1814	10	Jonathan W. Dyer	35		Upsetting in chase of an American Privateer.

Ship	Guns	Date	Commander	No. of Crew	Lost	Circumstances
Fleche	14	Nov. 12, 1795	Charles Came	86	None	Reef of Rocks off Fernelli Tower, Saint Fiorenzo's Bay, Mediterranean.
Fortune, Sloop	14	June 15, 1797	Valentine Collard	215	None	Ran on shore near Toreiro, coast of Portugal.
Fox	32	Sept. 18, 1799	James Wooldridge	60	None	In St. George's Sound, Gulf of Mexico.
Fulminante, Cutter	10	Mar. 24, 1801	Robert Corbett	343	None	Drifted on Shore at La Cruelle, coast of Egypt.
Forte	50	Jan. 28, 1801	Lucius F. Hardyman		None	On a sunken rock in the harbour of Jedda, Red Sea.
Fly, Sloop	16	Jan. 1802	Thomas Duval	121	All	Foundered, exact date unknown, coast of Newfoundland.
Fearless, Gun-boat		Jan. 19, 1804	Richard Williams	50	1	Driven on shore in Cawsand Bay.
Firebrand, Fireship		Oct. 13, 1804	William Maclean	18	1	Off Dover.
Fly, Sloop	18	Mar. 3, 1805	Pownole Bastard Pellew	121	None	On the Carysfort Reef, Gulf of Florida.
Felix, Schooner	18	Jan. 23, 1807	Robert Clarke	60	57	In St. Andero Bay.
Firefly		Oct. 17, 1807	Thomas Price	264	All except the Surg. & 3 men	Foundered in a hurricane off the Spanish Main.
Flora	36	Jan. 19, 1808	Loftus Otway Bland	50	9	On the coast of Holland.
Flying Fish, Schoon.	12	Dec. 15, 1808	J. Glassford Gooding	121	None	On reef to eastward of Point Salines, St. Domingo.
Fama, Sloop	18	Dec. 23, 1808	Chas. Topping	86	2	On Bornholm, Baltic.
Foxhound, Sloop	16	Aug. 31, 1809	James Mackenzie	40	All	Foundered on her return from Halifax.
Fleche, Sloop		May 24, 1810	George Hewson	50	None	On the Shaarhorn Sand, off Newark, Elbe.
Fleur de la Mer		Dec. 29, 1810	John Alexander	50	None	Foundered in lat. 15° 15′ long. 71° 2′.
Firm, Brig		June 28, 1811	John Little		None	On a bank off the coast of France.
Fancy, Gun-boat	10	Dec. 24, 1811	Alexander Sinclair	50	All	In the Baltic (foundered.)

Name of Ship.	Date.	Guns.	Commanding Officer's Name.	No. of men.	Number of lost.	Where lost.
Fly, Sloop	Feb. 28, 1812	16	Henry Higman	95	None	On Anholt Reef.
Fearless	Dec. 8, 1812	10	Henry L. Richards	50	None	Rocks off St. Sebastian.
Ferret, Sloop	Jan. 7, 1813	18	Fred. Alex. Halliday	121	None	On Newbiggin Point, Northumberland.
Fantôme, Sloop	Nov. 24, 1814	18	Thomas Sykes	121	None	On rocks near Prospect Harbour, Nova Scotia.
Fury	Aug. 1, 1825	5	H. P. Hoppner	75	None	In Regent's Inlet.
Firefly, Schooner	Feb. 27, 1835	6	Julius Mc Donnell	50	A few	Reef near Belize.
Fairy	1841		William Hewett	63	All	Foundered in the North Sea.
Garnet	Jan. 7, 1798		James Clark	195	None	On a reef off Cape François.
Garland	July 26, 1798	28	James Athol Wood	195	None	Coast of Madagascar.
Grampus, Store-ship	Jan. 19, 1799	20	John Hall	155	None	Near Woolwich.
Galgo	Oct. 9, 1800		Thomas Forrest		25 saved	Upset in a squall, in lat. 21° long. 61° west.
Grappler, Gun-boat	Dec. 20, 1803		Abel Wantn. Thomas	50	None	On the Isle de Chausey, Jersey.
Garland	Sept. 10, 1803	24	Frederick Cotterell	135	None	Caracol Reef, off St. Domingo.
Georgiana, G.-boat	Sept. 25, 1804		Joshua Kneeskarn	50	None	On a sand-bank near Harfleur.
Griper	Feb. 18, 1807	10	Edward Morris	50	All	Off Ostend.
Greyhound	Oct. 11, 1808	32	Hon. W. Pakenham	215	1	On the coast of Lemonia.
Glommen, Sloop	Nov. 1809	18	Charles Pickford	100	None	In Carlisle Bay, Barbados.
Guachapin, Brig	July 7, 1811	10	Michael Jenkins		None	On Rat Island, Antigua.
Grouper, Brig	Oct. 21, 1811	4	James Atkins	40	None	Off Guadaloupe.
Goshawk, Sloop	Sept. 21, 1813	16	Hon. W. J. Napier	95	None	To the eastward of the Mole Head, Barcelona.
Hussar	Dec. 24, 1796	28	James Colnett	195	None	In a gale of wind to the westward of the Island of Bass, France.

Ship	Commander		Date		Saved	Remarks
Helena, Sloop	Jeremiah J. Symons	14	Nov. 3, 1796	86	All	On the coast of Holland.
Hamadryad	Thomas Elphinstone	36	Dec. 24, 1797	264	None	Blown on shore in Algier Bay.
Hermes	William Malso	14	Jan. 1797	76	All	Place unknown.
Hunter, Sloop	Tudor Tucker	14	Dec. 27, 1797	80	75	Wrecked on Hog Island, off Virginia.
Hound, Sloop	Wm. Jas. Turquand	16	Sept. 26, 1800	235	None	Near Shetland.
Harwich	Phillip Bartholomew	16	Nov. 9, 1801	121	None	In St. Aubin's Bay, Jersey.
Hindostan, Store-sh.	John Le Gros	20	Mar. 20, 1804	140	3	Burnt in Bay of Rosas.
Hussar	Philip Wilkinson	38	Feb. 8, 1804	284	None	On the Saintes in the Bay of Biscay.
Hawke, Sloop	James Tippet	14	May, 1805	96	All	Foundered in the Channel.
Heureux	John Morrison	24	1806	155	All	Foundered, exact date unknown, in passage from West Indies to Halifax.
Hirondelle, Cutter	Joseph Kidd	12	Feb. 23, 1808	50	46	On shore on the coast of Barbary.
Harrier, Sloop	Thomas B. Ridge	18	1809	121	All	Foundered, date unknown, in the East Indies.
Hero	J. Newman Newman	74	Dec. 24, 1811	590	All	Off the coast of Jutland.
Halcyon, Sloop	J. Houlton Marshall	14	May 19, 1814	121	None	On reef of rocks in Annatto Bay, Jamaica.
Holly, Schooner	S. Sharpe Treacher	10	Jan. 29, 1814	50	44	Off St. Sebastian.
Herring, Gun-boat	John Murray	4	1814	20	All	Exact date unknown, in the Halifax station.
Illustrious	Thomas L. Frederick	74	Mar. 17, 1795	600	None	In a gale of wind on rocks near Avenga.
Jason	Chas. Stirling	38	Oct. 13, 1798	284	None	Unknown rock near Brest.
Impregnable	Jonathan Faulknor	74	Oct. 19, 1799	190	None	Striking on Chichester Shoals.
Invincible	John Rennie	74	Mar. 16, 1801	590	464	Ran on Hammond's Knowl, near Yarmouth.
Iphigenia	Hayard Stackpool	20	June 20, 1801	60	None	Burnt by accident in Aboukir Bay.
Jason	Hon. J. Murray	36	July 24, 1801	264	None	On a rock not laid down in the Charts, entrance of St. Maloes.
Julia	James Harley		Jan. 24, 1805		None	On Castle Rocks at the entrance of Dartmouth Harbour.
Imogene, Sloop	Henry Vaughan	18	Mar. 12, 1805	121	None	Foundered in passage from Leeward Islands.

Name of Ship.	Date.	Guns.	Commanding Officer's Name.	No. of men.	Number of lost.	Where lost.
Jupiter	Dec. 10, 1807	50	Hon. E. Reg. Baker	343	None	Reef of rocks in Vigo Bay.
Java	1807	32	George Pigot	50	All	Foundered with Blenheim.
Inveterate, Gun-boat	Feb. 18, 1807	14	George Norton	50	4	Off Etables, France.
Jackall, Gun-boat	May 29, 1807	14	Charles Stewart	32	None	Near Calais,
Ignition, Fire-ship	Feb. 19, 1807		Phillip Griffin	32	28	Wrecked off Dieppe.
Jaspar, Sloop	Jan. 20, 1817		Thomas Carew	76	72	Rocks under Mount Batten, entrance of Catwater.
Julia, Brig	Oct. 2, 1817		Jenkin Jones	95	55	Off Tristan d'Acunha, coast of Africa.
Jasper, Sloop	Oct. 11, 1828	10	L. C. Rooke	75	None	Grounded in running for Harbour of St. Maura.
Jackdaw	Mar. 11, 1835	4	Edw. Burnett	36	None	On reef off Old Providence.
Kangaroo, S.-vessel	Dec. 18, 1828	6	Anthony de Mayne	45	1	South-east of Reef of Hogsties.
Leda	Dec. 11, 1796	38	John Woodley	264	257	Foundered by upsetting in a heavy gale, lat. 38° 8' long. 17° 40'
Lively	April 12, 1798	36	Jas. N. Morris	254	None	On Rosa Point, near Cadiz.
Lord Mulgrave	April 10, 1799	26	Edward Hawkins	121	None	Arklow Bank, Irish Channel.
Latine	Oct. 9, 1799	32	Lancelot Skinner	240	1	Off the Vlie Island, coast of Holland.
Legère, Sloop	Feb. 2, 1801	16	Cornelius Quinton	121	None	Jamba Bay, east of Carthagena, S. America.
Lowestoffe	Aug. 10, 1801	32	Robert Plampin	215	None	On the Island of Great Heneaga, W. Indies.
Leveret, Sloop	Nov. 10, 1807	18	Jas. L. O'Connor	121	None	On the Albion Shoal, Galloper Rock.
Leda	Jan. 31, 1808	32	Robert Honyman	284	None	At the entrance of Milford Harbour.
Lark, Sloop	Aug. 3, 1809	18	Robert Nicholas	121	3	In a sudden squall off Point Palenqua, Island of Domingo.
Lively	Aug. 10, 1810	38	George M'Kinley	284	None	Point of Salina, South-east of Bay of St. Paul's, Malta.

Ship	Date	Guns	Commander	Crew	Saved	Remarks
Laurel	Jan. 31, 1812	38	Samuel C. Rowley	300	None	On a sunken rock in Teigneuse Passage, Quiberon Bay.
Laurestinus	Aug. 21, 1813	24	Thos. Graham	175	1	North end of the Island of Abaco, Halifax.
Leopard, Transport	June 28, 1814		Edward Crofton		Greater part saved	Near the Island of Anticosti, Gulf of St. Lawrence.
Lizard, Steam-vessel	July 24, 1843	3	Charles Postle	60	None	Off Carthagena, by being run foul of by a French man-of-war.
Musquito, G.-boat	1795		— M'Carty	50		Wrecked, exact date unknown, on the coast of France.
Malabar	Oct. 10, 1796	54	Thos. Parr	324	None	Foundered coming home from West Indies.
Medusa, Store-ship	Nov. 22, 1798		Alexander Becher	118	None	Drifting on shore in Rosier Bay, Gibraltar.
Mastiff, Gun-boat	Jan. 5, 1800		James Watson	50	Many	In Cockle Sands, Yarmouth Roads.
Marlborough	Nov. 4, 1800	74	Thomas Sotheby	590	None	In the Bervadeux Shoal, near L'Orient, France.
Martin, Sloop	October, 1800	16	Hon. Matth. St. Clair	76	All	Foundered in North Sea.
Meleager	June 9, 1801	32	Hon. T. Bladen Capel	215	None	In the Westernmost Triangle, G. of Mexico.
Minerve	July 2, 1803	40	Jaheel Brenton	294	None	On the western point of the Cones of Cherbourg.
Magnificent	March 25, 1804	74	Wm. Henry Jervis	500	None	Wrecked near the Pierres Noires, Brest.
Morne Fortunée	Dec. 5, 1804		John L. Dale	50	None	On Crooked Island, West Indies.
Mallard, Gun-boat	Dec. 24, 1804		John William Miles	121	None	Near Calais.
Martin, Sloop	1806	18	Thomas Prouse	121	All	Date unknown. In passage to Barbadoes.
Moucheron	1807	18	James Hawes		All	Wrecked, date unknown, in the Mediterranean.
Maria, Gun-boat	1807	10	John Henderson	50	All	Foundered, date unknown, in West Indies.
Melbrook, Schooner	March 25, 1808	12	James Leach	50	None	On the Burlings.
Muros	March 24, 1808	24	Archibald Duff	155	None	At the entrance of the Harbour of Bahia Honda, Cuba.

Name of Ship.	Date.	Guns.	Commanding Officer's Name.	No. of men.	Number of lost.	Where lost.
Meleager . . .	July 30, 1808	36	Fred. Warren . .	264	4	On Barebush Cay, Jamaica.
Magnet, Sloop . .	Jan. 11, 1809	18	George Morris . .	121	None	In the Baltic.
Morne Fortunée, Bg.	Jan. 9, 1809	10	John Brown . .	65	41	Off Martinique.
Minotaur . . .	Dec. 22, 1810	74	John Barrett . .	640	400	On the North Haaks, Texel.
Monkey, Brig . .	Dec. 25, 1810	10	Thomas Fitzgerald .	50		Rocks at Belle Isle, France.
Manilla . . .	Jan. 28, 1812	38	John Joyce . .	274		On Haaks, Texel.
Magnet, Sloop . .	1812	16	F. Moore Maurice .	95	8 men	Foundered, date unknown, near Halifax.
Magnet, Sloop . .	Aug. 4, 1814	16	G. I. Hawksworth .	90	All	Run on shore near Niagara.
Martin, Sloop . .	Dec. 8, 1817	18	— Mitchell . .	121	None	Western coast of Ireland.
Magpie, Schooner .	Aug. 27, 1826	3	Edward Smith . .	35	None	Colorados Roads, Island of Cuba.
Myrtle . . .	April 3, 1829	6	Samuel Sisin . .	29	33	Western head of Ragged Island, Nova Scotia.
Megæra . . .	March 4, 1843	2	George Oldmixon .	60	None	On Bare Bush Cay.
Mutine, Sloop . .	Dec. 21, 1848	12	J. Lewis Palmer .	120	1	Reef near Palestrina, Adriatic.
Narcissus . . .	Oct. 3, 1796	24	Percy Fraser . .	155	5	{ On Sandy Key, near Nassau, New Providence.
Nautilus . . .	Feb. 2, 1799	16	Henry Gunter . .	121	None	Near Flamborough Head.
Nassau . . .	Oct. 24, 1799	36	George Tripp . .	250	None	Haaks Sand, in the Helder.
Nautilus, Sloop .	Jan. 4, 1807	18	Capt. Palmer . .	122	42	On Cerrigoto, a barren rock in the Levant.
Netley, Schooner .	July 10, 1808	12	Charles Burman . .	65	58	On the Leeward Island Station.
Nymphe . . .	Dec. 18, 1810	36	Edward Sneyd Clay	254	56	Wrecked off Dunbar.
Nimble, Cutter . .	Oct. 6, 1812	10	John Reynolds . .	50	None	On Salo Beacon, coast of Sweden.
Nimrod, Sloop . .	Jan. 14, 1827	18	— Sparshott . .	115	None	Driven on shore in Holyhead Bay.
Nightingale, Schoon.	Feb. 17, 1829	2	George Wood . .	31	None	On ground in the Shingles.
Nimble, Schooner .	Dec. 4, 1834	5	Charles Bolton . .	50	None	{ On a reef between Key Verde and Old Bahama Channel.

Ship	Date	Guns	Commander	Tons	Lost	Fate
Orestes . . .	Unknown, 1799	16	William Haggett .	121	All	In a hurricane in the Indian Ocean.
Orestes, Sloop .	July 11, 1805	14	Thomas Brown . .	80	None	Splinter Sand, Dunkerque.
Orquino . . .	Nov. 7, 1805		Charles Balderson .		Many	In a sudden squall off Pt. Antonio, Jamaica.
Orpheus . . .	Jan. 23, 1807	36	Thomas Briggs . .	255	None	Running on shore at the entrance of Port Royal Harbour.
Osprey, Sloop .	March 11, 1846	12	Fred. Patten . .	110	None	At False Hokianga.
Pigmy, Cutter .	Dec. 16, 1793	4	A. Pullibank . .	60	10	On the Motherbank.
Placentia, Sloop	May 8, 1794	4	Alexander Sheppard		None	Saddle Back, Marticot Island, N. America.
Pylades, Sloop .	Nov. 26, 1794	16	Thomas Twysden .	125	None	Heraldswick Bay, Nest, Shetland.
Port Royal . .	March 30, 1797		Elias Man . . .		None	Running on shore near Cape St. Nicolas.
Providence, Sloop	May 17, 1797	14	W. R. Broughton .	96	None	On a reef in the Pacific.
Pandora . . .	1797	14	Samuel Mason . .	75	All	In the North Sea. Date unknown.
Pallas . . .	April 4, 1798	36	Hon. Henry Curzon	254	None	On Mount Batten Point, Plymouth Sound.
Pique . . .	June 30, 1798	32	David Milne . .	250	None	Running on shore on the French coast, after action with the French frigate, La Seine.
Proserpine . .	Feb. 1, 1799	28	James Wallis . .	195	14	On a sand-bank, near Newark Island, River Elbe.
Proselyte . .	Sept. 2, 1801	32	Henry Whitly . .	215	None	On shoal, Isle of St. Martin, West Indies.
Porpoise . . .	Aug. 17, 1803		Richard Fowler .		None	On a reef of coral, in the Pacific.
Pigmy, Cutter .	Aug. 9, 1805	10	William Smith . .	60	None	On Sillet Rock, St. Aubyn Bay, Jersey.
Pigeon . . .	Dec. 1805		John Luckraft . .		None	Running on sand-bank, off Texel.
Papillon, Sloop .	1806	18	William Woolsey .	121		Foundered in Jamaica station, exact date unknown.
Pert, Sloop . .	Oct. 16, 1807	14	Donald Campbell .	70	10	Driven on shore in a hurricane, Island of Mucarva, Spanish Main.
Prospero, Bomb.	Feb. 18, 1807	10	William King . .	67	All	Foundered in the North Sea.
Pigmy, Cutter .	March 2, 1807	10	Geo. M. Higginson .	60	None	Off Rochefort.

Name of Ship.	Date.	Guns.	Commanding Officer's Name.	No. of men.	Number of lost.	Where lost.
Pickle, Schooner	June 27, 1808	10	Moses Cannadey	40	None	On the Chipiona Shoal, Cadiz.
Proselyte, Bomb.	Dec. 5, 1808	12	James Hy. Lyford	78	None	On Anholt Reef, Anholt Island.
Primrose, Sloop	Jan. 22, 1809	18	James Mein	121	120	On the Manacle Rocks, near Falmouth.
Pelter, Brig	Dec. 1809	10	William Evelyn	50	None	Foundered in passage from Halifax to Leeward Islands.
Pigeon	Jan. 15, 1809		Richard Cox	215	2	Off Kingsgate Point, near Margate.
Pallas	Dec. 18, 1810	32	George Paris Monke	215	11	Wrecked off Dunbar.
Pandora, Sloop	May 13, 1811	18	John Ferguson	121	29	On the Skaw Reef, Kategat.
Pomone	Oct. 14, 1811	38	Robert Barrie	284	None	On a sunken rock in the Needles.
Porgey, Gun-boat	1812		Name unknown	20	All	Foundered, date unknown, in the West Indies.
Persian, Sloop	June 26, 1813	18	Charles Bertram	121	None	On the Silver Keys, West Indies.
Peacock, Sloop	Aug. 1814	18	Richard Coote	121	All	Off the southern coast of the United States.
Penelope		36	James Galloway	284	None	To the east of Magdalen River, Lower Canada.
Phœnix	Feb. 20, 1816	36	Charles John Austin	284	None	Near Smyrna.
Partridge	Nov. 27, 1825	10	G. Yonge	75	None	Stranded at the mouth of the Texel.
Parthian, Sloop	May 15, 1828	10	Fred. Hotham	75	None	Stranded 16 miles to the westward of Mayabout, Egypt.
Pincher, Schooner	March 6, 1838	5	F. Hope	40	All	In a squall off the Owers.
Queen Charlotte	Mar. 17, 1800	110	Andrew Todd	859	673	Burnt by accident off Leghorn.
Rose	June 28, 1794	28	Matthew H. Scott	200	None	Rocky Point, Jamaica.
Reunion, Cutter	Dec. 7, 1797	36	W. Henry Baynton	249	A few	In the Swim.
Resolution, Cutter	Unknown, 1797		W. Huggett	60	All	Foundered at sea.
Raven, Sloop	Feb. 3, 1798	16	John W. T. Dixon	121	None	On a sand-bank, Cuxhaven, in the Elbe.

Ship	Commander	Guns	Date	Men	Saved	Remarks
Rover	George Irvine	14	June 23, 1798	80	None	Running on shore on coast of Cape Breton.
Resistance	Edward Pakenham	44	July 24, 1798	294	290	Blown up in the Straits of Banca.
Repulse	James Alms	64	Mar. 10, 1800	491	3	Saints, Coast of France.
Railleur, Sloop	John Raynor	14	May 16, 1800	76	All	Foundered in the Channel.
Requiem, Brig	James Fowell	12	Feb. 1, 1801	59	None	On rocks in Quiberon Bay.
Resistance	Hon. P. Wodehouse	36	May 31, 1803	264	None	Running on rocks near Cape St. Vincent.
Raven, Sloop	Spelman Swaine	14	Jan. 5, 1804	86	None	Ran on shore, near Mayara Bay, Sicily.
Romney	Hon. John Colville	50	Nov. 10, 1804	343	None	In the Haaks, near the Texel.
Raven, Sloop	William Layman	18	Jan. 30, 1805	121	None	In Cadiz Bay.
Redbridge, Schooner	F. Blower Gibbs	10	Feb. 26, 1805	60	None	Foundered in Pedro Bay, Jamaica.
Redbreast, Gun-boat	J. Bayley Harrison	14	Feb. 24, 1807	50	None	Running on shore at the Needles.
Rhodian, Sloop	John George Boss	14	Feb. 2. 1813	76	None	On Little Plumb Point, Port Royal, Jamaica.
Racer, Schooner	H. F. G. Pogson	14	Oct. 10, 1814	178	None	In the Gulf of Florida.
Racehorse	Benjamin Suckling	18	Dec. 14, 1822	125	5	Ran on Langness Point, Isle of Man.
Redwing	D. C. Clavering	18	1827	125	All	Near Mataceney, coast of Africa (supposed).
Recruit, Gun-brig	T. Hodges	10	1832	52	All	Supposed to be lost in a hurricane off Bermuda.
Rapid, Brig	Hn. G.S.V. Kinnaird	10	Apr. 12, 1838	50	Commr.	Off Cape Biso, Mediterranean.
Spitfire, Sloop	J. W. Rich	16	Feb. 1794	125	All	Foundered or upset off St. Domingo.
Scourge, Gun-boat	W. Stap		Nov. 7, 1795	30	None	On Penconsand, coast of Friesland.
Salisbury	William Mitchell	50	May 10, 1796	343	None	On the Isle of Ash, West Indies.
St. Pierre	Christopher Paule		Feb. 12, 1796		None	Rocks off Point Negroe.
Spider, Hired Lug.	J. Oswald		April 4, 1796	121		Running foul of the Ramilies.
Swift, Sloop	Thomas Hayward	16	Unknown	121	All	{In the China seas (foundered), all perished, date unknown.
Sceptre	Valentine Edwards	64	Nov. 5, 1799	491	438	In Table Bay, Cape of Good Hope.
Stag	Robert Winthrop	36	Sept. 6, 1800	271	None	In Vigo Bay.

Name of Ship.	Date.	Guns.	Commanding Officer's Name.	No. of men.	Number of lost.	Where lost.
Scout . . .	Mar. 25, 1801	16	Henry Duncan .	121	None	Running on Shingles in British Channel.
Sensible, Troop-ship	March 3, 1802	16	Robert Sauce .	155	None	Stranded to southward of Moeltiva, Trincomalee.
Seine . . .	July 23, 1803	28	David Milne .	284	None	Running on sand-bank, off Schelling Island, Texel.
Suffisante, Sloop .	Dec. 25, 1803	14	Gilbert Heathcote .	86	None	Off Spike Island, Cork Harbour.
Shannon . .	Dec. 10, 1803	36	Edward L. Gower .	264	None	In a gale, under the batteries near Cape La Hogue.
Starling, Gun-brig	Dec. 24, 1804	32	George Skottowe .	50	None	Near Calais.
Severn . .	Dec. 20, 1804	44	Duke de Bouillon .	224	None	In Gronville Bay, Jersey.
Sheerness . .	Jan. 8, 1805	18	Lord G. Stuart .	294	2	In a hurricane off Trincomalee.
Seagull . .	1805	18	Henry Burke .	121	All	Foundered.
Serpent, Sloop .	1806	14	John Waller .	121	All	Foundered in Jamaica station.
Seaforth, Gun-brig	Feb. 1806		George Steel .		All	Foundered on the Leeward Island station.
Subtle . .	Oct. 26, 1807	10	W. Dower .	60	None	On a reef of rocks, near Somerset Island, Bermuda.
Speedwell, Cutter .	Feb. 18, 1807	14	L. W. Robertson .	50	All	Foundered off Dieppe.
Snipe, Gun-brig	1807	10				Near Lowestoffe.
Sparkler, Gun-brig	Jan. 29, 1808	32	Sam. Akid Dennis .	50	14	On a reef, S. W. of the Island of Schelling, Holland.
Sacorman . .	Dec. 23, 1808	4	Andrew Duncan .	215	None	Foundered in Baltic.
Solebay . .	July 11, 1809	16	E. H. Columbine. .	20		Coast of Africa.
Sealark . Brig	June 18, 1809	36	James Proctor .	95	All	In the North Sea.
Satellite, Sloop .	Dec. 1810		Willoughby Berkie.	274	All	In the Channel.
Saldanha . .	Dec. 4, 1811		Hon. W. Pakenham		All	Off Loughswilly, Ireland.

Ship	Date lost	Guns	Commander	Crew	Lives lost	Where and how lost
Shamrock, Brig	Feb. 25, 1811	10	W. Parsons Croke	40	1	On Cape Sta-Maria.
St. George	Dec. 24, 1811	98	R. Carthew Reynolds, R.-Adm., Daniel O. Guion, Captain	738	731	Off the Coast of Jutland.
Skylark, Sloop	May 3, 1812	16	James Boxer	95	None	Between Etaples & Cape Grisnez, France.
Southampton	Nov. 27, 1812	32	Sir James Lucas Yeo	215	None	Sunken rock off Island of Conception, Jamaica.
Sarpedon, Sloop	Jan. 1, 1813	10	Thomas Parker	76	All	Foundered.
Subtle, Schooner	Nov. 30, 1812	10	Charles Brown	50	All	Foundered off St. Bartholomew's, West Indies.
Statira	Feb. 27, 1815	38	Spelman Swaine	315	None	On a sunken rock off the S. E. Point of the Great Maque, West Indies.
Sylph, Sloop	Jan. 17, 1815	18	George Dickens	121	115	On Southampton Bar, North America.
Success	Nov. 29, 1829	28		61	All	In Cockburn Sound.
Spey, Packet			— James		None	In passage to Havanna.
Skipjack, Schooner			H. Wright		None	On the Lighthouse Reef, British Honduras.
Spitfire, St.-vessel	Sept. 10, 1842	3	H. E. S. Winthrop	40	None	Ran on shore, Kemeridge, Isle of Wight.
Skylark, Brig	April 25, 1845	6	Geo. Morris	50	None	On a reef, Coast of Africa, five miles from Mozambique.
Snake	Aug. 29, 1847	2	T. Bourneaster Brown	53	None	Forty-four miles south of Cape Henry.
Thetis		14	A. F. Cochrane	106	None	
Trompeuse, Sloop	July 15, 1796	14	J. Rowley Watson	130		On Dudley Point, Kinsale.
Tartar	July 1, 1797	28	The Hon. C. Elphinstone	195		Coming out of Port Plate, St. Domingo.
Tribune	Nov. 16, 1797	32	Scory Barker	244	238	Off Halifax, Nova Scotia.
Trompeuse, Sloop	May 16, 1800	16	Peter Robinson	86	83	Supposed to have foundered in Channel.
Tartarus	Dec. 20, 1804	10	Thomas Withers	67	1	On Margate Sands.
Tartar	Aug. 18, 1811	32	Joseph Baker	254	None	On a sand in the Baltic.
Thistle, Cutter	Mar. 6, 1811	10	George McPherson	50		Near New York.
Tweed, Sloop	Nov. 5, 1813	18	William Mather	121	64	In Shoal Bay, Newfoundland.

Name of Ship.	Date.	Guns.	Commanding Officer's Name.	No. of men.	Number of lost.	Where lost.
Tay	Nov. 11, 1816	20	Samuel Roberts .	135	None	On the Isles Alacranes, Gulf of Mexico.
Telegraph, Schooner	Jan. 20, 1817		John Little . .	50	None	Rocks under Mount Batten, entrance of Catwater.
Thetis . . .	Dec. 5, 1830	46	Samuel Burgess .	275	16	Off Cape Frio.
Tribune . .	Nov. 28, 1839	20	C. Hamlyn Williams	190	None	Off Port of Tarragona.
Thunderbolt, St.-ves.	Feb. 3, 1847	6	Alex. Boyle . .	148	None	Cape Recife, Algoa Bay.
Undaunted . .	Aug. 31, 1796	38	Robert Winthrop .	286	None	Morant Keys, West Indies.
Vanceau, Cutter .	Oct. 21, 1796		John Gourly . .	60		Running on sunken rock, Port Ferrajo, Elba.
Viper . . .	Jan. 2, 1797		H. Harding Parker	120	All	Off the Shannon.
Urchin, Gun Boat .	1800		T.Pearson Croasdale		116	In tow of the Hector, in Tetuan Bay.
Utile, Sloop .	Nov. 1801	14	Edward Jekyl Canes	76	All	Foundered in a gale in passage from Gibraltar to Malta.
Venerable . .	Nov. 24, 1804	74	John Hunter . .	590	None	In Torbay.
Volador, Sloop .	Oct. 22, 1808	18	Francis G. Dickens	121	1	Near Cape Arrekle, Spanish Main.
Unique, Brig .	May 31, 1809	10	Thomas Fellowes .	65		Burnt at Basse Terre, Guadaloupe.
Union, Schooner .	May 17, 1828		C. Madden . .	32	None	On a reef off the East End of Rose Island, West Indies.
Victor . . .	1843	16	Charles Otway . .	130	All	In passage from Vera Cruz to Halifax.
Weazel, Sloop .	Jan. 12, 1799	14	Hon. Henry Grey	86	85	In Barnstaple Bay.
Weazel, Sloop .	Feb. 29, 1804	12	William Layman .	70	None	On Cabreta Point, Gibraltar Bay.
Woodlark . .	Nov. 13, 1805	14	Thos. Innes . .	50	None	Near Calais.
Wolfe, Sloop .	Sept. 4, 1806	18	G. C. Mackenzie .	121	None	On Heneaga, one of the Bahama Islands,
Woodcock, Schooner	Feb. 13, 1807	10	I. C. Smith Collett	18	None	West of Villa France, Saint Michael's.
Wagtail, Schooner .	Feb. 13, 1807	10	William Cullis .	18	None	West of Villa France, Saint Michael's.

Ship	Date	Guns	Commander	Crew	Saved	Remarks
Widgeon, Schooner	April 20, 1808	6	George Elliot	20	None	On a reef of rocks, near Banff.
Wildboar, Sloop	Feb. 15, 1810	10	Thomas Burton	76	12	On the Rundel Stone, Scilly Islands.
Woolwich	Sept. 11, 1813	20	Thos. Ball Sullivan	135	None	Off Barbuda, West Indies.
Whiting, Schooner	Sept. 21, 1816	14	John Jackson	50	None	Near Dunbar.
Wolf, Sloop	Mar. 10, 1830	18	Robt. Russell, Esq.	116	None	Off Isle of Wight (Brock).
York	Jan. 1803	64	Henry Mitford	491	All	Foundered in the North Sea.
Zenobia	1806		Name unknown		All	Wrecked, exact date unknown, on the Coast of Florida.
Zebra, Brig	1841	16	J. S. Shepperd	115	None	In the Levant.

LONDON:
SAVILL AND EDWARDS, PRINTERS,
CHANDOS STREET.

NEW BOOKS AND NEW EDITIONS,

PUBLISHED BY

JOHN W. PARKER, WEST STRAND.

Young Italy.

By Alexander Baillie Cochrane, M.P.

CONTENTS:

Cannes—The First of March—Piedmont and the Battle of Novara—The Madonna of Genoa—The History of the Roman Republic—The Two Artists — The Mount Quirinal — The Feast of the Golden Rose—The Temporal and Spiritual Authority of the Pope—The Murder of Rossi—Monte Casino—The Prisons of Naples—The Pope's Return to Rome.

Post Octavo. 10s. 6d.

Gazpacho, or Summer Months in Spain.

By William George Clark, M.A.,

Fellow of Trinity College, Cambridge.

Post Octavo. 7s. 6d.

Auvergne, Piedmont, and Savoy.
A Summer Ramble.

By Charles Richard Weld,

Author of *History of the Royal Society.*

Post Octavo. 8s. 6d.

Wanderings in some of the Western Republics of America.

By George Byam, (late 43rd Light Infantry.)

Author of *Wild Life in the Interior of Central America.*

Post Octavo, with Illustrations. 7s. 6d.

NEW BOOKS AND NEW EDITIONS,

Hesperos:
Or, Travels in the West.
By Mrs. Houstoun,

Author of *Texas and the Gulf of Mexico*.

Two Volumes, Post Octavo. 14*s*.

Travels in the Track of the Ten Thousand Greeks:

A Geographical and Descriptive Account of the Expedition of
Cyrus, and of the Retreat of the Ten Thousand, as
related by Xenophon.

By W. F. Ainsworth, F.G.S.

Surgeon to the late Euphrates Expedition.

Post Octavo 7*s*. 6*d*.

The Handbook for New Zealand:

The most recent Information, compiled for Intending Colonists.

By a Late Magistrate of the Territory.

6*s*.

Port Phillip in 1849.

By J. B. Clutterbuck, M.D.

Nine Years Resident in the Colony.

With a Map. 3*s*.

Lunacy and Lunatic Life;

With Hints on the Personal Care and Management of those afflicted with
temporary or permanent Derangement.

By the late Medical Superintendent of an Asylum for the Insane.

3*s*. 6*d*.

PUBLISHED BY JOHN W. PARKER, WEST STRAND.

Journal of Summer Time in the Country.

By R. A. Willmott,

Incumbent of St. Catherine's, Bearwood, 5s.

The City of God:

A Vision of the Past, the Present, and the Future.

Being a Symbolical History of the Church of all Ages,
and especially as depicted in some of the Scenes of the Apocalypse.

By Edward Budge,

Rector of Bratton Clovelly. Post Octavo. 8s. 6d.

Neander's

Julian the Apostate and his Generation;

An Historical Picture.

Translated by George Valentine Cox, M.A.

Small Octavo. 3s. 6d.

Homeric Ballads,

The Greek Text, with a Metrical Translation and Notes,

By the late Dr. Maginn.

Collected from Fraser's Magazine, and carefully revised.
Foolscap Octavo. 6s.

Anschar: a Story of the North.

By R. J. King.

Foolscap Octavo. 7s.

Compton Merivale:

Another Leaf from the Lesson of Life.

By the Author of Brampton Rectory.

A COMPANION VOLUME. 8s. 0d.

Printed in the United States
139834LV00006BC/12/A